N O L O ' S

L I V I N G

T R U S T

Legal Manual
by Mary Randolph

User's Guide
by Albin Renauer

NOLO PRESS   Berkeley

Your responsibility when using a self-help law book

We've done our best to give you useful and accurate information in this book. But laws and procedures change frequently and are subject to differing interpretations. If you want legal advice backed by a guarantee, see a lawyer. If you use this book, it's your responsibility to make sure that the facts and general advice contained in it are applicable to your situation.

Keeping up to date

To keep its books up to date, Nolo Press issues new printings and new editions periodically. New printings reflect minor legal changes and technical corrections. New editions contain major legal changes, major text additions or major reorganizations. To find out if a later printing or edition of any Nolo book is available, call Nolo Press at 510-549-1976 or check the catalog in the *Nolo News,* our quarterly newspaper.

To stay current, follow the "Update" service in the *Nolo News*. You can get the paper free by sending us the registration card in the back of the book. In another effort to help you use Nolo's latest materials, we offer a 25% discount off the purchase of any new Nolo book if you turn in any earlier printing or edition. (See the "Recycle Offer" in the back of the book.)

FIRST EDITION

Second Printing   October 1992

BOOK DESIGN	Jackie Mancuso Eddie Warner	SOFTWARE DESIGN	Mary Randolph Albin Renauer
PACKAGE DESIGN	Toni Ihara		Michael Sexton
INDEX	Sayre Van Young	PROGRAMMING	Michael Sexton
PROOFREADING	Ely Newman	TESTING	Dave Middleton
PRINTING	Delta Lithograph		Adam Stanhope Eddie Warner
EDITORS	Steve Elias Ralph Warner Denis Clifford Dave Middleton	BOX PHOTO	Albin Renauer Richard Blair

ISBN 0-87337-163-1

Nolo's Living Trust License

This is a software license agreement between Nolo Press and you the purchaser, for the use of the *Nolo's Living Trust* program and accompanying manual. By using this program and manual, you indicate that you accept all terms of this agreement. If you do not agree to all the terms and conditions of this agreement, do not use the *Nolo's Living Trust* program or manual, but return both to Nolo Press for a full refund.

Grant of License

In consideration of payment of the license fee, which is part of the price you paid for *Nolo's Living Trust*, Nolo Press, as licensor, grants to you the right to use this manual and enclosed program to produce living trusts for yourself and your immediate family, subject to the terms and restrictions set forth in this license agreement.

Copy, Use and Transfer Restrictions

The *Nolo's Living Trust* manual and program are protected by copyright. You may not give, sell or otherwise distribute copies of the program to third parties, except as provided in the U.S. Copyright Act. Under this license agreement, you may not use the program to prepare living trusts for commercial or nonprofit purposes, or use the program to prepare living trusts for people outside your immediate family.

Commercial Use of This Product

For information regarding commercial licensing of this product, (including use by educational institutions and non-profit organizations) call Nolo Press during normal business hours at (510) 549-1976.

Disclaimer of Warranty and Limited Warranty

This program and accompanying manual are sold "AS IS," without any implied or express warranty as to their performance or to the results that may be obtained by using the program.

As to the original purchaser only, Nolo Press warrants that the magnetic disk on which the program is recorded shall be free from defects in material and workmanship in normal use and service. If a defect in this disk occurs, the disk may be returned to Nolo Press. We will replace the disk free of charge. In the event of a defect, your exclusive remedy is expressly limited to replacement of the disk as described above.

Your Responsibilities for Your Living Trust

We've done our best to give you useful and accurate information in this product. But laws and procedures change frequently and are subject to differing interpretations. If you want legal advice backed by a guarantee, see a lawyer. If you use this product, it's your responsibility to make sure that the facts and general advice contained in it are applicable to your situation. Any living trust you make using *Nolo's Living Trust* is yours, and it is your responsibility to be sure it reflects your intentions.

Term

The license is in effect until terminated. You may terminate it at any time by destroying the program together with all copies and modifications in any form.

Entire Agreement

By using the *Nolo's Living Trust* program, you agree that this license is the complete and exclusive statement of the agreement between you and Nolo Press regarding *Nolo's Living Trust*.

Contents

6   Creating a Shared Marital Trust

7   Signing, Storing and Registering the Trust Document

8 Transferring Property to the Trust

9 Living With Your Living Trust

10 After a Grantor Dies

11   If You Need Expert Help

User's Guide

Welcome to the User's Guide. This part of the manual explains the basics on how to use *Nolo's Living Trust* software.

Sections A through D of the manual cover installation of the program. Sections E through G cover general information about how the program works. Section H takes you step-by-step through the process of making a living trust. Section I covers printing and exporting the trust document. Sections J and K cover making changes to the trust document after you've printed it. Section L covers miscellaneous problems you may encounter.

If you have a legal question, use Part II of this manual (the Legal Manual). There you'll find discussions of the legal and practical aspects of making and maintaining a revocable living trust.

A. First Things

This section tells you what you need to do before you can begin working with *Nolo's Living Trust*. If terms such as "select" and "click" are not familiar to you, refer to the owner's guide that came with your Macintosh computer.

First, check to see that you have everything you need.

1. What You Will Need

To use *Nolo's Living Trust,* you'll need:

- A Macintosh Plus, Classic, SE, SE/30, LC, Portable, or II family of computers.

- A hard disk and a floppy disk drive, or two floppy disk drives (800K or 1.4MB).

- A System Folder, with System file version 6.01 or later.

- The *Nolo's Living Trust* application disk, which contains the *Nolo's Living Trust* application, two help files, an NLT Read Me First file, and *TeachText* (an application for reading the NLT Read Me First file).

- One blank, initialized (formatted) 800K disk for making a working copy of the application.

2. Read the NLT Read Me First File

The *Nolo's Living Trust* disk includes a file named NLT Read Me First that contains information and clarifications of problems that may have developed after this manual was printed. You should read this information before you go further.

To display the contents of this file on your screen double-click on it. The *TeachText* application will display the contents of the NLT Read Me First file on the screen. You can also print the NLT Read Me First file for future reference.

B. Making a Back-Up Copy

Make a copy of your *Nolo's Living Trust* diskette before running it. Never use original software disks for anything other than making copies. Make a copy even if you are installing *Nolo's Living Trust* onto a hard disk.

If you are already familiar with a particular copy process, use it to make your back up copy, then skip to Section D on *Starting Nolo's Living Trust.*

The copying process is slightly different if you have one or two floppy disk drives.

1. If Your Computer Has One Disk Drive

- Insert a system disk, version 6.01 or later, into the drive.
- Turn the computer on.
- When the desktop appears, eject the disk by choosing Eject (⌘E) from the File menu.
- Insert a blank, formatted disk into the disk drive. When the icon for this disk appears on the desktop, eject the disk by choosing Eject (⌘E) from the File menu.
- Insert the *Nolo's Living Trust* disk into the disk drive.

- Point, click and hold on the *Nolo's Living Trust* disk icon. Drag the *Nolo's Living Trust* disk icon to the icon of the blank formatted disk.

- You will have to swap diskettes back and forth into the disk drive to make the copy.

- When the copying procedure is complete, name the new disk "NLT working copy."

- Remove all diskettes.

- Label the copy and store the original diskette in a safe place.

- Use the copy as your working copy. Do not set the write protection tab on the disk; *Nolo's Living Trust* will not work if you do.

- Go to Section D for instructions on *Starting Nolo's Living Trust.*

2. If Your Computer Has Two Disk Drives

- Insert a system disk, version 6.01 or later, into the internal drive.

- Turn the computer on.

- Insert the *Nolo's Living Trust* disk into the external disk drive.

- Click on the icon of the system disk and eject that disk by choosing Eject (⌘E) from the File menu.

- Insert a blank, formatted disk into the internal disk drive.

 If the disk you put in the internal drive is not blank, all the information on it will be erased.

- When the icon appears on the desktop, point, click and hold on the *Nolo's Living Trust* disk icon. Drag that icon to the icon of the blank formatted disk.

- You may have to swap diskettes back and forth into the disk drives to make the copy.

- When the copying procedure is complete, name the new disk "NLT working copy."

- Remove all diskettes.

- Label the copy and store the original diskette in a safe place.

- Use the copy as your working copy. Do not set the write protection tab on the disk; *Nolo's Living Trust* will not work if you do.

- Go to Section D for instructions on *Starting Nolo's Living Trust*.

3. If Your Computer Has a Hard Drive With One Disk Drive

- Turn the computer on (and your hard disk if it is separate from your computer).

- When the desktop appears, place a blank, formatted disk into the disk drive.

 If the disk you put in the disk drive is not blank, all the information on it will be erased.

- When the icon appears on the desktop, eject the disk by choosing Eject (⌘E) from the File menu.

- Insert the *Nolo's Living Trust* disk into the disk drive.

- When the Icon appears on the desktop, point, click and hold on the *Nolo's Living Trust* disk icon.

- Drag the *Nolo's Living Trust* disk icon to the icon of the blank formatted disk.

- You will have to swap diskettes back and forth into the disk drive to make the copy.

- When the copying procedure is complete, name the new disk "NLT working copy."

- Remove all diskettes.

- Label the copy and store the original diskette in a safe place.

- Use the copy as your working copy. Do not set the write protection tab on the disk; *Nolo's Living Trust* will not work if you do.

- If you plan to run the program from your hard disk, go to Section C for instructions on *Installing Nolo's Living Trust Onto a Hard Disk*. Otherwise, go to Section D for instructions on *Starting Nolo's Living Trust*.

4. If Your Computer Has a Hard Drive With Two Disk Drives

- Turn the computer on (and your hard disk if it is separate from your computer).

- When the desktop appears, insert the *Nolo's Living Trust* disk into the internal disk drive.

- Place a blank, formatted disk in the external disk drive.

 If the disk you put in the external drive is not blank, all the information on it will be erased.

- When the icon appears on the desktop, point, click and hold on the *Nolo's Living Trust* disk icon. Drag that icon to the icon of the blank formatted disk icon.

- You will be asked if you really want to replace the contents of the blank disk with the contents of *Nolo's Living Trust*. Click OK or press the Return key.

- When the copying procedure is complete, name the new disk "NLT working copy."

- Remove all diskettes.

- Label the copy and store the original diskette in a safe place.

- Use the copy as your working copy. Do not set the write protection tab on the disk; *Nolo's Living Trust* will not work if you do.

- If you plan to run the program from your hard disk, go to Section C for instructions on *Installing Nolo's Living Trust Onto a Hard Disk*. Otherwise, go to Section D for instructions on *Starting Nolo's Living Trust*.

C. Installing Nolo's Living Trust Onto a Hard Disk

You will need approximately 700K of space on your hard disk to install *Nolo's Living Trust*.

- Start your computer and get to the desktop.
- Insert the copy of *Nolo's Living Trust* into a disk drive.
- Point, click and hold on the *Nolo's Living Trust* disk icon.
- Drag the *Nolo's Living Trust* disk icon onto the hard disk icon.
- A dialog box will alert you that the disks are of different types and the contents of *Nolo's Living Trust* will be placed in a folder on the hard disk.
- Click the OK button.
- After the copy process has ended, point, click and hold on the *Nolo's Living Trust* disk icon.
- Drag the disk icon to the Trash icon. This will eject the *Nolo's Living Trust* disk. Then store the disk in a safe place.

Note Installing *Nolo's Living Trust* in this manner places a copy of the *TeachText* application on your hard drive in the *Nolo's Living Trust* folder. If you already have a copy of *TeachText* on your computer, you can discard our copy.

Go to Section D for instructions on *Starting Nolo's Living Trust*.

D. Starting Nolo's Living Trust

To start *Nolo's Living Trust*, open your working copy of the application. The procedure varies slightly depending on whether or not you are using a hard disk.

With a Hard Disk

If you are using a hard disk:

- Turn on the Macintosh and/or the hard disk.
- Double-click the hard disk icon to open it.

- If necessary, double-click any folder icons to find the *Nolo's Living Trust* application icon.

- Double-click the application icon. It looks like this:

Nolo's Living Trust

Nolo's Living Trust application icon

The program will start and bring you to the Welcome screen. The title bar of the window should read "Nolo's Living Trust."

With Two Floppy Disk Drives

If you are using two floppy drives.

- Turn on the Macintosh.

- Insert your start-up disk into the internal (or upper) drive.

- Insert the *Nolo's Living Trust* working disk you prepared into the other drive.

- If necessary, double-click on the Nolo's Living Trust working disk icon to find the application icon. (For a picture of the icon see the previous section.)

- Double-click the application icon.

The program will start and bring you to the Welcome screen. The title bar of the window should read "Nolo's Living Trust." Click the Continue button to start the orientation to the program.

Nolo's Living Trust welcome screen

(For instructions on opening a trust you made earlier using this program, read Section G, *Entering and Saving Your Trust Data.*)

E. Nolo's Living Trust Information and Help

Nolo's Living Trust offers three kinds of online help.

- **Legal Help** provides assistance in making decisions involved in making a living trust.

- **Program Help** provides step-by-step instructions on how to run the program.

- A **Tutorial** provides a basic overview of how to use the program.

Here are more detailed instructions on how to use each kind of help:

1. Using Legal Help

To use legal help:

Legal Help icon and button

- Click the Legal Help icon, whenever you see it at the bottom of the screen, or
- Choose from the lists of Legal Help topics that appear on certain screens.

If there is no Legal Help topic list or icon on the screen, you'll need to use the legal manual to get the answer to your particular question. All information in Legal Help is in the Legal Manual as well.

Here's how to use Legal Help's topic lists and buttons:

How To Use Legal Help Topic Lists

Nolo's Living Trust provides a list of Legal Help topics whenever you're introduced to a new concept or legal term. These help topics address legal and practical considerations about what the program is about to ask you to do.

If a list contains more topics than can fit on the screen, click the scroll bar on the right side of the list to see any topics that are hidden from view.

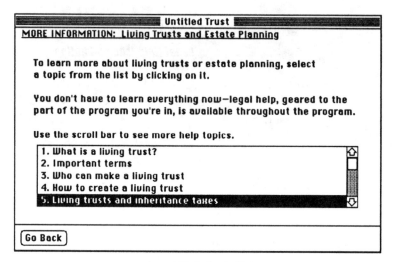

Legal Help topic list

To read about a particular topic, click once on it. The Legal Help window will open, and display the information on that topic.

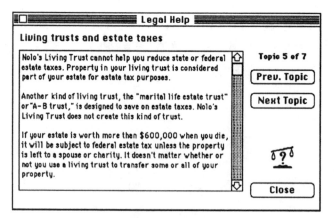

Legal Help topic screen

When the Legal Help window is open, you can also move to other topics in the list by clicking the Next Topic and Prev. Topic buttons.

When you're done reading Legal Help, click the Close button to return to the main program.

Legal Help Buttons

Some screens in *Nolo's Living Trust* offer Legal Help in the form of a button at the bottom of the screen. This button has a dotted outline, and appears next to a Legal Help icon (see example below).

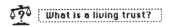

Legal Help icon and button

The button name describes the information you'll get when you click on the icon or the button. If the button name refers to a particular topic, the Legal Help window will open to a discussion of only that topic. If it says "Legal Help Topics" you'll get a list of Legal Help topics relevant to the part of the program you're using.

2. Using Program Help

Program Help covers the mechanical aspects of operating the *Nolo's Living Trust* software. Program Help is available at any time by:

- choosing Program Help from the Go menu, or

- typing an H while holding down the Command (⌘) key.

Program Help is context-sensitive. That means it "knows" what part of the program you are using. When you open it, it "guesses" what your problem is and opens to a relevant screen or list of topics. It may or may not guess correctly. If it guesses wrongly, click the Index button. You'll see a list of all Program Help topics. Browse through the topics to see if you can find the answer to your problem.

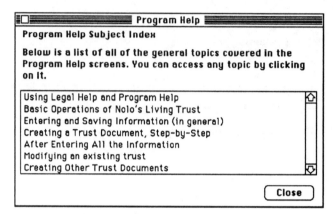

Program Help Subject Index

If you still can't find what you're looking for, check the manual. Look under all relevant items in the index of the manual. If you still can't figure out how to operate the program, call Nolo Technical Support at the number listed in the introduction to this manual. (If you are confused about some legal aspect of the program or manual, the Tech Support department cannot help you. Call Customer Service instead.)

3. Using the Tutorial

There is a short tutorial that explains the basics of how to run this program. It is available from any point in the program by choosing Tutorial from the Go menu. The tutorial is in a separate window and, if you have a large-screen monitor, you can drag the window to one side and leave it open while you use the program.

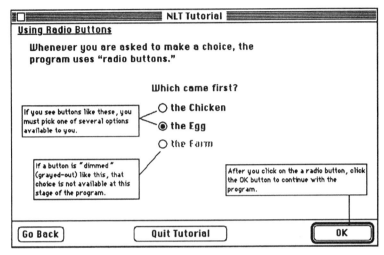

A program tutorial is available from any point in the program
by choosing the Tutorial command in the Go menu

To close the tutorial window, either click the close box in the title bar, or click
the Quit Tutorial button.

F. Basic Operations of Nolo's Living Trust

This section explains the basic kinds of tasks that are found throughout this
program. For more specific information on how to use a particular part of the
program, read Section H, *Creating a Trust Document, Step-by-Step*.

1. Creating a New Trust File

When you first start up *Nolo's Living Trust*, a new untitled trust file is
automatically opened. This file remains untitled until the first time it is saved.

If the AutoSave feature is on (this is the default setting of the program, see
Section G, below) the program will automatically save your trust file after you
have gone through the introductory screens and select the type of trust you
want to make.

The first time the trust file is saved, you can give it any name you want. The name of the currently opened file is always displayed in the title bar of the program window.

You can also create a new trust file at any time from within the program: First, close any currently opened file by choosing Close (⌘W) from the File menu. Then choose New Trust (⌘N) from the File menu. If AutoSave is on, you will be immediately prompted to enter the name of the new trust file.

2. Opening an Existing File

If you've already used the program before and created a trust file, you can open that file by first closing any open file (choose Close (⌘W) from the File menu), then choosing Open Trust (⌘O) from the File menu.

3. Moving From One Screen to the Next

Once a file is opened, or a new one created, *Nolo's Living Trust* takes you step-by-step through the process of making a living trust, explaining each step along the way. By the time you're finished, you will have stepped through 20 to 80 screens, depending on how complex you make your living trust document.

To move through these screens, follow the instructions below:

Information screens

Some screens do not require any input from you. These screens give you important information. Simply read the screen and advance to the next screen by clicking the Continue button at the bottom right corner of the screen.

Legal Help list screens

As described in Section E above, some screens offer a list of Legal Help topics. These topics explain the law and address particular questions about the part of the trust document you are working on.

To read about a particular topic, click once on it in the list. The Legal Help window will open and display the information on that topic.

When you've finished viewing all the topics you want to see, close the Legal Help window. Click the Continue button on the main screen to go on with the program.

Multiple-choice screens

On some screens, you must answer a multiple-choice question before you continue. Indicate your choice by clicking the appropriate radio button, and then click the OK button to continue with the program.

Input screens

On other screens, you must type in a name or other information before you can proceed. After you do so, click the OK button to go on with the program.

More information on input screens is in Section G, *Entering and Saving Information*.

4. Backing Up to a Previous Screen

As you go through the program, you may want to refer to a previous screen to read information or change something you entered in answer to a question. To do this, click the Go Back button at the bottom left corner of the screen. Go Back takes you back one screen at a time. Each input or multiple-choice screen you go back to will display your previous answer.

If you are at a data entry screen, clicking the Go Back button will pop up a warning that any data you entered on that screen may not be saved if you back up. (This is because data are not usually saved until you click the OK button.)

Go Back button

On some screens the Go Back button does not appear. You cannot go backwards from these screens.

Jumping Back to the Checklist Screen

After you complete each Part of the program you return to the Checklist screen (described below). If you want to jump directly back to the Checklist screen before you complete a Part, choose Return to Checklist from the Go menu.

Returning to the Checklist screen in this manner may lose any data you have just entered. A dialog box will alert you of this fact and offer you a chance to cancel the command.

Note You can't access this command from certain Parts of the program. If it is unavailable, the menu item will be dimmed.

5. Using the Checklist Screen

The Checklist screen is the base from which you enter the various Parts of the program. If you are just starting the program, you must go through some important introductory screens before you get to the Checklist screen.

The Checklist screen looks slightly different, depending on whether you are making a trust for an individual or a trust for a married couple. Although the screens differ, they both work the same way:

First, indicate the Part of the program you want to enter by clicking the radio button next to its name. Then click the OK button to enter that Part.

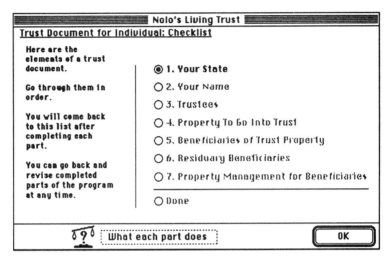

Individual trust Checklist screen before any data has been entered

Marital trust Checklist screen before any data has been entered

To re-enter a Part of the program you've already been through simply click the radio button again. Then click OK.

Why Some Buttons Are Dimmed

A button on the Checklist screen is dimmed if that Part of the program is not yet available to you. If you are just starting a new trust, the Your State button should be the only one available; all the other buttons should be dimmed.

Other parts of the program become available one by one, as you complete each Part of the trust document. As each part becomes available the buttons become activated. All are available by the time you finish making your trust.

What the Check Marks Mean

As you complete each Part, a check mark appears on the Checklist screen to show that the Part has been completed.

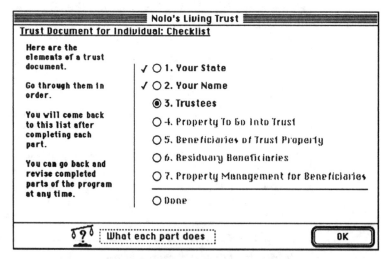

Checklist screen for individual trust
after Parts 1 and 2 have been completed

If you go through a Part of the program but leave all the input screens empty, then the check mark will not appear by that Part. You will not be able to continue with later Parts of the program until you complete the earlier Parts.

EXAMPLE You enter Part 4 but don't list any property. When you return to the checklist screen, Part 4 will not be checked, and you will not be able to go on to Part 5.

Re-entering a Part of the Program You've Already Been Through

You can re-enter any Part of the program you have already been through. Your prior answers will be on each input screen as you come to them again.

Note Part 5 of the program works slightly differently when you re-enter it. See the specific instructions for Part 5 in Section H below, *Creating a Trust Step-by-Step*.

After You've Completed All Parts

After you complete Parts 1 through 6 (the minimum information necessary to create a trust), the Done button becomes available. However, you should at least look at Part 7 if you have named any minor or young adult beneficiaries.

Clicking the Done button and then clicking OK takes you to a screen where you can display or print your trust document.

```
╔══════════════════════ A7 Individual Trust ══════════════════════╗
  Trust Document for Individual: Checklist
  
  Here are the
  elements of a trust
  document.                    ✓ ○ 1. Your State
  
  Go through them in           ✓ ○ 2. Your Name
  order.
                               ✓ ○ 3. Trustees
  You will come back
  to this list after           ✓ ○ 4. Property To Go Into Trust
  completing each
  part.                        ✓ ○ 5. Beneficiaries of Trust Property
  
  You can go back and          ✓ ○ 6. Residuary Beneficiaries
  revise completed
  parts of the program         ✓ ○ 7. Property Management for Beneficiaries
  at any time.
                               ◉ Done
  
         ♪?♪   ┌┈┈┈┈┈┈┈┈┈┈┈┈┈┈┈┈┈┐              ╭─────────╮
               ┊ What each part does ┊            │   OK   │
               └┈┈┈┈┈┈┈┈┈┈┈┈┈┈┈┈┈┘              ╰─────────╯
╚═════════════════════════════════════════════════════════════════╝
```

Individual trust Checklist screen after
all Parts have been completed

6. Quitting the Program

You can quit *Nolo's Living Trust* at any time by choosing Quit (⌘Q) from the File menu. If you've made any changes since the last time the trust file was saved, the program will ask whether you want to save those changes before you quit. The next time you open this trust file, the program will open to the Checklist screen so you can continue from where you left off.

7. Keyboard Shortcuts

List of keyboard shortcuts

Enter key .... Triggers OK or Continue button or "default button" (defined below), if any.

⌘-Return key .... Same as **Enter** key.

Return Key .... Triggers default buttons only.

Esc Key........................... Triggers Cancel, Close or No button if present in the top window.

⌘ **L** .... Show Names List.

⌘ **H** .... Program Help.

⌘ **S** .... Save Trust.

⌘ **X** .... Cut selected text.

⌘ **C** .... Copy selected text.

⌘ **V** .... Paste contents of clipboard.

⌘ **Z** .... Undo.

⌘ **W** .... Close the top window. (If the main screen is the top window, all windows, including help windows, will be closed.)

To Trigger Default Button:

Whenever you see a button with a heavy black outline, this is the default button. To activate the default button: press the **Return** key or press the **Enter** key

(The **Enter** key is on the numeric keypad of your keyboard. If your Mac does not have a numeric keypad, the **Enter** key is just to the right of the space bar.)

To Trigger OK or Continue Button:

Any OK or Continue button (whether or not it is a default button) can be activated by pressing the **Enter** key *if there is no other default button on that screen.*

(The **Enter** key is on the numeric keypad of your keyboard. If your Mac does not have a numeric keypad, the **Enter** key is just to the right of the space bar.)

You can also accomplish the same thing by holding down the ⌘ key and pressing the **Return** key.

Using the esc key to close windows or cancel dialogs

Keyboards for the Macintosh SE and later have an escape key labeled **esc**. On most keyboards this key is in the top left corner. On the LC and IIsi keyboards, it is just to the right of the spacebar. Pressing this key in *Nolo's Living Trust* is the same as clicking any button called Cancel, Close or No. If there is no such button on the screen, pressing the **esc** key has no effect.

Note   Some third-party (non-Apple) keyboards use **esc** key for other purposes, such as Undo. This **esc** key shortcut may not work if you are using such a keyboard.

G. Entering and Saving Your Trust Data

1. Saving Your Information to a Trust Data File

All data you enter into the program are saved in a separate trust data file, which you name. This file remains fairly small (about 3 to 15K) on your disk.

The program allows you to create an unlimited number of trust data files. However, if you are using this program to produce trusts for others, read the licensing agreement at the beginning of this manual.

Automatic Saving of Your Trust Data

This program is set up to automatically save your changes every time you leave a data-entry screen.

You can turn this AutoSave feature on or off by choosing the Preferences command in the File menu. In the Preferences dialog box, there is a box called Automatically save changes. If this box is checked, AutoSave is on.

With AutoSave on, you'll be asked to name your data file when you first begin to make your trust, and whenever you choose New Trust from the File menu. Your trust data file can have any name less than 31 characters long.

Since the program automatically saves your changes, the Save Trust command in the File menu will usually be unavailable. (The Save Trust command is available only if you have made changes since the last time the file was saved.)

Manual Saving (With AutoSave Turned Off)

If AutoSave is turned off, you must choose the Save Trust command from the File menu to save your information.

The Save Trust command in the File menu

The first time you choose the Save Trust command, the program will ask you to name your trust data file. You can use any name less than 31 characters long.

After the file has been saved, two things happen. First, the name you chose appears in the title bar of the program's main window. Second, the Save Trust item in the File menu becomes disabled, until you add or change information in your trust data file.

Be sure to save often, to guard against power failures or other computer problems that may interrupt your work.

If you try to quit the program before you have saved your data, the program will stop and ask whether you want to save your changes before you quit. If you click Yes your changes will be saved in the current file. If this is the first time you've saved, you will be asked to name the trust file. If you say No all changes you've made since the last time you saved will be lost.

Making a Backup Copy of Your Trust Data File

Floppy disks and hard disks can (and do) fail. Therefore, it's always a good idea to make one or two extra copies of all of your valuable computer files. To do this, after you quit the program, drag a copy of your trust data file to another floppy disk. Keep the copy in a safe place.

Making More Than One Trust Data File

If you want to make more than one trust, you must create a separate file for each trust you create. You can do this by choosing New Trust from the File menu. The first time you save a new file, you will be asked to give it a name. (If AutoSave is turned on, you are asked to name the file as soon as you create it.)

There is no limit to the number of trust files you can make, but you can only have only one open at a time. You must close any open trust files before you can open a new one.

 If you are using this program to create trusts for others, be sure you are complying with the license agreement in the beginning of this manual, as well as statutes governing the unauthorized practice of law.

2. Entering Names

Whenever you type in names in this program, keep these rules in mind:

- Use full names, first name first.
- Type only one name per line.
- If a field can hold only one line of text, type only one full name in the field.
- Names cannot exceed 255 characters.
- Use only one name; don't enter various versions of your name joined by aka (also known as).

- Check the online Legal Help for issues to consider which you might not otherwise think of.

Certain screens ask you to enter one or more names. On such screens, the cursor should be flashing in the field where the name(s) should go. If it isn't, point and click in the field.

If there is more than one field, pressing the Tab key takes you to the next field.

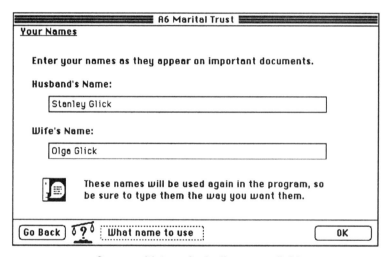

Screen with two single-line name fields

If a field can hold more than one line of text, type only one full name per line, and press the Return key after each name to make a new line.

```
╔══════════════ The Glick Trust ══════════════╗
║ Your Successor Trustee                        ║
║                                               ║
║   Name one or more persons or institutions    ║
║   you want to serve as successor trustee.     ║
║                                               ║
║   If you name more than one successor         ║
║   trustee, they will share responsibility.    ║
║   (On the next screen, you will be able to    ║
║   name an alternate, who will take over if    ║
║   none of these people can serve.)            ║
║                                               ║
║      Type only one name per line (press       ║
║         "return" to make a new line).         ║
║   ┌──────────────────────────────────┐ ▲     ║
║   │ Cecil Canseco                    │ │     ║
║   │ Sparky Larussa                   │ │     ║
║   │ |                                │ ▼     ║
║   │ ◁─────────────────────────────▷ │       ║
║   └──────────────────────────────────┘       ║
║                                               ║
║  ( Go Back )  Legal Help Topics     ( OK )    ║
╚═══════════════════════════════════════════════╝
```

Screen with a multi-line name field

Multi-line name fields can scroll both vertically and horizontally. Scroll the field vertically to enter an unlimited number of names. As a practical matter, however, the program will slow down noticeably if you have more than 500 different names in a single trust document.

Scroll the field horizontally only if you need to enter an especially long name. (The program can handle names up to 120 characters long.) Horizontal scroll bars do not appear unless the appropriate box in the Preferences dialog box is checked. Choose Preferences... from the File menu to change this setting.

Using the Same Name More Than Once in the Program

All names entered into your trust file are permanently stored in a master names list for that file. Names that are spelled differently are treated as two separate persons.

If you enter the same person's name more than once in this program, be sure to type it *exactly* the same way each time. Spelling and punctuation must match identically for the program to treat the two names as the same person. If the same person is listed under two separate spellings, this may cause confusion later, especially in Part 7 of the program.

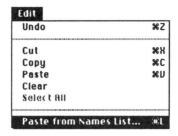

Paste from Names List command

If you are unsure how you spelled a name earlier, choose Paste from Names List… from the Edit menu. A dialog box will appear with all of the names you've entered so far.

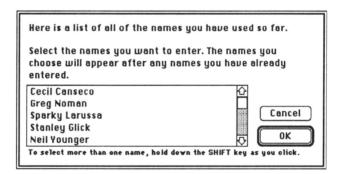

Names List dialog box

To paste one or more names from the list:

- Select one or more names from the list. (To select more than one name, hold down the Shift key as you click.)

- Click the OK button on the dialog box.

The name(s) will be inserted after the last name in the active field of the main program screen.

Note Misspelled names are permanently recorded in the names list for this file. They will appear in the Paste from Names List… dialog box, even if the names are no longer being used for any purpose.

Distinguishing Persons With Similar Names

If two persons have almost the same name, be sure to spell them differently somehow (for example, John Doe and John Doe, Jr., or John G. Doe and John C. Doe). If you do not distinguish the names in some manner, the program will treat them as the same person. This could cause confusion for your successor trustee when it's time to distribute your trust property.

When You Are Finished Entering Names

When you're finished entering names on a screen, click the OK button to go to the next screen. Your changes are not recorded in your trust data file until you click the OK button.

If You Leave a Screen Blank

Some parts of the program won't let you go further until you enter required information. If you try to go on, you will get a beep and a pop-up reminder telling you that you must enter the data.

If you don't want to enter the information because you are unsure of its spelling or you haven't decided on your choice, you have three options.

1. Use the Go Back button to return to earlier screens.

2. Go directly back to the Checklist screen by choosing Return to Checklist from the Go menu.

3. Enter the information as best you can, and then go back and change it later. (See Section F.5, *Using the Checklist Screen.*)

3. Entering Property Descriptions

Part 4 of the program asks you to enter descriptions of the property you plan to transfer to your living trust. Instructions on how to enter property descriptions are covered in Section H, *Creating a Trust Document, Step-by-Step.*

4. Multiple Choice Screens

Some screens ask you to answer a question by clicking on a radio button. The radio button is highlighted after you click on it, but your choice is not recorded until you click the OK button.

5. Lists

On some screens, you answer a question by clicking once on your choice on a list—for example, Part 1 (selecting your state), and Part 5 (selecting what property should go to a beneficiary).

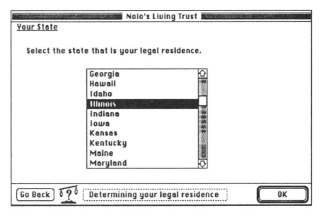

Example of entering information by selecting from a list

On most lists, you can only select one item at a time. However, in Part 5, you can select more than one item from the available property list by holding down the Shift key.

As with other data-entry screens, your selection is not recorded until you click the OK button.

Lists are used in other ways in *Nolo's Living Trust*. In Part 4, you build a list of trust property by entering property descriptions one at a time.

Lists are also used as a way of assigning alternate beneficiaries (in Part 5), and specifying property management for young beneficiaries (in Part 7).

How to use each of these particular lists is explained in detail in Section H of this manual, *Creating a Trust Document, Step-by-Step.*

6. Using the Cut, Copy and Paste Commands

On any screen that permits typing of text, you can use the Cut, Copy or Paste commands from the Edit menu.

However, to cut, copy or paste into dialog boxes, you must use the command-key equivalents; menus cannot be used while a dialog box is open.

7. Changing Your Answers Later

How you change the information in your trust depends on whether you have printed it out and signed it yet.

If You Have Already Printed and Signed Your Trust

If you have already printed and signed your trust, read the important information in Chapter 9 of the Legal Manual. There you will learn why you probably don't want to create a new trust to change provisions of the first trust. Instead, you probably want to make a document called a "trust amendment." See Section K of this manual on how to create a trust amendment.

If You Have Not Signed Your Trust Document

If you haven't printed your trust document, or if you have printed it but haven't signed it yet, you can simply tear up the unsigned printed copy. You can then change the data in your trust file and print out a new trust.

Simply re-enter the appropriate Part of the program from the Checklist screen and change the answers as they appear on the screen. When you've changed the answers the way you wish, click Done on the Checklist screen and print out the new trust. See Section I, *Displaying and Printing Your Trust Document*. Be sure to discard any earlier printed copies to avoid confusion.

H. Creating a Trust Document, Step-by-Step

This part of the manual takes you step-by-step through the process of creating a living trust using *Nolo's Living Trust*.

STEP-BY-STEP EXAMPLE

As we go through each step, we'll make a sample living trust, using the fictitious family of Olga and Stanley Glick. Feel free to make a trust file of your own and follow along.

---

1. Before You Begin

Before you start creating your living trust, you should browse the Legal Manual and think about the decisions you'll have to make. What property should you put in the trust? Whom do you want to receive it after your death? Do you even need a living trust at all? After you've thought about these questions, you're ready to create your trust document.

As you step through the rest of this section, you may also want to follow the step-by-step material in the Legal Manual (Chapter 5 for individual living trusts, and Chapter 6 for marital living trusts).

2. Opening a New Trust File

A new trust file is automatically opened when you start the program. The words "Untitled Trust" appear in the title bar of the main program window. The first time you go to save the trust, you will name the trust file. From that point on, the name you chose will appear in the title bar.

If a trust file isn't open already, choose New Trust from the File menu. If AutoSave is on, you will be asked to name the trust file as soon as you choose the New Trust command. (If the New Trust menu item is dimmed, then a trust file is opened already. You can only have one trust file open at a time.)

3. Reading the Introductory Information

Each time you open a new trust file, the program takes you through several introductory screens. These screens explain how the program works and give a general background on the law and practical uses of living trusts.

There is also an on-screen tutorial you can use to get general information on how the program works. This tutorial can be accessed from the introductory screens, or at any point in the program by choosing the Tutorial command from the Go window. When the tutorial is running, "NLT Tutorial" appears in the window title bar. This is a separate window. If you have a large-screen monitor, you can drag the tutorial to one side, and still see the main program screen underneath. If you have a regular sized Mac monitor, you'll probably want to close the tutorial window when you're not using it.

4. Selecting the Type of Trust

After the introductory screens, you come to a screen which asks you to select the type of trust you want to make. Your choices are:

- a trust for an individual or

- a shared trust for a married couple.

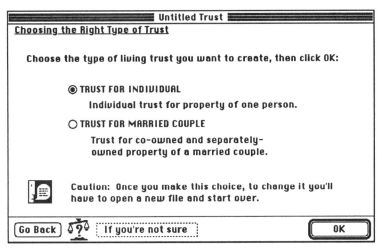

Trust selection screen

Use the Legal Help system and Legal Manual to help you decide which choice is best for your situation.

Changing from one trust type to the other

Once you've chosen to make one kind of trust and clicked OK, you can't later change this trust to the other kind of trust. That is, you can't change an individual trust to a shared marital trust, or visa versa.

The only way to make a different kind of trust after you leave this screen is to create a new trust file, by choosing New Trust from the File menu. (See above.)

Record your choice by clicking on the appropriate button, then click the OK button.

If the AutoSave feature is on, and your trust has not been saved yet, you will be asked at this time to type in the name of your trust file. This is the file in which all of your trust data will be stored.

STEP-BY-STEP EXAMPLE (continued)

Because Olga and Stanley are married and own property together, they click the "Trust for married couple" button, then click OK.

When the program asks them to save their trust, they name it "The Glick Trust." From that point on, that will appear in the title bar.

---

5. Using the Checklist Screen

The next screen you will see is the Checklist screen (described in Section F, above). This screen lists the seven steps involved in making your trust document, and is your branching-off point for the rest of the program. When you are making a new trust, only Part 1 will be available at first. Click the OK button to enter Part 1 of the program.

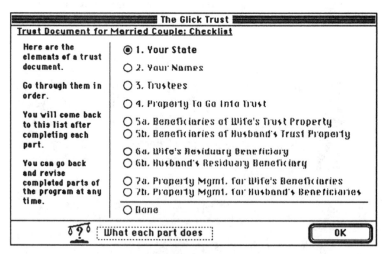

Marital trust checklist screen
before any data has been entered

6. Part 1. Selecting Your State

To select your state, scroll through the list on the Your State screen and click once on the name of your state. Then click OK to record your selection and return to the Checklist screen.

STEP-BY-STEP EXAMPLE (continued)

After clicking OK on the Checklist screen, the Glick family comes to the list of states. The Glick family lives in Illinois, so they scroll down to Illinois, click on it, and then click OK. This takes them back to the Checklist screen.

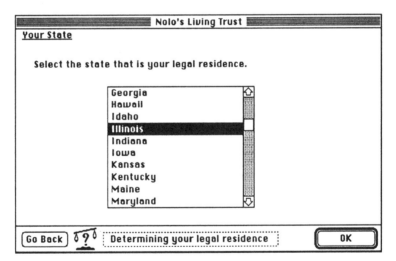

State selection screen

If You Change Your State Later

The state you choose determines the language of your trust document, and the sequence of screens you see as you go through the program. It particularly affects Parts 4 and 7. If you change your state after having already completed later parts of the program, you may get one or two pop-up warnings:

1. If you've completed Part 4 (Your Property), the program checks to see if the marital property laws in your new state differs substantially the old one. If the laws differ, you will be alerted to read the legal manual on the marital property laws for your new state.

2. If you've already completed Part 7 (Property Management for Young Beneficiaries), you may have to redo it. Laws regarding property management vary considerably from state to state. The program will inform you if the laws of your new state do not allow the same kinds of property management as the state you originally selected.

7. Part 2. Entering Your Name(s)

This step varies slightly depending on whether you are making an individual trust or a marital trust.

Note If you haven't done so already, read the standard rules about entering names set out in Section G above.

Individual Trust

Type your full name in the blank, then click on your sex, Male or Female. This information is needed for your trust to be grammatically correct. When the information is correct, click OK to return to the Checklist screen.

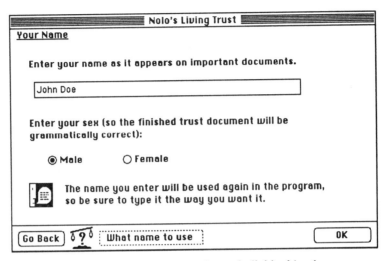

The Your Name screen for an individual trust

Marital Trust

Type the full name of each spouse in the appropriate blanks. When the information is correct, click OK to return to the Checklist screen.

The Your Name screen for a marital trust

STEP-BY-STEP EXAMPLE (continued)

The Glicks type Stanley Glick in the husband blank and Olga Glick in the wife blank.

---

8. Part 3. Naming Your Successor Trustees

This step begins with several introductory screens that explain what a successor trustee is and why you need one. Read these screens and the Legal Help topics carefully so you understand what the program is asking you to do.

After those screens, you come to the screen where you can name one or more persons to serve as successor trustee.

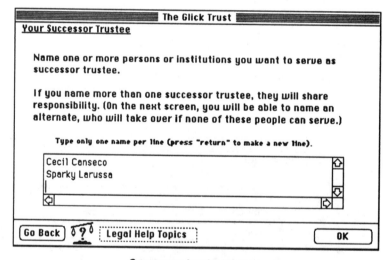

Successor trustee screen

If you type more than one name, press the Return key after each one to make a new line. Click OK to go to the next screen.

STEP-BY-STEP EXAMPLE (continued)

The Glicks type in the name of Olga's brother, Cecil Canseco, and a friend, Sparky Larussa, to be their successor trustee, and then click OK.

On the next screen, you enter the name(s) of the alternate successor trustee(s). This person or persons will serve if the person or persons you named in the previous screen are all unable to serve. (Read the Legal Manual or the on-line Legal Help for a complete explanation.)

Here again you can type one or more names (each on a new line). Click OK when you're finished to return to the Checklist screen.

STEP-BY-STEP EXAMPLE (continued)

The Glicks type in the name of a friend, Gordie Orr, to be their alternate successor trustee, and then click OK.

By now, if you've been following along and entering in data, your Checklist screen should have three check marks on it. Buttons 1 through 4 should be active, and the rest dimmed.

---

9. Part 4. Listing Your Trust Property

Every item of property you plan to transfer to your living trust should be listed in this section. You should do this before you name any beneficiaries. You can add property later, but you'll find your use of this program much more efficient if you list all of your property in advance.

There are important legal considerations regarding the kinds of property you should and should not transfer into a living trust. If you haven't done so already, read the Legal Manual on this subject. The Legal Manual also tells you how to describe the property you are transferring.

This part of the manual tells you only how to enter property items into the trust property list.

Why You Must List Your Trust Property

As explained in the Legal Manual, a living trust document requires that items be identified with greater specificity than in a will, because you are transferring ownership of the property to the trust.

Every item you include in this list will be identified in property schedules that you attach to your trust document. If the living trust document states that a particular item goes to a particular beneficiary, that clause will have no effect if the property is not listed on a property schedule.

Nolo's Living Trust automatically keeps track of all property you enter and makes sure that every item appears in the appropriate property schedule.

How To Add Property to the List

To add items to the trust property list, you must be at the List Trust Property screen in Part 4 of the program. This screen appears after a few introductory and explanatory screens.

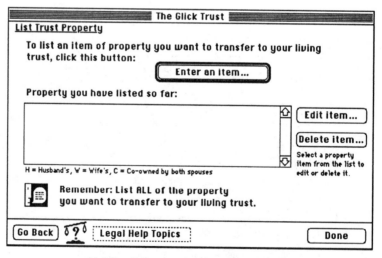

*List Trust Property screen for a marital
trust before any property has been entered*

Click the Enter An Item... button or press the Return or Enter key to bring up a dialog box. Type the description of the property in the dialog box.

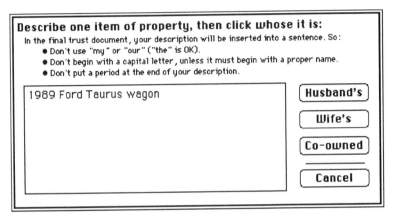

Property description dialog box for a marital trust

What happens next varies slightly depending on whether you're making an individual trust or a marital trust.

Individual trusts

When you've described the property item, press Enter or click OK. The item will appear on the list on the main screen.

Marital trusts

When you've described the property item, you must next identify its owner by clicking Husband's, Wife's or Co-owned.

(If you haven't read the on-line Legal Help or the manual on marital property laws, you should do so now. Some items you think are owned separately by one spouse may actually be owned by both spouses.)

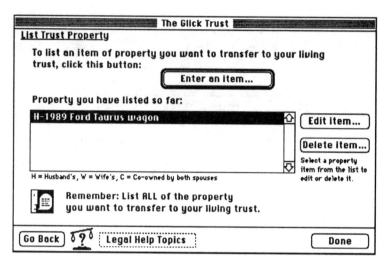

*List Trust Property screen after one item of
husband's property has been entered*

After you've clicked the owner of the property, the dialog box closes. The
item now appears on the property list on the main screen. A single-letter tag
describes whose property it is: **H** for husband's, **W** for wife's and **C** for co-
owned.

STEP-BY-STEP EXAMPLE (continued):

Olga and Stanley Glick own some property separately and some together. After
reading Legal Help and consulting the manual they decide to put only their two
cars and their house into the trust.

Stanley goes first. He clicks the Enter An Item... button, and then types in his
"1989 Ford Taurus Wagon" and then clicks the Husband's button.

Next, Olga clicks the Enter An Item... button, and types "1986 Honda Accord,"
and then clicks the Wife's button.

Next, they click the Enter An Item... button, and type "the house at 4553 Elm
Street, Anytown, Illinois" and then click the Co-owned button.

If you mistakenly click the wrong owner, you can change it by selecting the item from the list and clicking the Edit Item... button, and then clicking the correct owner in the dialog box. More on this in the next topic.

Editing Items Already on the List

To edit the description of an item of property already on the list, select the item and then click the Edit Item... button. The dialog box will reappear with the item already in it. Edit the description as desired.

What happens next varies slightly depending on whether you're making an individual trust or a marital trust:

Individual trusts

When you've finished editing the description, press Return or click OK to save your changes. The changes will appear on the list on the main screen.

Marital trusts

When you've finished editing the description, click Husband's, Wife's or Co-owned to save your changes. The existing owner designation for that item will be automatically set as the default button. To keep the same owner designation, click the default button. To change the owner designation click a different owner button.

Changing the property list after you name beneficiaries in Part 5:

If you come back to this property list after you go through Part 5 (where you name beneficiaries), any changes you make in the property list will have the following effects on the gifts already made in Part 5.

1. Changes in property descriptions will be reflected in the gifts you've made.

2. In a marital trust, if you change the listed owner from one spouse to the other, or from co-owned to solely-owned by one spouse, any gifts of this property made by the non-owning spouse will be erased.

3. If you change the owner designation of a listed item from one spouse to co-owned, the other spouse should re-enter Part 5 of the program to name beneficiaries for his or her share of the co-owned item.

STEP-BY-STEP EXAMPLE (continued):

Note This particular example is out of sequence. Do not try to follow along. Just read it for now.

Olga and Stanley Glick originally listed a 1989 Ford Taurus as "Husband's" property. Then they completed Part 5, where Stanley named beneficiaries for the car.

Suppose they then returned to Part 4 and changed the owner designation for the car to "Co-owned." Now Olga would have to return to Part 5 and name beneficiaries for her share.

Removing Items From the List

To delete an item from the list, select the item then click the Delete Item... button. You will be asked to confirm the deletion. If you say yes, the property will be deleted.

If a beneficiary has been chosen for the deleted property, that information is erased when the property is deleted.

When You Are Finished

When you are finished listing or editing items, click the Done button to return to the Checklist screen.

10. Part 5. Naming Beneficiaries of Trust Property

In this part of the program, you name beneficiaries for the trust property you listed in Part 4. This is the longest part of the program, but it's easy if you take it step-by-step. Also, there are shortcuts you can use if you are leaving all of your property to one person or a group of persons to share. These shortcuts, called "fast tracks," are explained shortly.

Before You Can Name Any Beneficiaries

Before you can name any beneficiaries, you must have created a list of trust property in Part 4 of the program. If you haven't listed your property in Part 4, you cannot start Part 5.

In a marital trust, a spouse cannot go through this Part of the program unless he or she owns or co-owns at least one item in the trust property list.

STEP-BY-STEP EXAMPLE (continued):

If the Glicks had listed only Stanley's solely-owned property in Part 4, Olga would not be able to name any beneficiaries because she would have nothing to give away.

If, however, since they listed some property as co-owned, each of them will get to name beneficiaries for their shares of that property.

"Fast Track" Options: Leaving All Trust Property to One or More Beneficiaries

Soon after you enter this part of the program, you come to a multiple-choice screen. This screen offers several options for naming beneficiaries:

1. You can name specific beneficiaries for specific items of property.

2. You can use a "fast track" option to leave *all* of your trust property to one person or to several beneficiaries to own together.

3. And, in a marital trust, you have the "fast track" option of leaving all the trust property to your spouse.

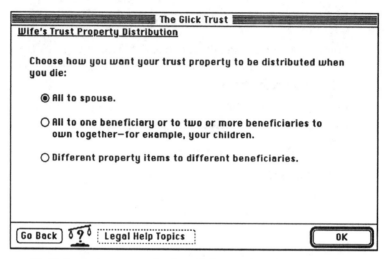

Multiple choice screen for beneficiary options in a marital trust

If you choose a fast track option, all the trust property will go to the beneficiary or beneficiaries you name. You will not be able to leave trust property to any other beneficiaries. You will, however, name alternates for the beneficiaries who are receiving all the trust property. (See below, *Naming Alternates for Your Beneficiaries.*)

STEP-BY-STEP EXAMPLE   (continued):

Stanley wants to leave all of his trust property to go to Olga after his death. So he enters Part 5b of the program, and then clicks the "All to spouse" button, then clicks OK. Stanley can now skip ahead to the section on naming alternates.

When Olga goes through this part of the program (Part 5a) she decides to leave some items to Stanley and some items to her cousins Louise and Laverne. So she clicks the "Different property items to different beneficiaries" button, and then clicks OK.

---

1. If you chose "All to spouse," you can now skip ahead to the section called *"Naming Alternates For Your Beneficiaries."*

2. If you chose "All to one beneficiary..." you can now skip ahead to the section called *"Entering Beneficiaries' Names."*

The Non-Fast Track Option: Leaving Specific Items to Specific Beneficiaries

If you forgo the fast track options, you will get to leave specific items of property to specific beneficiaries. To do this, you must loop through a series of steps:

• First, you select some property from a list.

• Next, you name beneficiaries for the property you selected.

• Finally, you name alternates for each beneficiary.

Each of these steps is described in detail in the pages that follow.

After you complete these steps, you come to a review screen. The review screen lets you review the gift you just made, change it if you like, or go on and make another gift. You repeat this loop until each item of the listed trust property has been assigned a beneficiary.

Selecting property items from the list of available property

If you are leaving specific items of property to different beneficiaries, you start by selecting one or more items of property from a list of available property.

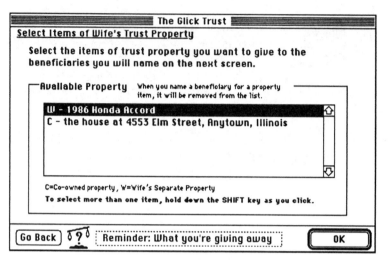

List of property available to be given to specific beneficiaries (marital trust)

In an individual trust, the available property list is the list you created in Part 4 of the program.

In a marital trust, the available property list does not include trust property owned separately by your spouse. It includes only property owned by you or co-owned with your spouse.

To select an item of property from the list, click on the item.

To select more than one item, hold down the Shift key as you click. Shift-clicking also lets you deselect an item that is already selected.

After you have selected the desired property, click OK to go on to the next step.

STEP-BY-STEP EXAMPLE (continued):

When Olga gets to the available property screen, her solely-owned property is listed, along with the property she co-owns with Stanley. In this case her Honda Accord and their home are listed on her available property list.

She wants Stanley to get her share of the house, but she wants her cousins to get the car, so she must make two gifts. She starts with the gift to her cousins, so she clicks on the car in the available property list and then clicks OK.

Entering Beneficiaries' Names

In this step, you name one or more beneficiaries who should receive the trust property you just selected (or all of your trust property, if you are using the fast track option).

 When naming beneficiaries, type the name of a specific person exactly the same way each time. You can also use the Paste from Names List... command in the Edit menu to ensure that names are spelled the same way. The program will treat different spellings of the same name as two different persons. This could lead to confusion and unintended results in your trust document.

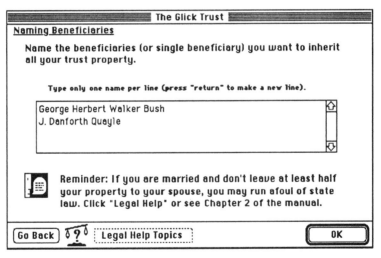

Naming beneficiaries for a fast track gift

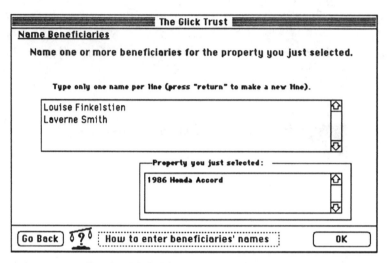

Naming beneficiaries for specific property

If you type more than one name, the order in which you type them doesn't matter. Each person you name will receive the property at the same time and share ownership of it.

After you've typed the names of your beneficiaries, click OK to continue.

STEP-BY-STEP EXAMPLE   (continued):

Olga is making her first gift (the car to Louise and Laverne). Since these names have not appeared previously in the program, she cannot use the Paste from Names List... command. Instead she types their full names: Louise Finkelstien, then the return key, then Laverne Smith. Then she clicks the OK button.

Setting Each Beneficiary's Share If You Name More Than One Beneficiary

If you enter more than one beneficiary to share the trust property, you will be brought to a screen that asks you how you want the property to be shared among them.

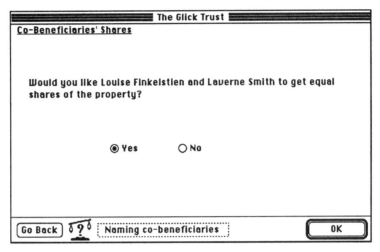

Co-beneficiaries shares of property can be
equal or split however you want them

If you want each beneficiary to have an equal share, click the Yes button and click OK.

If you would like to divide the property unequally, click the No button and click OK.

Specifying unequal shares for each beneficiary

If you choose to give co-beneficiaries unequal shares of the property, you come to a screen where you can enter the fractional share that each beneficiary should receive.

The Glick Trust

Unequal Shares for Co-Beneficiaries

Click on each beneficiary's name to enter the fractional share of property the beneficiary should receive.

Make sure the fractions don't add up to more than 1.

1/4 — Louise Finkelstien
3/4 — Laverne Smith

Go Back   Done

Screen for specifying unequal shares for co-beneficiaries you've named

The beneficiaries' names are presented in a list.

- Click on a beneficiary's name to set that beneficiary's share.

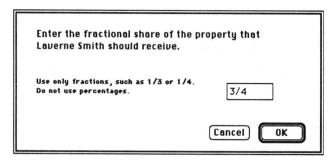

Enter the fractional share of the property that Laverne Smith should receive.

Use only fractions, such as 1/3 or 1/4.
Do not use percentages.   3/4

Cancel   OK

Enter each beneficiary's share in the pop-up dialog box

- Type a fraction (for example, 1/3) in the pop-up dialog box, then click OK to make the dialog box go away.

- Repeat this for each beneficiary on the list.

Make sure the fractions do not add up to more than 1. If they do, there will be confusion when it comes time to distribute the property, and it may lead to a legal dispute among the beneficiaries you have named.

STEP-BY-STEP EXAMPLE   (continued):

Olga wants Louise to get 1/4 ownership of the car, and Laverne to get 3/4. So, first she clicks No when the program asks whether she wants the beneficiaries to get equal shares. When she gets to the next screen, Louise and Laverne's names appear in a list.

To specify Louise's share, Olga clicks on Louise's name in the list. A dialog box pops up, Olga types "1/4" and clicks OK to close the dialog box. Then she clicks on Laverne's name, types "3/4" in the pop-up dialog box, and clicks OK to close the dialog box.

Louise's and Laverne's shares now appear in the list, before their names. Olga sees that they're correct, so she clicks OK to go on to the next screen.

Naming Alternates for Your Beneficiaries

The last step in naming beneficiaries for your trust property is to name alternates for each beneficiary. How you do this depends on whether you named one, or more than one, beneficiary.

For one beneficiary

If you named only one beneficiary, or if, in a marital trust, you selected your spouse to receive all your property, you will go through a few screens that discuss the issues involved in naming alternate beneficiaries.

Then you come to a screen where you can name one or more alternates for that beneficiary. When you get to that screen, type in the name(s) of the alternates for the beneficiary you named. Type only one name per line.

```
╔═══════════════════════ The Glick Trust ═══════════════════════╗
║ Name Alternate Beneficiary for Your Wife                       ║
║                                                                ║
║    Name the person(s) or institution(s) you want to be the     ║
║    alternate beneficiary for your wife.                        ║
║                                                                ║
║       Type only one name per line (press "return" to make a    ║
║       new line).                                               ║
║    ┌──────────────────────────────────────────────────┬──┐    ║
║    │ Alan Fielder                                      │ ⇧│    ║
║    │                                                   │  │    ║
║    │                                                   │  │    ║
║    │                                                   │ ⇩│    ║
║    └──────────────────────────────────────────────────┴──┘    ║
║                                                                ║
║    If you don't want to name an alternate, leave the box blank.║
║                                                                ║
║ ┌──────────┐  ⚖  ┌──────────────────┐        ┌──────────────┐  ║
║ │ Go Back  │     │ Legal Help Topics│        │     OK       │  ║
║ └──────────┘     └──────────────────┘        └──────────────┘  ║
╚════════════════════════════════════════════════════════════════╝
```

Screen for entering alternate beneficiaries for an "all-to-spouse" fast track gift

If you don't want to name alternates for this beneficiary, you can leave this
screen blank. (See the Legal Manual for an explanation of what happens to the
property if you don't name an alternate.)

Click OK when you're done to go to the review screen. The review screen is
described below in the section titled *Reviewing the Gift You Just Made.*

STEP-BY-STEP EXAMPLE (continued):

Note This example is out of sequence. Do not try to follow along. Just read the
example for now.

When Stanley gets around to giving all of his property to his spouse, here is
where he names the person who should get his property if Olga does not
survive him. He names his nephew, Alan Fielder.

Stanley then clicks the OK button which takes him to the review screen.

For more than one beneficiary

If you named more than one beneficiary, you will come to a multiple choice
screen that gives you the following options:

- have the program automatically designate the other co-beneficiaries as the alternates for each beneficiary

- specifically name alternates for each beneficiary, or

- elect not to have alternate beneficiaries.

(Read Legal Help or the legal manual for a discussion of the legal results of choosing these various options.)

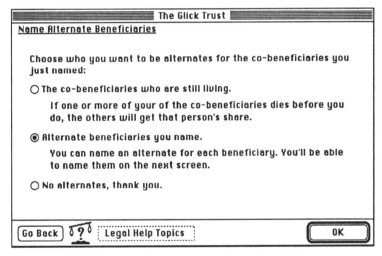

Options for naming alternates for co-beneficiaries

If you choose the Surviving Co-Beneficiaries option, or the No Alternates option, click OK and you will be taken directly to the review screen.

STEP-BY-STEP EXAMPLE (continued):

Olga decides that it would be impractical for her cousins to share ownership of her car with anyone except each other. So she simply clicks the "Co-beneficiaries who are still living" button to set the alternate beneficiaries. That way, if either cousin dies before Olga does, the other cousin will get the entire car to herself. (If both cousins don't survive Olga, the car will go to the person she names as her "residuary beneficiary" in Part 6, below.)

Olga then clicks the OK button which takes her to the review screen.

If you choose to name specific alternates for each beneficiary, here's what happens:

- First, you are presented a list of help topics that discuss the issues involved in naming alternate beneficiaries.

- Then you come to a screen with a list of the beneficiaries of the current gift.

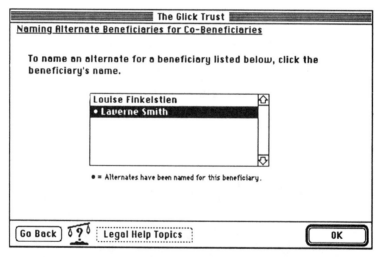

Screen for naming different alternates for co-beneficiaries

- Click once on the name of a beneficiary. A dialog box will pop up, prompting you for the names of your alternate beneficiaries for the selected beneficiary.

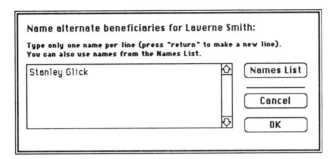

Pop-up dialog for naming alternates for the selected beneficiary

- Type the name(s) of one or more alternates for that beneficiary in the pop-up dialog box, one name per line. You can also select names from the Names List by clicking the Names List button.

- Click OK to close the dialog box.

A black dot appears next to the name of each beneficiary for whom you have named an alternate. You should name at least one alternate for each beneficiary listed.

If you want to change an alternate, click on the name again. The dialog box will appear with the alternates you previously entered. Edit the names any way you wish, and click OK to record your changes.

STEP-BY-STEP EXAMPLE (continued):

If Olga had decided to name her husband as the alternate for both of her cousins, she would have clicked the Alternate Beneficiaries You Name button to set the alternate beneficiaries. That would bring her to a screen where the names of her cousins will appear on a list. Now she names the alternates for one beneficiary at a time.

First she clicks on Lousie's name. A dialog box pops up asking for the names of the alternate beneficiaries. In this case, Stanley is the only alternate. To make sure his name is spelled exactly the same way, she clicks on the Names List button and then double-clicks on Stanley's name on the list. Stanley's name is inserted in the alternate beneficiary dialog box. She clicks OK to close the dialog box.

At this time a black dot should appear next to Louise's name, indicating that an alternate has been named for her.

Then she clicks on Laverne's name and repeats the same process.

Olga then clicks the OK button on the main screen which takes her to the review screen.

Reviewing the Gift You Just Made

After you have selected property and named beneficiaries and alternates, you come to a review screen. This screen lets you see how the gift you just made will be worded in your trust document.

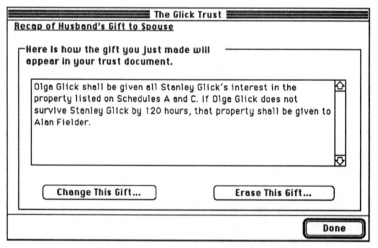

Review screen for a fast track gift

The review screen also lets you go back and change any portion of the gift you just made, or erase the gift and start over.

If you are not using one of the "fast track" options, you can also make additional gifts from the review screen.

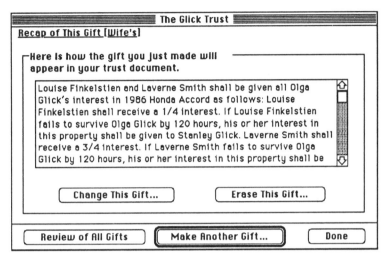

Review screen for a gift of a specific item to a specific beneficiary

The next several sections describe how each of these features work.

Changing the Gift You Just Made

The only thing you can change in this part of the program (Part 5) is the designations of beneficiaries to the particular items of property that you listed in Part 4. You cannot make any changes in the trust property descriptions or add items to the trust property list. Those changes can be made only in Part 4.

To edit the gift that appears on the review screen you must click the Change This Gift button.

What happens next depends on the kind of gift you have made.

If you left all of your property to your spouse

If you left all of your property to your spouse, the Change This Gift button returns you to the alternate beneficiary screen, where you can change the alternate beneficiaries for your spouse. That is the only change you can make for this kind of gift.

To make any other change—for example, to leave property to someone other than your spouse—you must click the Erase This Gift button and start over.

If you left all your property to one or more persons

If you left all your property to one or more persons, the Change This Gift button first returns you to the screen where you named those beneficiaries. The names you typed earlier will already appear on the screen. You can change these names or leave them the same. Then you proceed through each step you went through the first time, and make any changes you wish.

To make any other kind of change—for example, to leave different property to different beneficiaries—you must click the Erase This Gift button and start over.

If you left specific property items to specific beneficiaries

If you left specific property items to specific beneficiaries, the Change This Gift button takes you back to the beginning of the gift loop. This is the screen where you select from available property. From there you'll step through each screen again (property selection, beneficiaries and alternate beneficiaries).

At each step, your previous answers will already be displayed. You can change them if you wish, or leave them as they are. You must cycle through the entire loop (all the way back to the review screen) even if you want to change only one aspect of the gift.

Erasing the Gift You Just Made

If you left all of your property to your spouse

The Erase This Gift button erases the designation of your spouse as the recipient of all your trust property and erases the choices you made for her alternate beneficiary. It does not delete items from the trust property list.

After the gift is erased, you are returned to the multiple-choice screen that lets you leave all your property to your spouse, all to some other person or persons, or different items to different beneficiaries.

If you left all your property to one or more persons

The Erase This Gift button erases the designation of beneficiaries and alternate beneficiaries you named to receive of all your trust property.

After the gift is erased, you are returned to the multiple-choice screen that lets you leave all your property to your spouse (marital trusts only), all to some other person or persons, or different items to different beneficiaries.

If you left specific property items to specific beneficiaries

The Erase This Gift button erases the designation of beneficiaries and alternate beneficiaries for the property you selected. That property can then be given to other beneficiaries.

After the gift is erased, you remain at the review screen, but the Erase This Gift button is dimmed. Click the Make Another Gift button to make a new gift, or click Done to return to the Checklist screen.

Making Additional Gifts

If you are not making a fast track gift, there will be a Make Another Gift button on the review screen. This button lets you make additional gifts. You will be returned to the property selection screen where you can begin to make your next gift.

You can keep making gifts until there is no more trust property to give away. If all the property has been spoken for, the Make Another Gift button will be dimmed. You will not be able to make any more gifts.

Why the list gets shorter after you make each gift

When you return to the available property list, you'll notice that the property you have given away in previous gifts is no longer listed. This is because the property items you select for a gift are removed from the list and are no longer available for later gifts. This prevents you from giving away the same item more than once, and creating inconsistent clauses in your trust document.

> **STEP-BY-STEP EXAMPLE (continued):**
>
> After Olga finishes making her gift of the car to Louise and Laverne, and returns to this list, the car will no longer be on the list. The car is no longer available to be given away to anyone else. Only Olga's share of the house is still available.

Getting an item to reappear on the list

Suppose you want to give away an item of property that you've already given away in an earlier gift. You must erase or change the earlier gift so the property is no longer part of it. Once the earlier gift has been changed, the item will appear the next time you bring up the available property list. (For instructions on how to change earlier gifts, see *Reviewing and Changing Earlier Gifts,* below.)

> **STEP-BY-STEP EXAMPLE (continued):**
>
> If Olga had accidently left her cousins both the the car and the house, and wanted the house to reappear on the list, she would have to change the gift to her cousins first. The house would have to be deleted from from the items given to her cousins. Then when she returned to make a new gift, the house would be available for her to give to Stanley.

Note To add new items to the trust property list, you must return to Part 4.

Reviewing and Changing Earlier Gifts: Using the Review All Gifts Screen

The Review All Gifts screen allows you to review, change or delete any gifts you have made so far. This screen does not appear if you made a fast track gift, because a fast track gift takes care of all trust property in a single gift.

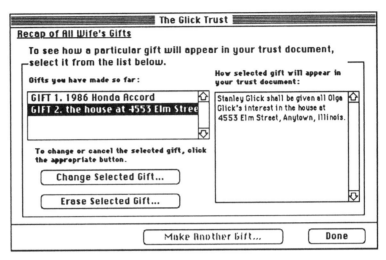

Review All Gifts Screen for non-fast track gifts

On the left had side of the screen is a numbered list of the gifts you've made in the order you made them. The first few words of the first property item given in each gift is also displayed.

Reviewing an earlier gift

To review a gift, select it from the list on the left. The box on the right will display how the gift will appear in the trust document.

Changing an earlier gift

To change any gift on the list, select it and then click the Change Selected Gift button. (This button is dimmed unless a gift is selected from the list.)

The program will take you back to the beginning of the gift loop. From there you'll step through each screen again, (starting with the property selection screen) with your answers for the selected gift already in place. You can change any answer you wish or leave them as they are.

Note on changing who gets a particular item of property Once you have named a beneficiary for an item of property, that property item will not be available for later gifts. To make that property available again you must either: a) erase the gift in which the item was given away, or b) change the gift to not include the item. Then the item will again appear on the list of available property for later gifts.

Erasing an earlier gift

The Erase This Gift button erases the designation of beneficiaries and alternate beneficiaries for the selected gift. The property that was part of that gift can then be given away in other gifts. Clicking this button DOES NOT delete any property from the trust property list. To do that, you must return to Part 4 of the program.

Making additional gifts

You make additional gifts by clicking the Make Another Gift button, but only if there is property left in the available property list.

This button takes you back to the property selection screen where you can begin making another gift.

If this button is dimmed there is no more property left—that is, all the property has been selected in earlier gifts.

When you are finished

If you don't want to make any changes or make any additional gifts, click the Done button to return to the Checklist screen.

Re-entering to Part 5 of the Program From the Checklist Screen

If you've been through Part 5 already and made at least one gift, the Checklist screen will have a check mark by the radio button for Part 5. (With a shared marital trust, there are two buttons, one for each spouse.)

If you choose to go back to Part 5 of the program when a check mark is visible, you will come to a screen that offers you three choices:

1. Make another gift (if you did not make a fast track gift and there is property still available)

2. Review the gifts you've already made, or

3. Erase all of your prior gifts and start over from scratch.

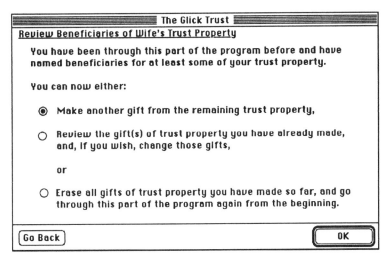

Your options if you re-enter Part 5 of the program after you've already named beneficiaries for some of your property

Review option

The review option takes you directly to the review screen, which displays the gift(s) you have already made. From there you can review, change, or delete gifts you have already made. If there is still property in the property list for which you have not named a beneficiary, you can also make additional gifts from the review screen.

Erase all and start over option

This option erases ALL of the beneficiary and alternate beneficiary designations you have made. This erasure cannot be undone, so make sure it's what you want before you click the OK button.

The trust property list that you made in Part 4 of the program will remain intact. Just the beneficiary designations for the property are erased.

11. Part 6. Naming Residuary Beneficiaries

This step begins with several introductory screens that explain what a residuary beneficiary is and why you need one. After those screens, you come to a screen where you name one or more persons to serve as your residuary beneficiary.

If you type more than one name, type a return after each one. Click OK to go to the next screen.

STEP-BY-STEP EXAMPLE (continued):

Olga Glick types in the name of her husband, Stanley Glick, to be the residuary beneficiary of all of her trust property, and then clicks OK.

On the next screen, you enter the names of the alternate residuary beneficiary. This person will be the residuary beneficiary if the person or persons you named in the previous screen are all unable to serve.

Here again you can type one or more names, one name per line. Click OK when you're finished to return to the Checklist screen.

STEP-BY-STEP EXAMPLE (continued):

Olga Glick types in the name of their friend Don Overton to be her alternate residuary beneficiary and then clicks OK. This returns her to the Checklist screen.

Stanley then goes through this same process, naming his wife, Olga, as his residuary beneficiary, and naming Don Overton as the alternate residuary beneficiary.

By now, if you've been following along, Parts 1 through 6 on your Checklist screen should have check marks by them, and the radio button for Part 7 should be highlighted.

---

12. Part 7. Setting Up Property Management For Minors and Young Adult Beneficiaries

This part of the program is optional, but anyone who has named young beneficiaries (under 35) is strongly urged to complete it.

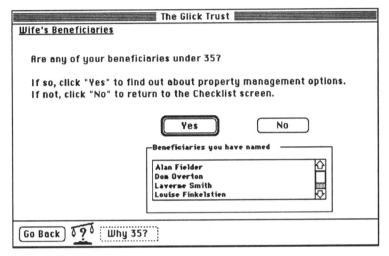

Second screen of Part 7, where you're asked
if any of your beneficiaries are under 35

When you first enter this part you are asked whether any of the beneficiaries you have named are under 35. If you answer No you are returned to the Checklist screen. If you answer Yes you are presented with more introductory information.

How this part of the program works varies depending on whether your state allows custodianships under the Uniform Transfers to Minors Act (UTMA). Consult the table in Part 7 of Chapter 5 of the Legal Manual to see if your state is one of them.

States That Have Adopted the UTMA

If your state allows custodianships under the UTMA, you will be brought to a screen that allows you to set up a subtrust or a custodianship for each young beneficiary you have named.

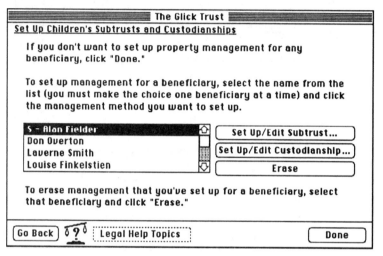

Screen for selecting property management for beneficiaries in a state that has adopted the UTMA

Each beneficiary can have either kind of property management, but you cannot set up both kinds for any one beneficiary.

To set up management for a beneficiary, do the following:

- Select the beneficiary's name from the list.

- Click on the Set Up Subtrust or the Set Up Custodianship button. A dialog box will appear, asking for the information required for the kind of management you have selected

- If you're setting up a subtrust, the only information required is the age at which the subtrust will end. The age cannot be greater than 35 or less than 18. (The trustee of the subtrust is automatically determined—see Legal Help on this subject.)

- If you're setting up a custodianship, you must name two persons: a custodian and an alternate custodian. If you live in a state that allows you to choose the age the custodianship shall end, you must also specify that age. In states that have a mandatory age, that age is automatically recorded for you.

What the Erase button does

Use the Erase button only if you want to delete property management that you have already set up for a beneficiary.

If you switch from one kind of management to the other

If you already have set up subtrust for a beneficiary and then set up a custodianship for that same person, the subtrust information will be erased and replaced by the custodianship information. The reverse is also true—setting up a subtrust for a beneficiary will erase any existing custodianship information for that person.

In either case, the program warns you of what is about to happen, and gives you a chance to cancel.

States That Have Not Adopted the UTMA

If you indicated that some of your beneficiaries were under 35, you will be brought to a screen that allows you to set up a subtrust for any of those beneficiaries.

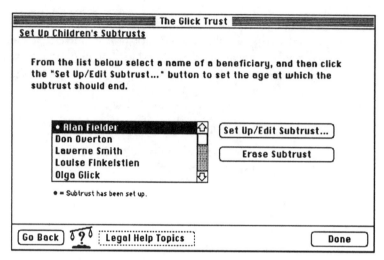

*Screen for selecting property management for
beneficiaries in a state that has not adopted the UTMA*

To set up a subtrust for a beneficiary, first select the name from the list, and
then click the Set Up Subtrust button. A dialog box will appear, asking for the
age at which the subtrust will end. (The trustee of the subtrust is automatically
determined—see Legal Help on this subject.)

What the Erase Subtrust button does

Use this button only if you want to delete a subtrust that you have already set
up for a beneficiary.

I. Displaying and Printing Your Trust Document

You can display your trust document after you have completed Parts 1
through 6 of the program. That is the minimum amount of information needed
to create a living trust with this program. However, you should complete
all seven Parts.

You'll know when you have entered enough information because the Done
button on the Checklist screen will no longer be disabled.

1. How To Display and Print the Trust Document

If the Done button on the Checklist screen is enabled, click it and then click OK. You will come to the screen shown below, which lets you display or print your trust document, called your "Declaration of Trust."

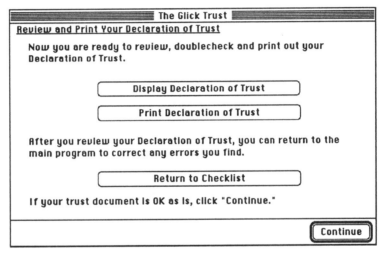

When you're done entering your trust information, you come to a screen where you can display and print your trust document

Click the Display Declaration of Trust button to display your trust. The program will then assemble your trust. This takes about a minute. A progress bar shows the progress as the trust is being assembled.

When the trust is fully assembled, a document window opens displaying the text of your trust document exactly as it will be printed. The first page is the instruction sheet. The actual trust language starts after the instructions.

You can print the document at any time while it is displayed, by choosing Print... from the File menu.

Two Ways To Display Your Trust Document

There are two ways to display your trust on the screen. The default setting shows the text as contiguous, with dotted lines indicating where the page breaks will be.

You can also show each page as a distinct page. Open the Preferences... dialog box from the File menu, and check the box shown below.

☐ **Display page borders in document windows**

For easier on-screen review of the text of your document, leave this box unchecked. If this feature is turned on, you will have to scroll the document from left to right to see all the text on a standard-sized Macintosh screen.

If you check this box, you must close and re-display the trust document to reflect any changes made.

Changing the Appearance of Your Trust Document

Nolo's Living Trust gives you a wide degree of control over the appearance of your trust document. To change the text font, the text size, line spacing or page margins, choose the Print Options... command in the File menu.

```
┌──────────────────────────────────────────────────┐
│                 PRINT  OPTIONS                     │
│  Page Margins:              Line spacing:          │
│                                                    │
│  Top  [1.25"]  Bottom [1.25"]   ○ Tight spacing    │
│                                 ◉ Standard spacing  │
│  Left [1.25"]  Right  [1.25"]   ○ Loose spacing    │
│                                                    │
│  Print font:  [ Courier      ▼]  ☒ Page number smaller │
│  Print size:  [10] [▼]                             │
│                               ( Cancel ) ( OK )    │
└──────────────────────────────────────────────────┘
```

The Print Options dialog box

Any changes you make in any of these settings will be immediately reflected in the display window.

Changing the text font and size

The Print Font pop-up menu lists all fonts available on your system.

The Print Size pop-up menu lists available sizes for the selected font.

Style Note   It is a good idea to keep your Declaration of Trust looking fairly plain. Most legal documents these days are printed in plain old Courier font. Strange or overly fancy fonts are not typical in modern legal documents, and therefore may raise unnecessary questions about the validity of your trust.

Changing the line spacing

The three radio buttons on the right half of the dialog box control the line spacing of the document. You have a choice of "Tight, Standard and Loose." This roughly translates to single space, space-and-a-half and double space.

Changing the page margins

The page margin settings can be set to any value as low as .5 inch. However, we suggest a right and left margin of 1.25 inches. This creates a standard, six-inch wide print area that can be easily viewed on any Macintosh screen.

2. Exporting the Text of Your Trust Document

Nolo's Living Trust allows you to export your final trust document to a plain text (ASCII) file, which you can then open in your word processor to add formatting if you wish.

 If you export the text of your Declaration of Trust, do not make any changes in the trust language. Even changes that seem insignificant could create confusion, contradictions and legal problems. To be safe, print out a copy directly from *Nolo's Living Trust* for reference. Then compare this copy to any copies you print from your word processor. If you aren't happy with the trust document, take it to an experienced estate planning attorney and get advice on how to accomplish your goals.

To export the text of the trust document to a plain text (ASCII) file, first display the trust document, following the instructions above. Then, while the trust text is displayed, choose Export Trust Text... from the File menu. A dialog box will appear for you to name the text file.

After the text file has been created, quit *Nolo's Living Trust* and start your word processing software. Consult the manual that came with your word processing software for instructions on how to open a plain text (sometimes called ASCII) file.

Consult the manual that came with your word processing software for instructions on how to format the document once the text file is open. Use a copy of the trust document printed out from *Nolo's Living Trust* for reference of how the final document should look.

Do not call Nolo Press Technical Support for instructions on how to use your word processing software. We are happy to answer questions on how to format your trust using *Nolo's Living Trust's* built-in formatting options. However, we are not equipped to offer tech support of other publisher's word-processing software. Call the tech support department of the word-processing software publisher if you need assistance running their software.

J. Changing Your Trust Before You've Signed It

If you haven't signed your trust document yet, you can simply tear it up, throw it away and print out a new one. Until you sign it, the document is just a piece of paper with no legal effect.

1. Changing an Unsigned Living Trust Document Created With Nolo's Living Trust

If the program is not currently running, you can double-click on the Trust Data file icon in the Finder. Your data will be loaded into the program.

If the program is already running, first, close any trust files that are currently open. Then choose Open from the File menu and select your trust data file from the list of files displayed.

If you previously have printed your trust, you will be taken to a screen that asks whether you have signed the document. Click No then click OK. This will return you to the Checklist screen.

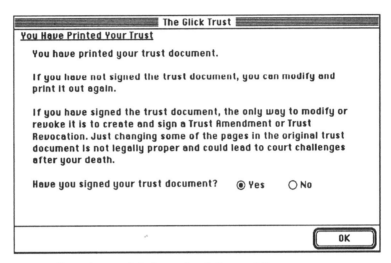

*If you have printed your trust, the next time you open
your trust file you will be asked if you have signed the document*

If you haven't printed your trust document, you will be taken to the Checklist screen, showing which parts of the trust document have been completed. You can click on the radio buttons to go back into any parts of the program and change your answers as you normally would.

When you're finished making your changes, you can display or print out the trust document.

2. Modifying an Unsigned Living Trust Document Made Some Other Way

If you created a revocable living trust document using some other software, or using Nolo's book *Plan Your Estate With a Living Trust*, but haven't signed it yet, you can simply tear up the document and start over using *Nolo's Living Trust*.

If you had the document drawn up by an attorney, do not tear it up or make any new living trust until you have consulted with the attorney who drew up the original document. If the attorney assures you that the document has not been signed and that no property has been transferred to the trust, you can then tear up the old document and start over, using *Nolo's Living Trust*.

K. Amending or Revoking Your Trust After You've Signed It

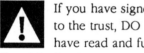 If you have signed a living trust document and transferred property to the trust, DO NOT print out a new trust document unless you have read and fully understood the discussion in the Legal Manual about the legal consequences of making a new trust.

In most cases, after you have signed your living trust document, any changes should be made by creating a separate document called a Trust Amendment.

1. Amendments

Chapter 9 of the Legal Manual has complete instructions regarding how and when you should amend your trust document. Refer to it for the correct wording of any amendments you must make, and for which parts of the document should and should not be amended.

This part of the manual tells you only the mechanics of making amendments and printing revised property schedules.

Using Nolo's Living Trust To Amend Your Trust Document

After you have printed your trust document, the next time you open that trust file the program will ask you whether or not you have signed the document.

If you answer Yes, you will come to a screen that lets you create and print out amendments and revised property schedules.

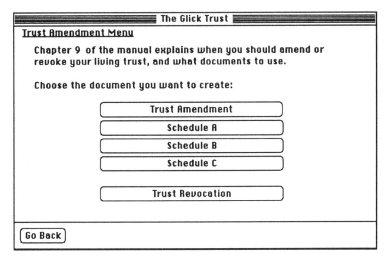

Trust Amendment/Revocation screen

Amending a Trust Document

Nolo's Living Trust includes several text file templates which you can use to create Trust Amendments, Revocations and revised Property Schedules.

Be sure to read Chapter 9 of the Legal Manual for a discussion of the legal effect of amending or revoking your living trust before using these templates.

To open an Amendment template, click on the Trust Amendment button. A dialog box will appear with a list of Trust Amendment templates.

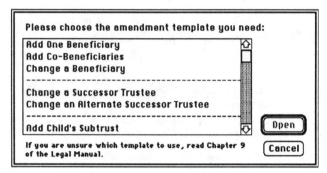

Trust amendment templates dialog box

Refer to Chapter 9 of the legal manual to determine which amendment template you need. Select the template from the list, and click Open.

Two windows will open. First, a copy of your original trust document will be assembled and displayed in a window. Then, on top of that window, another window will open displaying the amendment template you've chosen.

The amendment template window is fully editable: you can type in it and cut, copy or paste in it. The trust document window is a "Copy only" document: you can select text in it for copying, but you can't change its text.

Using amendment templates

Amendment templates have instructions written in them as part of the template. You will have to delete these instructions from the template before you print them.

Some templates offer a choice of clauses to use. Be sure to delete the clauses you are not using.

If you are using a template to change a provision of the original trust document, the template may instruct you to paste in language from the original trust document. To do this, follow these steps:

- Click on the trust document window to bring it to the front.

- Select the text you want to change.

- Choose Copy from the Edit menu.

- Click on the trust amendment template window to bring it to the front.

- Move the cursor to where you want to insert (paste) the copied text. (This is probably indicated in the template by the phrase "[PASTE PARAGRAPH YOU WANT TO DELETE FROM TRUST DOCUMENT]").

- Choose Paste from the Edit menu.

- Go to the part of the template where you are are adding the replacement language. Fill in any blanks, as instructed in the Legal Manual.

- Delete all instructional language—that is, all language in the square brackets—from the template.

Saving a Trust Amendment

After you have the amendment the way you want it, you can save two different ways:

1. As an NLT Amendment file (choose Save Amendment... from the File menu). Files saved in this manner retain all formatting and can be reopened later from within this program. However, these files cannot be opened in your word processor.

2. As a text file (choose Export Amendment Text... from the File menu). Files exported to a text file lose all formatting, cannot be opened in *Nolo's Living Trust*, but can be opened using your word processing software.

You can save your amendment in each format by choosing the above-mentioned commands while the amendment is displayed in the top window.

Reopening an Amendment You Created Earlier

You may want to reopen an amendment you created earlier, if you are amending trust text that has already been amended before. You can open the earlier amendment to copy language from it, and paste it into the new amendment as language you want to change.

If you created an amendment earlier and saved it as a *Nolo's Living Trust* amendment file, you can open it from the amendment screen.

Choose Open Amendment... from the File menu. This command is available only while you are at the amendment/revocation screen.

2. Revising Property Schedules

Read Chapter 9 of the Legal Manual for instructions on how and when to revise your property schedules. This part of the manual tells you only the mechanics of how to do it.

To delete property from a schedule:

- Click on the button that corresponds to the schedule you want to revise. A document window will open, showing the property schedule.

- Select the entire line you want to delete.

- Press the delete key on your keyboard or choose Cut from the Edit menu.

- While the schedule is still displayed, choose Print... from the File menu to print the revised schedule.

To add property to a schedule:

- Click on the button that corresponds to the schedule you want to revise. A document window will open, showing the property schedule.

- Click the mouse after the last character on the property schedule.

- Type a return if necessary to create a new line.

- Type the next number in the sequence, then enter the description of the property.

- While the schedule is still displayed, choose Print... from the File menu to print the revised schedule.

To move property from one schedule to another:

This requires changing two property schedules and printing out each one.

- Click on the button that corresponds to the schedule that currently lists the property. A document window will open, showing the property schedule.

- Select the entire line that contains the property description.

- Choose Cut from the Edit menu.

- While the schedule is still displayed, choose Print... from the File menu to print the revised schedule.

- Close the document window.

- Open the schedule to which the property is to be transferred.

- Click the mouse after the last character on the schedule.

- Type a return if necessary to make a new line.

- Choose Paste from the Edit menu. The property you cut from the other schedule should appear.

- Renumber the pasted items if necessary.

- While the schedule is still displayed, choose Print... from the File menu to print the revised schedule.

Saving Your Revised Schedules

Nolo's Living Trust prompts you to save any changes you make to the property schedules, and saves them as NLT amendment files. The next time you go to revise your property schedules, open the amended schedules (not the orignal ones) and your most recent changes will be intact.

3. Revoking the Trust

Consult Chapter 9 of the Legal Manual for instructions on when and how to revoke your trust. This part of the manual tells you how to create a revocation document.

- While at the amendment/revocation menu screen (see above) click on the button titled Revocation of Trust. A template for a trust revocation appears.

- Follow the instructions in Chapter 9 of the Legal Manual regarding what language to type into the template.

- While the revocation is still displayed, choose Print... from the File menu to print the revocation.

To save your revocation document, follow the instructions above for saving amendments.

L. Troubleshooting

This section of the manual will help you solve problems you may have getting *Nolo's Living Trust* to operate properly.

1. Table of NLT Error Messages

Use the table that is on the next several pages to diagnose your problem if you encounter an error message while running *Nolo's Living Trust*.

ERROR MESSAGE	WHAT IT MEANS	WHAT TO DO
The 'NLT Legal Help' file was not found; Legal Help will not be available this session.	The legal help file has either been renamed or has been dragged out of the NLT folder.	Find the file called NLT Legal Help and drag it back into the same folder as the NLT application. If the file has been renamed, change the name back to NLT Legal Help. If you can't find the file on your hard disk, recopy this file from your original master disk.
The 'NLT Program Help' file was not found; Program Help will not be available this session.	The program help file has either been renamed or has been dragged out of the NLT folder.	Find the file called NLT Program Help and drag it back into the same folder as the NLT application. If the file has been renamed, change the name back to NLT Program Help. If you can't find the file on your hard disk, recopy this file from your original master disk.
That disk is too full.	The program is trying to save information to a disk that does not have enough free space on it.	Save the trust file to a different disk with more free space. Choose the Save As... command from the File menu and then click the Drive button to switch to a different disk. Then click the Save button.
That disk seems to be damaged.	The program is trying to save information to a disk that appears to be defective.	Save the trust file to a different disk. Choose the Save As... command from the File menu and then click the Drive button to switch to a different disk. Then click the Save button.
That disk is write protected.	The program is trying to save information to a floppy disk that is locked—that is, the write protection tab on the floppy is in the open position.	Either unlock the disk, or save the trust file to different disk. To save the file to a different disk, choose the Save As... command from the File menu and then click the Eject button to eject the floppy disk. Then either insert a different floppy, or slide the write-protection tab on the floppy to the closed position and insert the disk again. Then click the Save button.

The file is locked or is on a locked disk. To use it, you must first unlock it.	The program is trying to open a file that is locked or is on a floppy disk that is locked—that is, the write protection tab on the floppy is in the open position.	Quit NLT. Then do one of the following: 1. If disk is unlocked, but the file is locked, you must unlock the file. Return to the Finder, click once on the file, then choose Get Info... from the File menu. A window will appear, with a check-box in the upper right corner that says "Locked." If there is an x in this box, click once on it to make the x go away. Then restart NLT and try again. 2. If the floppy is write-protected, eject the disk and slide the write-protection tab on the floppy to the closed (unlocked) position and insert the disk again, and retry what you were attempting.
There isn't enough memory to complete that operation.	Your computer is not giving NLT enough memory (RAM) to proceed further. NLT requires at least 512K of RAM.	Quit NLT, then do one of the following: 1. If you are running MultiFinder, find the NLT application on your disk, and click once on it. Then choose Get Info... from the File menu. At the bottom of the information window, where it says application memory size, type 512. 2. If you are not running MultiFinder, try disabling some of your INITs or dragging them out of your System folder, and then restart your computer.
The file wasn't found.	This should not occur under normal operations. It may be a problem with one of your INITs.	Quit NLT, and try restarting your computer. If that doesn't work, try disabling some of your INITs or dragging them out of your System folder, and then restart your computer.
Sorry. You are trying to open too many files at once.	To many files are open on your Macintosh; this could be caused by having too many INITs open. NLT will open approximately five files.	Quit NLT and your other applications. Try removing a few INITs, and restart your computer.

The disk wasn't found.	The disk or volume on which an operation was supposed to be performed has been ejected or taken off-line without the computer knowing it. This could happen if you turn off a hard disk, or eject a floppy while the program is running.	Insert any disk you may have removed while running NLT and try the operation again.
The printer wasn't found. Please use the Chooser to select a printer.	The LaserWrtiter or ImageWriter wasn't found by the application.	Use the Chooser (in the Apple Menu) to choose your printer.
The clipboard is too large to paste into this window.	There is too much text on the clipboard to paste in the document window.	Try copying and pasting a smaller amount of text. If this message persists and you are running under MultiFinder, try quitting NLT and increasing the application's memory size. (See the solution for the "not enough memory" message, above.)
Sorry. The contents of the clipboard can't be pasted here.	The amount of text in the clipboard is more than the field can hold. Most fields can hold only 255 characters.	Try copying and pasting a smaller amount of text.
Please choose a font size less than 127 points.	The Mac cannot deal with fonts larger than 126 points.	Choose a smaller font size.
Sorry. The file is severely damaged and cannot be opened.	A trust data file is severely damaged. It's toast. It's unusable.	There is no solution. The file is unusable. You'll have to make a new file, or use a backup copy.
Sorry. The file has been damaged and can't be opened.	The checksum for the file is off; this can be caused by a minor disk error, or an error in transferring data from disk to disk, or via modem.	Do not use this file if you can avoid it. Some data may well have been lost or scrambled. Use a backup copy. However, if you must access the file for some reason, hold down the option key as you open the file. The file will be opened regardless of the error, but you may well have problems with the file later.

A required resource was not found.	The application may have been damaged and is missing one of it's needed resources.	Try using a fresh copy of the program.
Sorry, an internal error has occurred.	We hope you never see this message… It means you've found a bug in our software.	You might try increasing the application memory size, to see if that clears up the problem. If that doesn't work, the bug is more severe and we will want to investigate it further. It would be helpful to us if you could send us a copy of your trust data file, your application, a complete description of your computer setup and a detailed note on what you were doing when the problem occurred. Please include your phone number so we can reach you if we have more questions.

2. Table of System "Bomb" Messages

The following errors may appear when your Macintosh "bombs." These errors are generated by your Macintosh system software, not by NLT. Generally they are caused by a problem with your Macintosh or a defective floppy or hard disk.

SYSEM BOMB	WHAT IT MEANS	WHAT TO DO
2	Address error	Reboot your computer and try again. If the problem is still there, disable any INITs or reboot from another system and try again.
25	Out of memory	If your computer has the required amount of RAM (1 meg), turn off all of your 'NITs and try again.
15 or 26	Segment loader error.	Probably caused by a defective disk. Recopy the NLT application from your master disk onto you working copy. If the problem persists, your master disk may be defective. Contact Nolo Press for a replacement disk.
28	Stack has moved into application heap	Reboot the computer and try again. If the problem persists, reinstall the system from a locked system disk. If running MultiFinder, try making the application memory size larger.
Freeze	If your machine froze but is working properly with other software, the problem is most likely the NLT disk.	Try running from a new backup or a new original. Also try rebooting without any INITs.

3. If a Virus Is Detected on Your Original NLT Disk

All disks shipped by Nolo Press are checked for viruses before they are duplicated. If your virus detection software detects a virus on your original NLT disk, it may be an an anomaly in your virus detection software. Contact the company that made your virus detection software to see if they are aware of any such problem. If they are not, contact Nolo Press Technical Support and we will investigate the problem further.

4. If the Original NLT Disk Is "Unreadable"

When you insert the original NLT disk, if you receive a message that the disk is "unreadable" you will be asked whether you want to format it. Answer No. Eject the disk and try reinserting it.

If you get the same message again, you may have received a defective disk. Eject the disk, and return it to Nolo Press for a free replacement. Complete instructions for receiving replacement disks are in the introduction to this manual.

If you get this message when you insert your working copy of the program, use a backup copy, or make a new copy of the master disk to use as your working copy.

5. Opening a Damaged Data File

As noted in the NLT Error Message table above, if you receive a message that your trust data file has been damaged, you may be able to open it by holding down the option key as you open the file from within the program. You will be asked whether you want to "check" the file. If you say yes, the file is checked for any damage. If any damage is found, minor repairs are performed, which may result in the loss of some data. You should check all of your data carefully before using this file further.

6. Getting Rid of Unused Names in the Names List Dialog

Every time you type a new name into *Nolo's Living Trust,* it is added to the file's names list. It remains in the list whether or not you later delete the name within the program.

Occasionally, you may want to purge the names list of all names that are not used anywhere in the trust document. You can do this by holding down the option key as you open the file from within the program. As noted above, holding down the option key also causes the program to check the file for any damage. If any damage is found you may lose some data as the problem is corrected.

LEGAL

MANUAL

1 Before You Begin

Nolo's Living Trust is a straightforward, easy-to-use piece of software. You will go through the program step by step, answering a series of questions about your property and who you want to inherit it. Your answers will be incorporated into a Declaration of Trust. When signed and notarized, this trust document creates your living trust.

Along the way, the program offers on-screen legal help. A list of Legal Help topics will appear before you're asked to enter each new kind of information. You can look at as many of the help topics as you wish, or skip them altogether.

You'll have an easier time of it, however, if you don't rely solely on the on-screen legal help. We suggest that you take time now to use this manual, to get familiar with living trusts and think about how you want to use yours.

Keep in mind that creating a living trust has important, long-term consequences for your family and their finances. It's worth doing right, which means educating yourself about your options so you can make well-informed decisions.

Before you begin, you should read at least two chapters in this manual:

- Chapter 2, *About Living Trusts* and

- *What Kind of Living Trust Do You Need?* (Chapter 4).

Here are the key decisions to think about before you ever sit down at the computer:

- what kind of living trust (individual or shared) to make;

- what property you want to put in trust;

- who you want to receive it after your death;

- who you want to distribute the property after your death; and

- what you want to do about property inherited by young beneficiaries.

If you're really prepared, you can probably breeze through the program and be ready to print your trust document in less than an hour. (You don't have to finish the program all at one sitting; you can quit and save whatever you've done.) As you use the program, consult either Chapter 5, *Creating an Individual Trust*, or Chapter 6, *Creating a Shared Marital Trust*. Each follows the program step by step.

CHECKLIST FOR CREATING A VALID LIVING TRUST

√   Prepare the trust document with *Nolo's Living Trust*.

√   Print out the trust document and sign it in front of a notary public.

√   Transfer ownership of the property listed in the trust document into the name of the trust.

√   Update your trust document when needed.

---

2 About Living Trusts

A revocable living trust lets your family inherit your property without going through the probate court process, which is notoriously slow, expensive and, for most people, unnecessary.

In the probate process, a deceased person's will is proved valid in court, the person's debts are paid and the remaining property is distributed to its inheritors. In most instances, where there is no dispute about the validity of a will, no fears of huge creditors' lawsuits and no fights among relatives, formal probate court proceedings are a waste of time and money.

If you set up a living trust while you are alive, the people who inherit your property don't have to bother with a probate court proceeding. And that means they won't have to spend any of your hard-earned money to pay for court and lawyer fees.

A. What Is a Trust?

A trust can seem like a mysterious creature, dreamed up by lawyers, wrapped in legal jargon and used for mysterious purposes. But in practice, a trust isn't complicated. Here are the basics.

1. The Concept of a Trust

A trust, like a corporation, is an entity that exists only on paper but is legally capable of owning property. You can create a trust simply by preparing and signing a document called a Declaration of Trust.

Once the trust has been created, you can transfer property to it. The trust becomes the legal owner. There must, however, be a flesh-and-blood person actually in charge of the property; that person is called the trustee. The trustee manages the property on the behalf of someone else, called the beneficiary.

Those, then, are the essential elements of every trust: the trust, the property, the trustee and the beneficiary.

There are many kinds of trusts. Some are designed to save on taxes, others to manage property. The kind of trust you create with *Nolo's Living Trust* is a "probate-avoidance revocable living trust."

2. Probate-Avoiding Revocable Living Trusts

A revocable living trust is primarily designed to reduce or eliminate the need for probate court proceedings.

First, an explanation of the name. It's called "revocable" because you can revoke it at any time. And it's called a "living" trust because it's created when you're alive, not at your death like some other kinds of trusts. (Sometimes living trusts are known by their Latin name: "inter vivos" (among the living) trusts.)

When you create a revocable living trust, you transfer ownership of some or all of your property to the living trust. You also appoint yourself trustee of your living trust, with full power to manage trust property. So you keep absolute control over the property in your living trust, even though technically it's owned by the living trust.

EXAMPLE Ashley, an unmarried woman, creates a revocable living trust and transfers her valuable property—a house and some stocks—into the trust's name. She names herself as trustee of the trust. As trustee, she can sell, mortgage or give away the trust property, or take it out of the trust and put it back into her name.

After you die, the person you named in your trust document to be "successor trustee" takes over. He or she is in charge of transferring the trust property to the family, friends or charities you named as the trust beneficiaries. No probate is necessary for property that was transferred to the living trust. In most cases, the whole thing can be handled within a few weeks. When the property has all been transferred to the beneficiaries, the living trust ceases to exist.

Because a probate-avoidance living trust lets your property go, after your death, to the relatives, friends or charities you choose, it performs the same function as a will. The crucial difference is that property left through a will must go through probate, while property in a living trust can go directly to your inheritors.

 "Back-up" wills . Every living trust should be backed up by a will, to handle property not transferred to the living trust and for several other reasons. See Chapter 3, *A Living Trust as Part of Your Estate Plan.*

A MINI-GLOSSARY OF LIVING TRUST TERMS

Unfortunately, you can't escape legal lingo entirely when you deal with living trusts. Keeping it to a minimum, here's what you need to know:

The person who sets up the living trust (that's you, or you and your spouse) is called a **grantor, trustor** or **settlor**. (These terms mean the same thing and are used interchangeably.)

The property you transfer to the trust is called, collectively, the **trust property, trust principal** or **trust estate**. (And, of course, there's a Latin version: the trust *corpus*.)

The person who has complete power over the trust property is called the **trustee**. The person who sets up the trust (the grantor) is the original trustee of a living trust, thus keeping total control over property in the trust. If a married couple creates one shared marital trust, both are trustees.

The person the grantor names to take over as trustee after the grantor's death (or, with a shared marital trust, after the death of both spouses) is called the **successor trustee**. The successor trustee's job is to transfer the trust property to the beneficiaries, following the instructions in the Declaration of Trust. The successor trustee may also manage trust property inherited by young beneficiaries (that's explained in Section B, below). Often, the successor trustee is a grown child of the grantor or another trusted relative or friend who inherits a large share of the trust property.

The people or organizations who get the trust property when the grantor dies are called the **beneficiaries** of the trust. (While the grantors are alive, they are technically the only beneficiaries of the trust.)

B. Important Features of a Living Trust

The main reason for setting up a revocable living trust is to save your family time and money by avoiding probate. But there are other advantages as well. Here is a brief rundown of the major features of a living trust.

1. Property in a Living Trust Doesn't Go Through Probate

As mentioned, property left by a will must go through probate before it can be transferred to the beneficiaries. And if you don't make a will or some other arrangement to designate who gets your property (living trust or joint tenancy, for example), the property also goes through probate. It is distributed to close relatives according to state "intestate succession" law.

During the probate process, a court oversees the distribution of a deceased person's property. The cost of probate varies widely from state to state, but probate attorney, court and other fees often eat up about 5% (or more) of your estate (the property you leave at death), leaving that much less to go to the people or charities you want to get it. If the estate is complicated, the fees can be even larger. Lawyer fees, set by statute or local custom, often bear no relation to the actual work done by the attorney.

Value of property in estate	Approximate cost of probate
$200,000	$10,000
$400,000	$20,000

At least as bad as the expense of probate is the delay it causes. Often, probate takes a year or two, during which time the beneficiaries generally get nothing unless the judge allows the decedent's immediate family a "family allowance." In some states, this allowance is a pittance—only a few hundred dollars. In others, it can amount to thousands.

From the family's point of view, probate's headaches are rarely justified. If the estate contains standard kinds of property—a house, stocks, bank accounts, a small business, cars—and no relatives are fighting about it, the property merely needs to be handed over to the new owners. In the vast majority of cases, the probate process entails nothing more than tedious paperwork, and the attorney is nothing more than a very highly paid clerk.

Even England—the source of our antiquated probate laws—abolished its elaborate probate system years ago. It survives in this country because it is so lucrative for lawyers; they can charge a hefty fee for what is, for the most part, just routine paperwork.

Given the needless drawbacks of probate, it's not surprising that people have sought ways around it. The living trust, which functions like a will but avoids the probate process, is the most popular.

2. Out-of-State Real Estate Doesn't Have To Be Probated in That State

The only thing worse than regular probate is out-of-state probate. Usually, an estate is probated in the probate court of the county where the decedent was living before he or she died. But if the decedent owned real estate in more than one state, it's usually necessary to have a whole separate probate proceeding in each. That means the surviving relatives must probably find and hire a lawyer in each state, and pay for multiple probate proceedings.

With a living trust, out-of-state property can be transferred to the beneficiaries without probate in that state.

3. You Can Avoid the Need for a Conservatorship

A living trust can be useful if the person who created it (the grantor) becomes incapable, because of physical or mental illness, of taking care of his or her financial affairs. The person named in the living trust document—a relative, friend or anyone else—to take over as trustee at the grantor's death can also take over management of the trust if the grantor becomes incapacitated, as certified in writing by a physician. When a couple sets up a trust, if one person becomes incapacitated, the other takes sole responsibility. The person who takes over has authority to manage all property in the trust, and to use it for the grantor.

EXAMPLE Margaret creates a living trust, appointing herself as trustee. The trust states that if she becomes incapacitated, and a physician signs a statement saying she no longer can manage her own affairs, her daughter Elizabeth will replace her as trustee.

If there is no living trust and no other arrangements have been made for someone to take over property management if you become incapacitated, someone else must get legal authority, from a court, to take over. Typically, the spouse or adult child of the person seeks this authority and is called a conservator or guardian.

You should also give your successor trustee (or spouse) the authority to manage property that has not been transferred the trust if you become incapacitated. The best way to do that is to prepare and sign a document called a Durable Power of Attorney for Financial Management.

In addition, if you are concerned about dying a natural death without the unauthorized use of life support systems, you'll want to prepare and sign some other documents. Planning for incapacity is discussed in more detail in Chapter 3, *A Living Trust as Part of Your Estate Plan.*

4. Your Estate Plan Remains Confidential

When your will is filed with the probate court after you die, it becomes a matter of public record. A living trust, on the other hand, is a private document in most states. Because the living trust document is never filed with a court or other government entity, what you leave to whom remains private.[1]

Some states require that you register your living trust with the local court. But there are no legal consequences or penalties if you don't. (Registration is explained in Chapter 7, *Signing, Storing and Registering Your Trust Document.*)

The only way the terms of a living trust might become public is if—and this is unlikely—someone files a lawsuit to challenge the trust or collect a court judgment owed by the grantor. (See Section D, below.)

5. You Can Change Your Mind at Any Time

You have complete control over your revocable living trust and all the property you transfer to it. You can:

- sell, mortgage or give away property in the trust
- put ownership of trust property back in your own name
- add property to the trust
- change the beneficiaries

---

[1]There is one exception: Records of real estate transfers are always public.

- name a different successor trustee (the person who distributes trust property after your death)
- revoke the trust completely

If you and your spouse create the trust together, both spouses must consent to changes, although either of you can revoke the trust entirely. (See Chapter 9, *Living With Your Living Trust*.)

6. You Can Name Someone To Manage Trust Property for Young Beneficiaries

If there's a possibility that any of your beneficiaries will inherit trust property while still young (not yet 35), you may want to arrange to have someone manage that property for them until they're older. If they might inherit before they're legally adults (18, in most states), you should definitely arrange for management. Minors are not allowed to control significant amounts of property, and if you haven't provided someone to do it, a court will have to appoint a property guardian.

When you create a living trust with *Nolo's Living Trust*, you can arrange for someone to manage property for a young beneficiary. In most states, you have two options:

- Have your successor trustee (or your spouse, if you created a shared marital trust) manage the property in a "child's subtrust" until the child reaches an age you designate.

- Appoint someone as a "custodian" to manage the property until the child reaches an age specified by your state's Uniform Transfers to Minors Act (21 in most states, but up to 25 in California and Alaska).

Both methods are explained in Chapters 5 and 6.

C. Drawbacks of a Living Trust

A living trust does have unique problems and complications. The drawbacks aren't significant to most people, but you should be aware of them before you create a living trust.

1. Recordkeeping and Paperwork

Setting up a living trust isn't difficult or expensive, but it requires some paperwork. The first step is to use *Nolo's Living Trust* to create and print out a trust document, which you should sign in front of a notary public. So far, the amount of work required is no more than writing a will.

There is, however, one more essential step to making a living trust effective. You must make sure that ownership of all the property you listed in the trust document is legally transferred to the living trust.

If an item of property doesn't have a title (ownership) document, listing it in the trust document is enough to transfer it. So, for example, no additional paperwork is required for most books, furniture, electronics, jewelry, appliances, musical instruments and many other kinds of property.

But if an item has a title document—real estate, stocks, mutual funds, bonds, money market accounts or vehicles, for example—you must change the title document to show that the property is owned by your living trust. For example, if you want to put your house into your living trust, you must prepare and sign a new deed, transferring ownership from you to your living trust.

After a revocable living trust is created, little day-to-day recordkeeping is required. No separate income tax records or returns are necessary as long as you are both the grantor and the trustee.[2] Income from property in the living trust should be reported on your personal income tax return.

You must keep written records whenever you transfer property to or from the trust, which isn't difficult unless you transfer a lot of property in and out of the trust. (Chapter 9, *Living With Your Living Trust*, discusses transferring property in and out of your living trust.)

EXAMPLE Monica and David Fielding put their house in a living trust to avoid probate, but later decide to sell it. In the real estate contract and deed transferring ownership to the new owners, Monica and David sign their names "as trustees of the Monica and David Fielding Revocable Living Trust."

---

[2]IRS Reg. § 1.671-4.

2. Transfer Taxes

In most states, transfers of real estate to revocable living trusts are exempt from transfer taxes usually imposed on real estate transfers. But in a few states, transferring real estate to your living trust could trigger a tax. (See Chapter 8, *Transferring Property to the Trust.*)

3. Difficulty Refinancing Trust Property

Because legal title to trust real estate is held in the name of the trust—not your name—a few banks and title companies may balk if you want to refinance it. They should be sufficiently reassured if you show them a copy of your trust document, which specifically gives you, as trustee, the power to borrow against trust property.

In the unlikely event you can't convince an uncooperative lender to deal with you in your capacity as trustee, you'll have to find another lender (which shouldn't be hard) or transfer the property out of the trust and back into your name. Later, after your refinance, you can transfer it back into the living trust.

4. No Cutoff of Creditors' Claims

Most people don't worry that after their death, creditors will try to collect large debts from property in the estate. In most situations, the surviving relatives simply pay the valid debts, such as outstanding bills, taxes and last illness and funeral expenses. But if you are concerned about the possibility of large claims, you may want to let your property go through probate instead of a living trust.

If your property goes through probate, creditors have only a set amount of time to file claims against your estate. A creditor who was properly notified of the probate court proceeding cannot file a claim after the period—about six months, in most states—expires.

On the other hand, when property isn't probated, creditors still have the right to be paid (if the debt is valid) from the property. There is no formal claim procedure, however. The creditor may not know who inherited the deceased debtor's property, and once the property is found, the creditor may have to file a lawsuit, which may not be worth the time and expense.

EXAMPLE Elaine is a real estate investor with a good-sized portfolio of property. She has many creditors and is sometimes named in lawsuits. It might be to her advantage to have assets transferred by a probate court procedure, which cuts off the claims of creditors who are properly notified of the probate proceeding.

 If you want to take advantage of probate's creditor cutoff, you must let *all* your property pass through probate. If not, there's a good chance the creditor could still sue (even after the probate claim cutoff) and try to collect from the property that didn't go through probate and passed instead through your living trust.

D. When Living Trusts Can Fail

Living trusts usually work easily and smoothly to transfer property at death.

Court challenges to living trusts, like challenges to wills, are rare. When living trusts fail, it is usually because the property listed in the trust document was not actually transferred to the trust. If property that has a title document (such as real estate, stocks or vehicles) isn't owned in the trust's name, the terms of the Declaration of Trust have no effect on it. At the owner's death, it passes under the terms of his or her will or, if there is no will, under the state "intestate succession" law. (How to transfer property to a living trust is explained in Chapter 8, *Transferring Property to the Trust.*)

This section discusses, briefly, the kinds of legal challenges that can be made to living trusts. You don't need to concern yourself with them unless you think a close relative might have an axe to grind after your death.

1. Challenges to the Validity of the Trust

Someone who wanted to challenge the validity of a living trust would have to bring a lawsuit and prove that:

- when the grantor made the trust, he or she was mentally incompetent or unduly influenced by someone; or

- the trust document itself is flawed—for example, because the signature was forged.

It's generally considered more difficult to successfully challenge a living trust than a will. That's because your continuing involvement with a living trust after its creation (transferring property in and out of the trust, or making amendments) shows that you were competent to manage your affairs.

2. Lawsuits From Spouses

Most married people leave much, if not all, of their property to their spouses. But if you don't plan to leave your spouse at least half of your property, your spouse may have the right to go to court and claim some of your property after your death. Such a challenge wouldn't wipe out your whole living trust, but might take some of the property you had earmarked for other beneficiaries and give it to your spouse.

The rights of spouses vary from state to state. The most important differences are between community property states and non-community property states.

 Wherever you live, if you don't plan to leave at least half of the property in your estate to your spouse, you should consult a lawyer experienced in estate planning.

a. Community property states

Arizona	Louisiana	Texas
California	Nevada	Washington
Idaho	New Mexico	Wisconsin

In these states, the general rule is that spouses together own all property that either acquires during the marriage, except property one spouse acquires by gift or inheritance. Each spouse owns a half-interest in this "community property."

You are free to leave your separate property and your half of the community property to anyone you choose at death. Your spouse—who already owns half of all the community property—has no right to inherit any of it. But if you don't want to leave anything to your spouse, you should make a will and include in it a specific statement to that effect. If you don't, in certain situations your spouse may be able to claim at least some—possibly all—of your half of the community property after your death.

b. Non-community property states

Alabama	Kentucky	North Dakota
Alaska	Maine	Ohio
Arkansas	Maryland	Oklahoma
Colorado	Massachusetts	Oregon
Connecticut	Michigan	Pennsylvania
Delaware	Minnesota	Rhode Island
District of Columbia	Mississippi	South Carolina
Florida	Missouri	South Dakota
Georgia	Montana	Tennessee
Hawaii	Nebraska	Utah
Illinois	New Hampshire	Vermont
Indiana	New Jersey	Virginia
Iowa	New York	West Virginia
Kansas	North Carolina	Wyoming

In these states, you cannot disinherit your spouse. A surviving spouse who doesn't receive one-third to one-half of the deceased spouse's property (through a will, living trust or other method) is entitled to insist upon that much. The exact share depends on state law. In short, a spouse who doesn't receive the minimum he or she is entitled to under state law (the "statutory share") may be entitled to some of the property in your living trust.

Even property given away *before* death may legally belong to the surviving spouse under these laws. For example, take the case of a man who set up joint bank accounts with his children from a previous marriage. After his death, his widow sued to recover her interest in the accounts. She won; the

Kentucky Supreme Court ruled that under Kentucky's "dower" law, a spouse is entitled to a half-interest in the other spouse's personal property (everything but real estate). Her husband had not had the legal right to give away her interest in the money in the accounts.[3]

State law may also give your spouse the right to inherit the family residence, or at least use it for his or her life. The Florida constitution, for example, gives a surviving spouse the deceased spouse's residence.[4]

 Plan Your Estate with a Living Trust, by Denis Clifford (Nolo Press) contains a state-by-state list of surviving spouses' rights.

3. Lawsuits by a Child

Children usually have no right to inherit anything from their parents. There are two exceptions: laws that give minor children certain rights and laws that are designed to protect children who are unintentionally overlooked in a will.

a. Minor Children

State law may give your minor children (less than 18 years old) the right to inherit the family residence. The Florida constitution, for example, prohibits the head of a family from leaving his residence in his will (except to his spouse) if he is survived by a spouse or minor child.[5]

---

[3] *Harris v. Rock,* 799 S.W.2d 10 (Ky. 1990). Most non-community property states have similar dower or "curtesy" laws.

[4] Fla. Const. Art. 10, § 4.

[5] Fla. Const. Art. 10, § 4.

b. Overlooked Children

State laws protect offspring who appear to have been unintentionally over-looked in a parent's will (the legal term is a "pretermitted heir"). Although these laws mention only wills, not living trusts, it's possible that a court could apply them to a living trust, reasoning that the living trust is serving the function of a will. And as living trusts become more widespread, state legislatures may expand their laws to include children not mentioned in living trusts.

Typically, these laws protect a child who is born after the parent's will is signed, and who of course is not mentioned in a parent's will. The law presumes that the parent didn't mean to cut that child out, but simply hadn't yet gotten around to writing a new will. The child will be entitled to a share (the size is determined by state law) of the deceased parent's estate, which may include property in a living trust.

It's also possible that a disinherited—and angry—child could challenge a will, even though he or she was alive when the will was signed.

If you don't want to leave any property to one or more of your children—perhaps they already have plenty of money, or you've already given them their inheritances—the easy way to avoid any later misunderstandings, hurt feelings or legal claims is to make a will and mention each child in it. You can simply mention the child, leave a token amount ($1 is common) or include a brief explanation of why you're not leaving him or her any property. (See Chapter 3, *A Living Trust as Part of Your Estate Plan*.)

Overlooked grandchildren.   Children have no right to inherit from their grand-parents unless their parent has died. In that case, the grandchildren essentially take the place of the deceased child and are entitled to whatever he or she would have been legally entitled to.

E. Creditors

A living trust does not provide any protection from creditors, at least while you're alive. Technically, the trust owns the trust property. But because you keep the power to transfer the property back to yourself or revoke the trust entirely, the law doesn't allow you to shield trust property from creditors. So if a creditor sues you and wins, and a court issues a judgment against you, the creditor can seize trust property to pay off the judgment.

As a practical matter, a living trust can, however, provide some protection after your death. When property in your living trust is distributed to the trust beneficiaries after your death, creditors are not notified. They may never find out where the property went, and it may not be worth their while to file lawsuits to try to collect from the property. When property goes through probate, on the other hand, creditors must receive written notice of the court proceeding, which gives them a chance to file claims.

F. Estate Taxes

Nolo's Living Trust cannot help you reduce federal or state estate taxes. Neither can other probate-avoidance techniques such as joint tenancy or pay-on-death bank accounts. The taxing authorities don't care whether or not your property goes through probate; all they care about is what you owned at your death. Property you hold in joint tenancy or leave in a revocable living trust is still considered part of your estate for federal estate tax purposes.

Another kind of living trust, the "marital life estate trust" or "A-B trust," however, is designed to save on estate taxes. *Nolo's Living Trust* does not create this kind of trust.

If your estate is worth more than $600,000 when you die, it will be subject to federal estate tax unless the property is left to a spouse or charity. (For information on marital life estate trusts and other ways to reduce federal estate taxes, see Chapter 3, *A Living Trust as Part of Your Estate Plan.*)

3 A Living Trust as Part of Your Estate Plan

A revocable living trust can accomplish most people's main estate planning goal: leaving their property to their loved ones while avoiding probate. But it is not, by itself, a complete estate plan. For example, a living trust such as the one produced by *Nolo's Living Trust* doesn't afford any estate tax savings. And parents of young children can't use a living trust to appoint a personal guardian to care for their minor children.

This chapter outlines estate planning methods that you may want to explore in addition to the living trust. If you want more information, consult one of the books or software packages listed below, or see a lawyer who has experience in estate planning.

Basically, estate planning includes:

- Deciding who will get your property when you die

- Deciding who will take care of your children and their finances if you die while they are young

- Setting up procedures and devices to minimize probate fees at your death

- If your estate is large, planning to reduce estate taxes

- Arranging for someone to make financial and health care decisions for you if at some time you can no longer do so yourself

NOLO PRESS ESTATE PLANNING RESOURCES

Nolo Press publishes several books and software packages that give detailed estate planning information and hands-on help. We think they are the best available. All of them are good in every state but Louisiana.

Plan Your Estate with a Living Trust, by Denis Clifford.

This book covers all the estate planning methods briefly discussed in this chapter, and more. Even allowing for a bit of bias on our behalf, it is by far the best book on estate planning for people whose estates are worth up to $1 million.

WillMaker, by Nolo Press.

This software for Macintosh and IBM (and compatible) computers can create a legally valid back-up will to complement your living trust. *WillMaker* allows you to name personal guardians for your minor children and direct your executor to use certain of your property to pay your last debts and taxes, things you can't do with *Nolo's Living Trust.*

Nolo's Simple Will Book, by Denis Clifford.

If you don't want to use a computer to prepare your will, this book includes all the instructions and forms you need to do it on paper.

Elder Care: A Consumer's Guide to Choosing & Financing Long-Term Care, by Joseph Matthews.

This book is a compendium of alternatives for evaluating and paying for long-term health care. It will help everyone involved—the older person in need of care, as well as the spouse, family and friends—deal with difficult decisions. It's especially valuable for older couples who want to be able to care for one spouse without bankrupting the other.

Who Will Handle Your Finances If You Can't, by Denis Clifford and Mary Randolph.

With this book you can arrange for someone to manage, if you become incapacitated, any property that you have not transferred to your living trust. (Remember that if your successor trustee takes over for you because you are incapacitated, he or she has authority over property only if it is owned by your living trust.)
The key is a document called a "Durable Power of Attorney for Finances."

Nolo's Personal Recordkeeper, by Carol Pladsen and Ralph Warner.

This software (Macintosh and IBM) lets you make a thorough record of what you own and what estate planning steps you've taken. It's organized into 27 categories, including real estate, pensions, bank accounts and emergency in-formation. It will be invaluable to the people who will be in charge of winding up your affairs after your death.

A. What a Revocable Living Trust Can't Do

The revocable living trust you create with *Nolo's Living Trust* is designed to avoid probate.

- This trust is *not* designed to save on federal estate taxes. It is not an "A-B" or "spousal life estate" trust, designed to make the most of each spouse's $600,000 estate tax exemption. (This sort of trust is useful pri-marily for elderly couples who own more than $600,000 worth of prop-erty; see Section D, below.)

- This trust is *not* designed to let you express your wishes about dying a natural death free of life-prolonging medical technology—for that, you need a "living will" or a Durable Power of Attorney. (See Section F, below.)

To accomplish other estate planning goals, including saving on estate taxes or making sure your doctors know your wishes about medical treatment, you'll need other documents and other techniques.

B. Using a Back-Up Will

Even though you create a living trust, you will almost certainly need a simple back-up will, too. Like a living trust, a will is a document in which you specify what is to be done with your property when you die.

1. Why Make a Back-Up Will

Having a will is important for several reasons.

First, a will is an essential back-up device for property that you don't get around to transferring to your living trust. For example, if you acquire property shortly before you die, you may not think to transfer ownership of it to your trust—which means that it won't pass under the terms of the trust document. But in your back-up will, you can include a clause that says who should get any property that you don't specifically transfer to your living trust or leave to someone in some other way.

If you don't have a will, any property that isn't transferred by your living trust or other probate-avoidance device (such as joint tenancy) will go to your closest relatives, in an order determined by state law. These laws are called "intestate succession laws," and they may not distribute property in the way you would have chosen. For example, if you die leaving a spouse and children, all the property that isn't subject to a living trust or will may be divided among your spouse and children. If your children are minors, that means there must be a court proceeding to get a guardian appointed to manage the property for them.

How a Back-Up Will Works

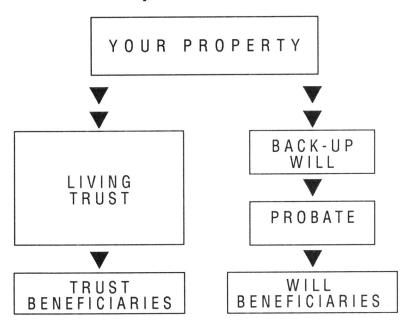

Second, in a will you can name someone to be the personal guardian of your minor child, in case you and the child's other parent die while the child is still under 18. You can't do that in a living trust.

Finally, if you want to disinherit your spouse or a child, you must make your wishes clear in a will. (State law may restrict your freedom to disinherit a spouse or minor child; see Chapter 5 or 6.)

HOW TO MAKE A BACK-UP WILL

Making a will is a fairly simple process. *Plan Your Estate With a Living Trust, Nolo's Simple Will Book* and *WillMaker* each contain complete instructions.

Unless your needs are unusually complicated, you probably don't need a lawyer. You must, however, be sure that you follow the will-making formalities required by law.

HOW TO USE *WILLMAKER* TO MAKE A BACK-UP WILL

If you have already made a will with *WillMaker*:

- Review your previous entries about name, state, county, marital status and children.

- Review your specific bequest entries and eliminate any that involve property being transferred to your living trust.

- Review your choice for residuary beneficiary to make sure this is the person you want to get all property not transferred to the living trust or left to a specific beneficiary.

- If you have minor children, review your choice for a personal guardian.

- If any beneficiary is a minor, review your previous choice for management. If the minor is also a beneficiary under your living trust, select the UTMA option if it is available in your state. If it isn't, use the children's trust option. If you use the UTMA option both in your living trust and in your back-up will, make your choices consistent.

- Review your choices for payment of debts and taxes. If most of your property has been placed in the living trust, it's probably best to use the "state law" option. If you identify assets to be sold, select non-trust assets.

- Review your choice for personal representative. If possible, choose the same person as your successor trustee, or your spouse if you're making a shared living trust.

- Carefully follow the instructions in the *WillMaker* manual for making your will valid in your state.

If you have never used *WillMaker*:

After providing some introductory information, *WillMaker* uses a question-and-answer format. On-screen help specific to each screen is available throughout the program.

To make a back-up will, focus on a few parts of the program. Your main job is to make sure that the terms of your will are consistent with your living trust. After the introductory material (name, state, marital status, children), focus on:

- your residuary beneficiary

- your choice for personal guardian of your minor children (if any)

- property management for minor children (if any). If you provide management for these same children in your living trust, use the UTMA option if it's available for your state. If you haven't, use either the UTMA or children's trust option (on-screen help is available)

- your personal representative. If possible, choose the same person as your successor trustee or your spouse, if you're making a shared living trust.

You may bypass the specific bequest part of the program as well as selecting who will pay your debts and taxes.

Carefully follow the instructions in the manual for making your will valid.

---

2. Avoiding Conflicts Between Your Will and Living Trust

When you make both a living trust and a back-up will, pay attention to how the two work together. If your will and your trust document contain conflicting provisions, at the least you will create confusion among your inheritors, and at the worst, bitter disputes—maybe even a lawsuit—among friends and family.

Here are some no-no's:

- Don't leave the same property in your living trust and will, even if it's to the same beneficiary. If you transfer the property to your living trust and name a beneficiary in the trust document, that's all you need to do. Mentioning the property in the will raises the possibility of probate.

- Don't leave the same property to different beneficiaries in your will and your living trust.

- Don't name different people to be executor of your will and successor trustee of your living trust, especially if you think they might quarrel about how your affairs should be handled. There's one important exception: If you make a shared marital trust, you may name your spouse as executor of your will, but not as successor trustee—the successor trustee takes over only after both spouses have died. (See Chapter 5 or 6, Part 3.)

3. Pour-Over Wills

Some lawyers urge people who make living trusts to make "pour-over wills" as well. A pour-over will takes all the property you haven't gotten around to transferring to your living trust and, at your death, leaves it to the trust.

Pour-over wills (named because everything is "poured over" from the will to your living trust) do *not* avoid probate. All property that is left through a will—any kind of will—must go through probate. It makes no difference that the beneficiary of the will is a living trust. If the value of the property left through a pour-over will is small, some states exempt it from probate or offer streamlined probate procedures. But the same is true whether or not the will is a pour-over one.

How a Pour-Over Will Works

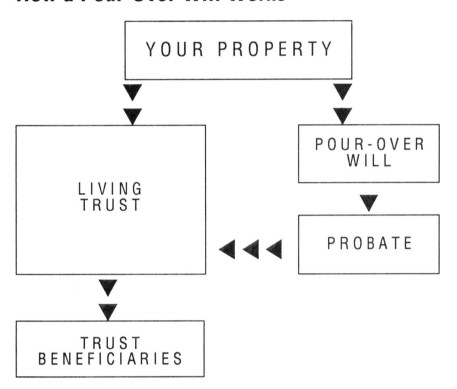

Pour-over wills are not usually a good idea. It's better to simply use a standard back-up will to take care of this property. In the back-up will, you can name the people you want to get the property, and skip the unnecessary extra step of pouring the property through the living trust after your death.

When used as a back-up will, a pour-over will actually has a disadvantage that standard wills don't: It forces the living trust to go on for months after your death, because the property left through the will must go through probate before it can be transferred to the trust. Usually, the property left in a living trust can be distributed to the beneficiaries, and the trust ended, within a few weeks after the person's death.

EXAMPLE Joy transfers her valuable property to her living trust. She also makes a pour-over will, which states that any property she owns at death not specifically left to someone in the will goes to the living trust. When Joy dies, the property left through her will goes to the trust and is distributed to the residuary beneficiary of her living trust, her son Louis. The living trust must be kept going until probate of the will is finished, when property left by the will is poured over into the living trust.

If Joy had simply named Louis as the residuary beneficiary of a plain back-up will, the result would have been the same, but the process would have been simpler. The living trust would have been ended a few weeks after Joy's death. And after probate was finished, Louis would have received whatever property passed through Joy's will.

There is, however, one situation in which you might want to use a pour-over will. If you set up a child's subtrust for a young beneficiary in your living trust, you may want any property that child inherits through your will to go into the subtrust. Otherwise, you would create two trusts for the beneficiary; one in the will and one in your living trust.

EXAMPLE Jessica makes a living trust and leaves the bulk of her property to her 12-year-old son. She arranges, in the trust document, for any trust property her son inherits before the age of 30 to be kept in a subtrust, managed by Jessica's mother.

Jessica also makes a back-up will, in which she also leaves everything to her son and again arranges for a subtrust to be set up if she should die before her son reaches age 30. So if Jessica dies before her son reaches 30, two subtrusts will be set up to manage property for him.

If Jessica used a pour-over will, any property her son inherited through the will would go into the subtrust created by her living trust. Only half the paperwork of maintaing the subtrust would be necessary.

C. Other Probate-Avoidance Methods

A living trust is not the only way to transfer some kinds of assets without probate, and it's not always the best. For example, it would probably be cumbersome to have your personal checking account held in the name of your living trust.

Fortunately, you can mix and match probate-avoidance techniques. Just put whatever property you want in your living trust, and choose other transfer methods—which also avoid probate—for the rest of your property.

You might, for example, want to put your checking account into joint tenancy with your spouse; at your death, your spouse would automatically take sole ownership of the account. Some helpful probate-avoidance methods are discussed below.

PROBATE-AVOIDANCE METHODS

Method	Advantages	Disadvantages
Revocable living trust	Flexible, private. Easy to create. You keep control over property during your life.	Some paperwork involved. May need attorney if yours is a complicated estate.
Pay-on-death accounts (revocable trust accounts)	Easy to create, using a form provided by the institution or agency.	Limited to bank accounts and some government securities.
Naming beneficiary of pension plan or retirement account	Easy to do. Beneficiary inherits all funds in the account at your death.	None, unless particular program imposes limits.
Life insurance	Good way to provide quick cash for beneficiaries or to pay estate taxes. Proceeds don't go through probate.	Family members may not need much immediate cash if they don't rely on you to support them, so expense of policy may not be justified.

Method	Advantages	Disadvantages
Joint tenancy with right of survivorship	Easy to create.	Not available in a few states. If you don't already own property in joint tenancy, you may not want to add another owner, who could sell his share. (For larger estates, there are negative gift tax consequences, too.) Can be a problem if a co-owner becomes incapacitated. No probate avoidance if all joint owners die at once.
Gifts of property made while you're alive	Reduces amount of property in your estate, which avoids both probate and estate taxes.	You lose control over property given away. Large gifts use up part of your federal gift/estate tax exemption. Insurance policies must be given away at least three years before death, or proceeds are included in your taxable estate.
State laws that allow simplified probate proceedings	Exempts certain property from formal probate.	Applies only to small estates; you may still need an attorney to explain the technicalities of your state's laws.
Transfer-on-death designation for motor vehicles	Easy to do. All you do is name, on your registration form, someone to inherit your vehicle.	Currently available only in California and Missouri, but other states are considering similar programs.
Transfer-on-death registration for securities	Easy to do. All you do is name, on the registration form, someone to inherit the securities at your death.	Currently available only in Colorado and Wisconsin.

1. Pay-on-Death Accounts (Banks and Government Securities)

Setting up a pay-on-death account, also called an informal bank account trust or revocable trust account, is an easy way to transfer cash at your death, quickly and without probate. All you do is designate one or more persons you want to receive the money in the account when you die.

You can use any kind of bank account, including savings, checking or certificate of deposit accounts. You can also register ownership of certain kinds of government securities, including bonds, Treasury Bills and Treasury Notes, in a way that lets you name a beneficiary to receive them at your death.

EXAMPLE   Terry opens a savings account in the name of "Terry Kelinkoff, trustee for Lynn Harris." When Terry dies, whatever money is in the account will go to Lynn.

During your life, the beneficiary has no right to the money in the account. You can withdraw some or all of the money, close the account or change the beneficiary, at any time. When you die, the beneficiary can claim the money by showing the bank the death certificate.

Like other bank accounts, a pay-on-death account may be temporarily frozen at your death, if your state levies death taxes. The state will release the money to your beneficiaries when shown that your estate has ample funds to pay the taxes.

Most banks have forms for setting up this kind of account, and they don't charge more for keeping your money this way. Before you open a pay-on-death account, ask your bank if there are any special state law requirements about notifying the beneficiary. In a few states, a pay-on-death provision isn't effective unless you have notified the beneficiary that you've set up the account. Your bank should be able to fill you in on your state's rules.

2. Pension Plans and Retirement Accounts

Retirement accounts such as IRAs and Keogh accounts weren't designed to be probate avoidance devices, but they can easily be used that way. All you have to do is name a beneficiary to receive the funds still in your pension plan or retirement account at your death, and the funds will not go through probate.

After age 70, however, federal law requires you to withdraw at least a certain amount every year or face a monetary penalty. The amount is refigured every year, based on your current life expectancy.

3. Life Insurance

Life insurance is a good way to provide surviving family members with quick cash for debts, living expenses and, in larger estates, estate taxes. And because you name the beneficiary in the policy itself, not in your will, life insurance proceeds don't go through probate.

The only circumstance in which life insurance proceeds are subject to probate is if the beneficiary named in the policy is your estate. That's done occasionally if the estate will need immediate cash to pay debts and taxes, but it's usually counterproductive. It's almost always a better idea to name your spouse, children or other beneficiary who can take the money free of probate and use it to pay debts and taxes.

Although the proceeds of a life insurance policy don't go through probate, they are included in your estate for federal estate tax purposes. If you think your estate will be liable for federal estate taxes (which usually means that it must be worth more than $600,000 at your death), you can reduce the tax bill by giving ownership of the policy to the beneficiary at least three years before your death. When ownership of the policy itself is transferred, gift tax may be assessed based on the present value of the policy. But at your death, the proceeds will not be counted as part of your taxable estate.

For help with choosing a life insurance policy from the bewildering array now available, see *How To Buy the Right Life Insurance Policy at the Right Price* (Consumer Reports Books).

LIFE INSURANCE TO PROVIDE FOR YOUR CHILDREN

If you have young children but not much money, consider buying a moderate amount of term life insurance, which would provide cash to support your children if you died while they were still young. Because term life insurance pays benefits only if you die during the covered period (often five or ten years), it's far cheaper than other types of life insurance. You can stop renewing the insurance when by the end of the term, the children will be on their own or your estate will be large enough to support them until they are.

---

4. Joint Tenancy

Joint tenancy is one of the most popular probate-avoidance devices around. It's an efficient and practical way to transfer some kinds of property, but for other kinds of property, a living trust is a better choice.

a. How Joint Tenancy Works

Joint tenancy is a way two or more people can hold title to property they own together. It is available in almost all states (see list below).

STATE LAW RESTRICTIONS ON JOINT TENANCY

Alaska	No joint tenancy in real estate, except for husband and wife
Pennsylvania	No joint tenancy in real estate (but this rule has been questioned in court decisions)
Tennessee	No joint tenancy except for husband and wife
Texas	No joint tenancy in any kind of property unless there's a written joint tenancy agreement signed by the owners

For estate planning purposes, the most important characteristic of joint tenancy is that when one joint owner (called a joint tenant) dies, the surviving joint owners automatically get complete ownership of the property. This is called the "right of survivorship." The property doesn't go through probate court—there is only some simple paperwork to fill out to transfer the property into the name of the surviving owner.

EXAMPLE Evelyn and her daughter own a car in joint tenancy. When Evelyn dies, her half-interest in the car will go to her daughter without probate. Her daughter will need only to fill out a simple form to transfer ownership of the car into her own name.

Joint tenancy certainly has the virtue of simplicity. To create a joint tenancy, all the co-owners need to do is pay attention to the way they are listed on the document that shows ownership of property, such as a deed to real estate, a car's title slip or a card establishing a bank account. In the great majority of states, by calling themselves "joint tenants with the right of survivorship," the owners create a joint tenancy.[1] All joint tenants must own equal shares of the property.

A joint tenant cannot leave his or her share to anyone other than the surviving joint tenants. So even if Evelyn, in the preceding example, left a will giving her half-interest in the car to her son instead of her daughter, the daughter would still get the car.

This rule isn't as ironclad as it may sound. A joint tenant can, while still alive, break the joint tenancy by transferring his or her interest in the property to someone else (or, in some states, to himself, but not as a "joint tenant"). The new owner isn't a joint tenant with the other original owners.

EXAMPLE David, Jan and Loren own property together in joint tenancy. David sells his one-third interest to Paul. Paul is not a joint tenant with Jan and Loren; he is a "tenant in common," free to leave his property to whomever he wants. Jan and Loren, however, are still joint tenants with respect to their two-thirds of the property; when one of them dies, the other will own the two-thirds.

---

[1]In a few states, additional specific words are necessary. If you want to set up a joint tenancy and aren't sure how to word a title document, ask a real estate lawyer or someone at a land title company.

Joint bank accounts. If you and someone else want to set up a joint tenancy account together, so that the survivor will get all the funds, normally you can do it in a few minutes at the bank. But in a few states, you may need to comply with certain formalities. Texas state law, for example, requires a written agreement—not just a signature card—to set up such an account.[2] Your bank should be able to tell you about any requirements.

b. When To Consider Joint Tenancy

Joint tenancy often works well when couples (married or not) acquire real estate or other valuable property together. If they take title in joint tenancy, probate is avoided when the first owner dies.

But there are advantages to transferring the property to your living trust, even if you already own it in joint tenancy.

First, a living trust, unlike joint tenancy, allows you to name an alternate beneficiary—someone who will inherit the property if the first beneficiary (your spouse) doesn't survive you. If you own property in joint tenancy, and you and your spouse die at the same time, the property will go to the residuary beneficiary named in your will—but it will have to go through probate first.

Second, if you transfer joint tenancy property to a living trust, you will avoid probate both when the first spouse dies and when the second spouse dies. With joint tenancy, probate is avoided only when the first spouse dies. The second spouse, who owns the property alone after the first spouse's death, must take some other measure—such as transferring it to a living trust—to avoid probate.

---

[2]A dispute over such an account ended up in the Texas Supreme Court. Two sisters had set up an account together, using a signature card that allowed the survivor to withdraw the funds. When the surviving sister withdrew the funds, the estate of the deceased sister sued and won the funds. *Stauffer v. Henderson*, 801 S.W.2d 858 (Tex. 1991).

c. When To Think Twice About Joint Tenancy

Joint tenancy is usually a poor estate planning device when an older person, seeking only to avoid probate, puts solely owned property into joint tenancy with someone else. Doing this creates several potential problems that don't occur with a living trust:

You can't change your mind. If you make someone else a co-owner, in joint tenancy, of property that you now own yourself, you give up half ownership of the property. The new owner has rights that you can't take back. For example, the new owner can sell or mortgage his or her share. And even if the other joint tenant's half isn't mortgaged, it could still be lost to creditors.

EXAMPLE Maureen, a widow, signs a deed that puts her house into joint tenancy with her son to avoid probate at her death. Later, the son's business fails, and he is sued by creditors. His half-interest in the house may be taken by the creditors to pay the court judgment, which means that the house might be sold. Maureen would get the value of her half in cash; her son's half of the proceeds would go to pay the creditors.

By contrast, if you put property in a revocable living trust, you don't give up any ownership now. You are always free to change your mind about who you want to get the property at your death.

There's no way to handle the incapacity of one joint tenant. There can be serious problems if one joint tenant becomes incapacitated and cannot make decisions. The other owners must get legal authority to sell or mortgage the property. That may mean going to court to get someone (called a conservator, in most states) appointed to manage the incapacitated person's affairs. (This problem can be partially dealt with if the joint tenant has signed a document called a "Durable Power of Attorney," giving someone authority to manage his affairs if he cannot. See Section F, below.)

With a living trust, if you (the grantor) becomes incapacitated, the successor trustee (or the other spouse, if it's a shared marital spouse) takes over and has full authority to manage the property. No court proceedings are necessary.

Gift taxes may be assessed. If you create a joint tenancy by making another person a co-owner, federal gift tax may be assessed on the transfer. This probably isn't a reason not to transfer property; making a gift can be a sound estate planning strategy. But be aware that if gifts to one person (except your spouse) exceed $10,000 per year, you must file a gift tax return with the IRS.[3] (See Section D, below.)

Surviving spouse misses an income tax break. If you make your spouse a joint tenant with you on property you own separately, the surviving spouse could miss out on a potentially big income tax break later, when the property is sold.

When it comes to property owned in joint tenancy, the Internal Revenue Service rule is that a surviving spouse gets a stepped-up tax basis only for the half of the property owned by the deceased spouse.[4] (You may not face this problem if you live in a community property state.[5]) When the property is later sold, this means higher tax if the property has gone up in value after the joint tenancy was created but before the first spouse died.

5. Tenancy by the Entirety

"Tenancy by the entirety" is a form of property ownership that is similar to joint tenancy, but is limited to married couples. It is available only in the states listed below.

---

[3]There's one other exception: If two or more people open a bank account in joint tenancy, but one person puts all or most of the money in, no gift tax is assessed against that person. A taxable gift may be made, however, when a joint tenant who has contributed little or nothing to the account withdraws money from it.

[4]The tax basis is the amount from which taxable profit is figured when property is sold.

[5]If property held in joint tenancy property is actually community property, it will still qualify for a stepped-up tax basis if the surviving spouse can show the IRS that it was in fact community property. But it's up to you to prove it; when one spouse dies, the IRS presumes that property held in joint tenancy is not community property.

STATES THAT ALLOW TENANCY BY THE ENTIRETY

Alaska*	Maryland	Ohio
Arkansas	Massachusetts	Oklahoma
Delaware	Michigan*	Oregon*
District of Columbia	Mississippi	Pennsylvania
Florida	Missouri	Tennessee
Hawaii	New Jersey*	Vermont
Indiana*	New York*	Virginia*
Kentucky*	North Carolina*	Wyoming*

*allowed for real estate only

Tenancy by the entirety has almost the same advantages and disadvantages of joint tenancy and is most useful in the same kind of situation: when a couple acquires property together. When one owner (spouse) dies, the surviving co-owner (the other spouse) inherits the property. The property doesn't go through probate.

If property is held in tenancy by the entirety, neither spouse can transfer his or her half of the property alone, either while alive or by will or trust. It must go to the surviving spouse. (This is different from joint tenancy; a joint tenant is free to transfer his or her share to someone else during his life.)

EXAMPLE   Fred and Ethel hold title to their house in tenancy by the entirety. If Fred wanted to sell or give away his half-interest in the house, he could not do so without Ethel's signature on the deed.

6. Gifts

If you make gifts while you're alive, there will be less property in your estate to go through probate when you die. But if probate avoidance is your goal, usually it's better to use one of the other methods discussed above, which let you keep control over your property while you're alive, than to give away everything before you die.

Making sizeable gifts may be a good strategy if you and your spouse expect to have a combined estate worth more than $600,000 at your death, and you want to reduce the eventual federal estate tax bite. (See Section D, below.)

7. Simplified Probate Proceedings

Many states have begun, albeit slowly, to dismantle some of the more oner-ous parts of probate. They have created categories of property and benefi-ciaries that don't have to go through a full-blown probate court proceeding. If your family can take advantage of these procedures after your death, you may not need to worry too much about avoiding probate.

Almost every state has some kind of simplified (summary) probate or out-of-court transfer process for one or more of these categories:

Small estates. For "small estates," many states have created an out-of-court procedure that lets people collect the property they've inherited by filling out a sworn statement (affidavit) and giving it to the person who has the property. Typically, the beneficiary must also provide some kind of proof of his or her right to inherit, such as a death certificate and copy of the will. What qualifies as a small estate varies from state to state; the maximum goes from $5,000 to $60,000.

Personal property. In some states, the only property that qualifies for simpli-fied transfer procedures is personal property—that is, anything except real estate.

Property left to the surviving spouse. In some states, if a surviving spouse in-herits less than a certain amount of property, no probate is necessary.

Most people leave property that is worth more than can be passed without probate under state probate simplification laws. In many states, if the value of your entire estate exceeds the maximum set by law for simplified probate, you cannot use simplified probate procedures—even if most of your prop-erty is being passed through probate-avoidance devices such as a living trust.

EXAMPLE At her death, Jane has an estate worth $300,000. Her major asset is her home, worth $200,000, which she passes to her daughter through a living trust. She also passes $80,000 worth of other property through other probate-avoidance de-vices. That leaves $20,000 of property. In Jane's state, the maximum estate size for streamlined probate procedures is $25,000. But Jane's heirs can't use the simplified procedures for the last $20,000 of property, because Jane's total estate exceeds the limit.

In some states, however, even if your total estate is too large, you can still make use of the simplified procedures if the amount that actually goes through probate is under the limit. So, to continue with the example, in some states, the $20,000 of Jane's estate that isn't taken care of by other probate-avoidance devices could go through the simplified probate procedure.

 Every state's approach is listed in *Plan Your Estate With a Living Trust*, by Denis Clifford (Nolo Press).

D. Federal Gift and Estate Tax

The revocable living trust you make with *Nolo's Living Trust* won't help you save on estate taxes. If you and your spouse expect to have a combined estate worth more than $600,000, or you have already given away large amounts of property (more than $10,000 in one year to one beneficiary), consult a lawyer or tax planner about ways to reduce your federal estate taxes.

This section briefly discusses the basics of the federal estate and gift tax.

1. How the Federal Gift and Estate Tax Works

The federal government taxes both gifts made during life and at death. That's why the proper name of the federal estate tax is the "unified gift and estate tax." Congress reasoned that if only gifts made at death were taxed, everyone would give away as much property as they could during their lives. No tax is paid until your death (unless you give away an enormous amount of property while you're alive), when your combined gift and estate tax liability is calculated.

The tax won't affect you unless you give away or leave a substantial amount of property. First, many gifts are exempt from tax (see Section 2, below). In addition, you can transfer up to another $600,000 of property, either by gifts while you are alive or at your death (by living trust, will or other method), without incurring federal gift and estate tax.

EXAMPLE Susan doesn't make any taxable gifts during her life and leaves $500,000 worth of property at her death, using a living trust and back-up will. Her estate owes no federal gift and estate tax.

How the Unified Gift and Estate Tax Works

In addition to the $600,000 exemption, property you leave to your spouse (as long as he or she is a U.S. citizen) is not taxed, regardless of amount.[6] This is called the marital deduction. There is no comparable estate tax exemption for unmarried couples.

---

[6]Property left to a non-citizen spouse is not exempt from estate tax. You may want to see an estate planning attorney about using a "Qualified Domestic Trust" to leave a non-citizen spouse property without paying federal estate tax.

The marital deduction trap. Older couples who have a combined estate of more than $600,000 and rely on the marital deduction will probably be in for big estate tax bills on the death of the second spouse, who gets no marital deduction. (See Section 2.b, below.)

2. Reducing Estate Tax Liability

A living trust, or any other probate-avoidance technique, has no effect on estate tax liability. Property you leave in joint tenancy or in a living trust is still considered part of your estate for federal estate tax purposes. There are, however, a few strategies to reduce the tax bill. We discuss them briefly here.

 If you want to take steps to reduce eventual estate taxes, see a knowledgeable attorney.

a. Gifts

If you don't need all your income and property to live on, making sizeable gifts while you're alive can be a good way to reduce eventual federal estate taxes.

Tax-exempt gifts. Only gifts larger than $10,000 made to one person or organization in one calendar year count toward the $600,000 exemption. You can give smaller gifts tax-free.

EXAMPLE Allen and Julia give their two daughters each $20,000 every year for four years. They have transferred $160,000 without becoming liable for gift tax.

Other gifts are exempt regardless of amount, including:
- gifts between spouses who are U.S. citizens[7]
- gifts for medical bills or school tuition
- gifts to tax-exempt charitable organizations

---

[7]Gifts to spouses who are not United States citizens are exempt only up to $100,000 per year.

If you make gifts subject to tax during your life, they are counted toward the $600,000. But though you will have to file a gift tax return, you don't pay any tax when you make a gift unless you give away more than $600,000 worth of property during your life. Otherwise, your combined gift and estate tax liability is paid after your death, out of the property in your estate.

EXAMPLE Harry gives his daughter $25,000 one year. Although he must file a federal gift tax return, he does not pay tax on the $15,000 that is not tax-exempt. At his death, if his taxable gifts and the property he leaves exceed $600,000, his estate will have to pay tax.

Gifts made within three years of death. A few types of gifts made in the last three years of someone's life are considered part of that person's taxable estate—that is, they don't qualify as gifts for tax purposes. The most important, for most people, are gifts of life insurance policies and gifts made directly from a revocable trust—that is, from the trustee to the recipient.[8]

For that reason, it's important not to give away property directly from your living trust if you are concerned about estate tax. If you give away trust property within three years before your death, the IRS considers the property part of your estate at your death—which means estate taxes may be due on it.[9] To get around this rule, simply transfer the property from the living trust to yourself, and then give it away. That way, the property you give away won't be considered part of your taxable estate when you die.

---

[8] IRS Technical Advice Memorandum 8609005.

[9] IRS Letter Ruling 9049002 (1990).

How to choose property to give away. It's usually wise to give away property that you think will go up in value substantially before your death. That way, you may avoid gift tax now—if the gift is worth less than $10,000—and you may avoid estate tax later, because the increased value of the property won't be included in your estate when you die. Also, if the recipient (other than a child age 14 or under) is in a lower tax bracket, you may want to give away income-generating property, so that the income will be taxed at the recipient's lower tax rates.[10]

You may not, however, want to give away property that has already appreciated greatly in value. Usually, it's wiser to hold onto it until death to take advantage of the "stepped-up tax basis" rules discussed in Section C, above.

Gifts of Life Insurance

Life insurance policies you own on your own life and give away at least three years before your death are excellent gifts, from an estate planning view. Your gift tax liability is determined by the current value of the policy, which is far less than the amount the policy will pay off at death. For many policies, it will be less than the $10,000 annual gift tax threshold, which means that no gift tax will be assessed.

To give away a life insurance policy, you must comply with some fairly technical IRS rules, which should be available from your insurance company. You must make an irrevocable gift of the policy. If you keep the right to revoke the gift and get the policy back, the proceeds will be taxed as part of your estate.

And if you buy a policy that requires future premium payments, you'll want to make more gifts to the new owner of the policy to cover the payments. (As an alternative, you can pay for some kinds of policies all at once; they are called single-premium policies.)

---

[10]Any income over $1,000 per year received by a child 14 years or under from any gift (whether from parents or anyone else) is taxed at the parents' rate.

EXAMPLE Sarah buys three single-premium life insurance policies (that is, she pays the entire premium in advance) for $50,000 each and transfers ownership of the policies to her three children. She must file a gift tax return because the value of the gifts exceeds the $10,000 per person per year tax exemption, but the gift tax is not due until her death. When Sarah dies, each policy pays $200,000. The $600,000 is not taxed as part of her estate; only the $120,000 that exceeded the gift tax exemption is taxed.

The process of transferring ownership is simple. Insurance companies have forms you can use to make the transfer.

To get around the three-year limitation, some lawyers advocate use of an irrevocable life insurance trust. Instead of buying the life insurance policy directly and then giving it away, you set up the trust and give the trustee money to buy the policy. If you want to try this, see an estate planning attorney.

b. Marital Life Estate Trusts

Despite the marital deduction, which eliminates estate tax on property left to a surviving spouse who is a U.S. citizen, most elderly couples who have a combined estate of more than $600,000 should avoid leaving large sums to one another. The marital deduction really just postpones estate tax until the second spouse dies.

Say, for example, a husband leaves all his property to his wife. At the husband's death, no estate tax is due. But when the widow dies, the marital deduction won't apply. Her estate will have to pay a much larger tax than if the husband had left his property directly to children or other beneficiaries.

If the surviving spouse is not elderly, this isn't a problem. She has plenty of time to enjoy or give away the property. But for older couples, piling lots of money into the survivor's estate can be a real tax trap.

One way around this trap is for each spouse to put their property in a "marital life estate trust," sometimes called a "spousal trust" or "A-B trust." When one spouse dies, his or her half of the property goes to the children—with the crucial condition that the surviving spouse gets the right to use the deceased spouse's half of the property for life and is entitled to any income it generates. When the second spouse dies, the property goes to the children outright. Using this kind of trust keeps the second spouse's estate half as small as it would be if the property were left to the spouse—which means that estate taxes may be avoided altogether.

These examples show how a marital life estate trust can cut back drastically on estate taxes.

EXAMPLE 1: No life estate trust. Thomas and Maria, husband and wife, are in their mid-70s, and each has an estate worth $550,000. Thomas dies in 1993. He leaves all his property to Maria, so no estate tax is assessed because of the marital deduction. But the size of Maria's estate rises to $1,100,000 (plus any appreciation). At Maria's death, all property worth more than $600,000 that is not exempt (because it was given to a tax-exempt charity or for some other reason), is heavily taxed. The tax bill: $155,800.

EXAMPLE 2: With life estate trust. Thomas and Maria each establish a marital life estate trust, with the income to go to the survivor for life and the principal to the children at the survivor's death. When Thomas dies, Maria's estate remains at $550,000, plus any income she receives from the trust property.

Maria dies in 1994. Because $600,000 can be left to anyone free of estate tax, there is no estate tax liability either from Maria's $550,000, which now goes to the children, or from Thomas's $550,000, which now goes to the children under the terms of the trust.

Unlike a probate-avoidance revocable living trust, a marital life estate trust controls what happens to property for years after the first spouse's death. A couple who makes one must be sure that the surviving spouse will be financially and emotionally comfortable receiving only the income from the money or property placed in trust, with the children (or other persons) as the actual owner of the property.

Marital life estate trusts have other uses besides saving on estate taxes; see Section G, below.

Nolo's Living Trust does not create a marital life estate trust. If you want such a trust, see an experienced estate planning lawyer.

c. Generation-Skipping Trusts for Grandchildren

A "generation-skipping" trust won't reduce your own estate tax liability; it can, however, exempt up to $1 million from tax in the next generation.

With this kind of trust, your children are entitled to receive income from trust property but can't touch the principal. The principal goes to your grandchildren at the death of your children. The property you leave in such a trust is included in your taxable estate when you die. But it's not included in your children's taxable estate when they die.

E. State Death Taxes

Twenty-four states and the District of Columbia have effectively abolished state death taxes. The rest impose death taxes on:

- all real estate owned in the state, no matter where the deceased lived; and

- all other property of residents of the state, no matter where it's located.

STATES WITHOUT DEATH TAXES

Alabama	Georgia	North Dakota
Alaska	Hawaii	Oregon
Arizona	Illinois	Texas
Arkansas	Maine	Utah
California	Minnesota	Vermont
Colorado	Missouri	Virginia
District of Columbia	Nevada	West Virginia
Florida	New Mexico	Washington
		Wyoming

1. Your Residence for State Death Tax Purposes

State death taxes apply to all persons who live permanently in that state. If you divide your time between a state that doesn't impose inheritance tax (or has very low ones) and one with high death taxes, you'll want to establish your permanent residence in the lower tax state.

EXAMPLE A couple divides the year between Florida and New York. Florida effectively has no death taxes. New York imposes comparatively stiff estate taxes, with rates ranging from 2% for $50,000 or less to 21% for $10,100,000 or more. Other things being equal, it makes sense for the couple to make Florida their legal residence.

To establish your legal residence in a particular state, you should should register all vehicles there, keep bank and other financial accounts there and vote there.

Establishing residence in a no-tax state can be tricky if you also live in a high-tax one, because the high-tax state has a financial incentive to conclude that you really reside there. If you have a large estate, and a complicated two-or-more-state living situation, consult a knowledgeable tax lawyer or accountant.

2. Estate Planning for State Death Taxes

If you live or own real estate in a state that has death taxes, consider the impact of those taxes on your estate. In many instances, the bite taken from estates by state death taxes is annoying but relatively minor.

In some states, however, tax liability is significant, especially for property given to non-relatives. For example, Nebraska imposes a 15% death tax rate if $25,000 is left to a friend, but only 1% if it's given to a spouse.

Death tax rules for all states are summarized in *Plan Your Estate With a Living Trust* (Nolo Press). More detailed information is available from state tax officials.

F. Planning for Incapacity

A living trust can be a big help if you become unable to manage your own affairs, because your successor trustee (or your spouse, if you make a shared marital trust) can take over management of trust property. That person, however, has no power over any of your other financial or health affairs. For that reason, you should prepare some other documents as well and coordinate them with your living trust.

1. Durable Powers of Attorney

The best way to plan for the management of your financial affairs not covered by your living trust is to use a document called a "Durable Power of Attorney for Finances." This document gives a trusted person you choose, called your "attorney-in-fact," the legal authority to manage your finances (except for property owned by your living trust) on your behalf.

You may also want to appoint a trusted person (not necessarily the same person) to make health care decisions for you. You can do this with a document called a "Durable Power of Attorney for Health Care."

Both documents can be worded so that they only take effect if you become incapacitated.

Instructions and forms for preparing durable powers of attorney for finances are in *Who Will Handle Your Finances If You Can't?*, by Denis Clifford and Mary Randolph (Nolo Press).

2. Living Wills

If you're concerned about being hooked up to life support systems, and other issues surrounding dying a natural death, you may also want a "living will." (Despite the confusingly similar names, living wills and living trusts are completely different animals.)

A living will is a document addressed to your doctors. In it you state your preferences about treatment, including life support systems. You may also, depending on state law, be able to name a "proxy"—a trusted relative or friend who can make certain health care decisions for you. The extent to which doctors must follow your instructions depends on your state's law and what you specify in the living will. Some states, for example, do not require a doctor to stop artificial feeding even if a patient's living will requested it. And in some states, living wills are effective only after you have been diagnosed with a terminal illness.

But even if not legally binding, your living will can serve as valuable evidence of your wishes if family, friends or doctors disagree about the treatment you should receive.

Many states are passing laws governing living wills or developing their own living will forms. Up-to-date information about state requirements is available from Concern for Dying, 250 W. 57th St., Suite 323, New York, NY 10107.

Reminder. Whatever arrangements you make concerning your wishes in case of incapacity, be sure to let your family know what your wishes are, what documents you have signed and where you keep them.

G. Long-Term Property Distribution Methods

In certain circumstances, you may want to dictate how your property is to be distributed over many years. You may want to leave property to people who, for one reason or another, may not be able to manage it for themselves. Or you may want to leave property to your spouse for his or her life, but be sure it eventually goes to your children. This is especially true if you marry later in life and have children from a former marriage.

Here, we briefly discuss a few methods to accomplish these goals, but you'll need a lawyer's help.

For instructions on how to leave property to a minor or young adult, and have someone manage it until the beneficiary is older, see Chapter 5 or 6, Part 7.

1. Marital Life Estate Trusts

If you are in a second or subsequent marriage and have children from a previous marriage, you may want your current spouse to have some of your property during his or her life, but be sure that it eventually goes to your children. That way, children receive a fair share of your property, and your spouse receives income for the rest of his or her life.

The technique is for each spouse to leave his or her property in a "marital life estate trust," discussed as a tax-saving device in Section D, above. The survivor receives interest income from trust property, and often the use of real estate in the trust. The property itself goes to the first spouse's children when the surviving spouse dies.

Whether or not this arrangement is a good one depends on your situation. If relations could become strained between your children and your current spouse, you may very well not want to set things up so that they essentially share ownership of property for many years.

2. Spendthrift Trusts

If you want to leave property to an adult who just can't handle money, a "spendthrift trust," which doles the money out little by little, is a good idea. A spendthrift trust keeps the money from being squandered by the beneficiary or seized by the beneficiary's creditors.

3. Trusts for Disabled Persons

A person with a physical or mental disability may not be able to handle property, no matter what his or her age. Often, the solution is to establish a trust with a competent adult as trustee to manage the trust property.

The trust should be carefully prepared by an expert familiar with the state law, so that the trust won't jeopardize the beneficiary's eligibility for government benefits.

4. Flexible Trusts

You may want the determination of how your property is spent after your death to be decided in the future, not before you die. The usual way to do this is to create a "sprinkling trust," authorizing the trustee to decide how to spend trust money for several beneficiaries.

4 What Kind of Living Trust Do You Need?

Nolo's Living Trust makes two kinds of revocable living trusts: one for an individual and one for a married couple. Your first decision—probably an easy one—is to decide which is right for you.

A. If You Are Single

If you are single, you must use the individual trust. You can use it to transfer any of your property—both property you own in your name alone and your share of co-owned property, including partnership property.

If you and someone else own valuable items of property together—a house, for example—you can each transfer your half-interest to a separate living trust. An alternative, if you both want the survivor to inherit the property, is to use another probate-avoidance method, such as holding title to the property in joint tenancy. (But this may have adverse tax consequences; see Chapter 3, *A Living Trust as Part of Your Estate Plan.*)

B. If You Are Married

If you are married, you and your spouse have a choice: You can create a shared living trust or separate individual ones. Or you could make a shared trust and individual trusts.

Most couples prefer to make one shared trust, because that way they don't have to divide property they own together. But you may want to make separate trusts if you and your spouse own most of your property separately. Another reason to make separate trusts is if both spouses want to keep complete control over their own trust property. With a shared trust, either spouse has authority over all trust property while both spouses are alive. (See Chapter 6, *Creating a Shared Marital Trust.*)

Before you make this decision, make sure you understand the marital property laws of your state. This section briefly explains the two systems of marital property laws: community property and non-community property.

If You're Unsure of Your Marital Status

Most people are quite certain of their marital status. If you're not, here's what you need to know.

The divorce decree. Don't assume you're divorced until you have a final decree of divorce (or dissolution, as it's called in some states) issued by a state court in the United States.

If you think you're divorced but never saw the final decree, contact the court clerk in the county where you think the divorce was granted. Give the clerk your name, your ex-spouse's name and the date, as close as you know it, of the divorce.

Legal separation. Even if a court has declared you and your spouse legally separated, and you plan to divorce, you are still married. It's not over until you get the divorce decree.

Foreign divorces. Divorces issued to U.S. citizens by courts in Mexico, the Dominican Republic or another country may not be valid if challenged, especially if all the paperwork was handled by mail. In other words, if you or your spouse got a quickie foreign divorce, you may well be still married under the laws of your state. If you think that someone might make a claim to some of your property after your death based on the invalidity of a foreign divorce, see a lawyer.

Common law marriages. In some states, a couple can become legally married by living together, intending to be married and presenting themselves to the world as a married couple. Even in states that allow such common law marriages, most couples who live together don't have common law marriages. If you really do have a valid common law marriage, you must go to court and get a divorce to end it—there's no such thing as a common law divorce.

Common law marriages can be created in Alabama, Colorado, District of Columbia, Georgia, Idaho, Iowa, Kansas, Montana, New Hampshire (for inheritance purposes only), Ohio, Oklahoma, Pennsylvania, Rhode Island, South Carolina and Texas. If a common law marriage is created in one of these states, and the couple moves to another state, they are still legally married.

Gay or lesbian couples. No state allows marriage between two people of the same sex, even if a religious ceremony has been performed.

1. Community Property States

Arizona	Louisiana	Texas
California	Nevada	Washington
Idaho	New Mexico	Wisconsin

In these states, the general rule is that spouses share everything 50-50. All property earned or otherwise acquired by either spouse during the marriage, regardless of whose name is on the title slip, is community property. Each spouse owns a one-half interest in it. Property acquired by one spouse by gift or inheritance, however, or before marriage, is not community property; it is the separate property of that spouse.

For example, if while married you bought real estate with money you earned during marriage, your spouse legally owns a half interest in it, unless you both signed an agreement keeping it separate.

Typically, most property owned by spouses is community property, especially if they have been married for a number of years. So it usually makes sense to make one shared marital trust.

EXAMPLE Rob and Cecile live in Nevada, a community property state. They have been married for 20 years. Except for some bonds that Cecile inherited from her parents, virtually all their valuable property—house, stocks, car—is owned together. The money they brought to the marriage in separate bank accounts has long since been mixed with community property, making it community property too. Rob and Cecile decide to make a shared living trust.

Making two individual living trusts would require splitting ownership of the co-owned assets, which can be a clumsy process. For example, to transfer a co-owned house into two separate trusts would require the spouses to sign and record a deed transferring half-interests in the house to separate trusts. And to transfer household furnishings to separate trusts, spouses would have to allocate each item to a trust or each risk transferring a half-interest in a couch to separate trusts.

There is another advantage to making a shared trust if the spouses want to leave significant trust property to each other. With a shared trust, property left by one spouse to the survivor stays in the living trust when the first spouse dies; no transfer is necessary when the first spouse dies. With separate trusts, property left to the surviving spouse must usually be transferred first from the trust to the surviving spouse, and then (to avoid probate) to the surviving spouse's living trust.

If you and your spouse own most of your property together but each have some separate property, a shared marital trust is fine. You can transfer all of it to the trust, and each spouse can name beneficiaries (including each other) to receive his or her separate property.

If, however, you and your spouse own most of your property separately, you may want to make individual trusts. Most couples in this situation fit one of these profiles:

- You and your spouse signed an agreement stating that each spouse's earnings and other income are separate, not community property, and you have kept your property separate.

- You are recently married and have little or no community property.

- You each own mostly separate property acquired before your marriage (or by gift or inheritance), which you conscientiously keep from being mixed with community property. Couples who marry later in life and no longer work often fit into this category. Not only is the property they owned before the marriage separate, but federal social security benefits and certain retirement plan benefits are also separate, not community, property.

If you and your spouse decide on separate living trusts, each of you will transfer your separately owned property to your individual trust. If you own some property—a house, for example—together, you can each transfer your portion to your trust.

2. Non-Community Property States

Alabama	Kentucky	North Dakota
Alaska	Maine	Ohio
Arkansas	Maryland	Oklahoma
Colorado	Massachusetts	Oregon
Connecticut	Michigan	Pennsylvania
Delaware	Minnesota	Rhode Island
District of Columbia	Mississippi	South Carolina
Florida	Missouri	South Dakota
Georgia	Montana	Tennessee
Hawaii	Nebraska	Utah
Illinois	New Hampshire	Vermont
Indiana	New Jersey	Virginia
Iowa	New York	West Virginia
Kansas	North Carolina	Wyoming

It's increasingly common for couples, especially if they are older and have children from a prior marriage, to sign an agreement (before or during the marriage) to own property separately. Or they may not make a formal agreement, but carefully avoid mixing their property together. If you and your spouse each own substantial amounts of separate property and want to make sure it is kept that way, you may prefer to make individual living trusts.

In a non-community property state, it's usually fairly easy for spouses to keep track of who owns what. The spouse whose name is on the title document (deed, brokerage account paper or title slip, for example) owns it.

EXAMPLE Howard and Louisa live in Indiana, a non-community property state. Both have grown children from prior marriages. When they married, they moved into Howard's house. They both have their own bank accounts and investments, and one joint checking account which they own as joint tenants with right of survivorship.

Each makes an individual living trust. Howard, who dies first, leaves his house to Louisa, but most of his other property is left to his children. The funds in the checking account are not included in his living trust, but pass to Louisa, also without probate, because the account was held in joint tenancy. Howard's other accounts go to his children, under the pay-on-death arrangement he has with the bank.[1]

 Spouse's or minor child's right to inherit. Your spouse or minor child may have the right, under state law, to inherit some of your property after your death. A living trust does not let you evade those laws. (See Chapter 2, *About Living Trusts.*)

---

[1]Joint tenancy, pay-on-death accounts and other probate-avoidance methods are discussed in Chapter 3, A Living Trust as Part of Your Estate Plan.

5 Creating an Individual Trust

When you create your living trust document with *Nolo's Living Trust*, you have only a few choices to make. Basically, you must decide five things:

- Whether to make an individual living trust or a shared trust with your spouse.

- What property you want to put in your living trust.

- Who you want to receive the trust property at your death. These people or organizations are the beneficiaries of your living trust.

- Who is to be the successor trustee—the person you want to distribute trust property at your death.

- How you should arrange for someone to manage trust property inherited by beneficiaries who are too young to handle it without supervision.

You may already have a good idea of how you want to decide these issues. This chapter discusses the factors you should think about as you make each decision. It is organized the same way as the program is (Parts 1 through 7), so that you can easily refer to it while you're actually running *Nolo's Living Trust*. It's a good idea, though, to read through this chapter before you sit down at the computer—it will make the whole process clearer and easier.

CHECKLIST FOR CREATING A VALID LIVING TRUST

√ Prepare the trust document with *Nolo's Living Trust*.

√ Print out the trust document and sign it in front of a notary public.

√ Transfer ownership of the property listed in the trust document into the name of the trust.

√ Update your trust document when needed.

AN OVERVIEW: HOW AN INDIVIDUAL TRUST WORKS

Here, in brief, are the important points about how an individual trust works:

Control of trust property. You will be the trustee of your living trust, so you'll have control over the property in the trust.

Amendments or revocation. At any time, you can revoke the trust, add property to it, remove property from it, or modify any term of the trust document.

After your death. After you die, the person named in the trust document as successor trustee takes over. He or she is responsible for distributing trust property to the beneficiaries and managing any trust property left to a young beneficiary in a child's subtrust (explained later).

Here's an example to show you how the trust works.

EXAMPLE Lenora sets up a revocable living trust to avoid probate. In the trust document, she makes herself the trustee, and appoints her son Ben as successor trustee, to take over as trustee after her death. She transfers her valuable property—her house, savings accounts and stocks—to the living trust.

The trust document states that Lenora's grandson, Max, is to receive the stocks when she dies. She provides that if Max is not yet 21 when she dies, the stocks will stay in a "child's subtrust," managed by the successor trustee Ben. Everything else goes to her son, Ben.

When Lenora dies, Ben follows the terms of the trust document and in his capacity as trustee, distributes all the trust property except the stocks to himself, without probate.

He also manages the stocks inherited by Max, who is 16 at Lenora's death, until his 21st birthday. When all the property in the subtrust is given to Max or spent on his behalf, the subtrust ends.

How an Individual Living Trust Works

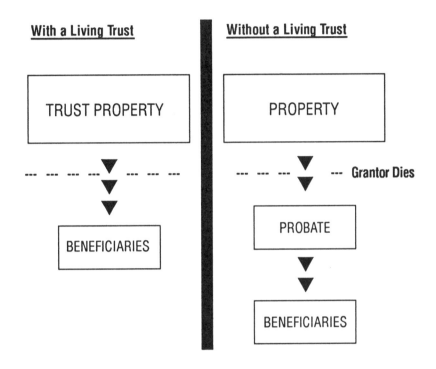

With a Living Trust	Without a Living Trust
TRUST PROPERTY	PROPERTY
BENEFICIARIES	PROBATE
	BENEFICIARIES

Grantor Dies

Part 1. Your State

In this part of the program, you choose the state that is your legal residence, also called your "domicile." That's the state where you live now and intend to keep living.

Your choice affects many aspects of your living trust, including the ways you can set up management for any trust property young beneficiaries may inherit and, if you are married, what property belongs to each spouse.

(You may notice that the list of states on the screen doesn't include Louisiana. We didn't forget it—but because Louisiana law is different from all other states, you can't use this program if you live there.)

A. If You Live in More Than One State

If during the course of a year you live in more than one state, your residence is the state with which you have the most significant contacts—where you vote, register vehicles, own valuable property, have bank accounts or run a business.

If you might be justified in claiming more than one state as your legal residence, you may want to arrange your affairs so that your legal residence is in the state with the most advantageous state estate tax laws. Some states (such as New York) impose stiff inheritance taxes; others (California and Florida, for example) have essentially no inheritance tax. If you have significant contacts with more than one state and a substantial estate, it may pay to have a lawyer with tax and estate planning experience advise you.

EXAMPLE Geraldine spends about half the year in Florida and the other half in New York. She has bank accounts and real estate in both states.

To take advantage of Florida's lack of a state inheritance tax, she registers her car in Florida, votes there and moves her bank accounts there. This leaves her owning nothing in New York but a condominium near where her son lives. She decides to sell him the condo and lease it back six months of every year, severing her last important property ownership contact with New York.

B. If You Live Outside the United States

If you are living outside the U.S., your residence is the state you still have contacts with and expect to return to. If you don't maintain ties with a particular state and have a large estate, see a lawyer to discuss what state you should declare as your residence.

If you are in the Armed Forces and living out of the country temporarily, your legal residence is the state you declared as your Home of Record—the state you lived in before going overseas, or where your spouse or parents live.

PART 2. YOUR NAME

The first information the program asks you for is easy: your name. The name you enter in this part of the program will form part of the name of your trust. For example, if you enter "William S. Jorgensen," your trust will be named "The William S. Jorgensen Revocable Living Trust." Your name will also automatically appear as the original trustee of your living trust (see Part 3, below).

Enter your name the way it appears on other formal business documents, such as your driver's license or bank accounts. This may or may not be the name on your birth certificate.

EXAMPLE Your birth certificate lists your name as Rose Mary Green. But you've always gone by Mary, and always sign documents as Mary McNee, your married name. You would use Mary McNee on your living trust.

Use only one name; don't enter various versions of your name joined by "aka" (also known as).

If you go by more than one name, be sure that the name you use for your living trust is the one that appears on the ownership documents for property you plan to transfer to the trust. If it isn't, it could cause confusion later, and you should change the name on your ownership documents before you transfer the property to the trust.

EXAMPLE You use the name William Dix for your trust, but own real estate in your former name of William Geicherwitz. You should prepare and sign a new deed, changing the name of the owner to William Dix, before you prepare another deed to transfer the property to your living trust.

PART 3. TRUSTEES

To be legally valid, every trust must have a trustee—a person or institution to manage the property owned by the trust. When you create a living trust with this program, you are the trustee now. Someone else, who you named in the trust document to be the successor trustee, takes over after both you and your spouse have died.

A. The Original Trustee

You will be the original trustee of your living trust. As trustee, you will have complete control over the property that will technically be owned by the trust.

As a day-to-day, practical matter, it makes little difference that your property is now owned by your living trust. You won't have any special duties as trustee of your trust. You do not even need to file a separate income tax return for the living trust. Any income the property generates must be reported on your personal income tax return, as if the trust did not exist.

You have the same freedom to sell, give away or mortgage trust property as you did before you put the property into the living trust. The only difference is that you must now sign documents in your capacity as trustee. It's that easy.

EXAMPLE   Celeste wants to sell a piece of land that is owned in the name of her living trust. She prepares a deed transferring ownership of the land from the trust to the new owner, and signs the deed as "Celeste Tornetti, trustee of the Celeste Tornetti Revocable Living Trust dated February 4, 1991."

 Naming someone else as trustee. In the unlikely event you don't want to be the original trustee of your living trust, you cannot use the trust created by *Nolo's Living Trust;* you need to see an estate planning lawyer to draw up a more specialized living trust. Naming someone else as trustee has important tax consequences and means you give up control over trust property.

B. The Successor Trustee

You must also choose a successor trustee—someone to act as trustee after your death or incapacity.[1] The successor trustee has no power or responsibility while you are alive and capable of managing your affairs.

1. The Successor Trustee's Duties if You Are Incapacitated

If you become physically or mentally incapacitated, as certified in writing by a physician, and unable to manage your affairs, the successor trustee takes over management of the property in your living trust.

In this situation, the successor trustee has authority to use trust property for your health care, support and welfare. The law requires him or her to act honestly and prudently in managing the property. And because you are no longer the trustee, the new trustee must file an income tax return for the trust. At your death, any remaining trust property is distributed to beneficiaries.

The successor trustee has no power over property not in your living trust, and no authority to make health care decisions for you. For this reason, it's also wise to create a document called Durable Powers of Attorney, giving the successor trustee authority to manage property not owned in the name of the trust and to make health care decisions. (See Chapter 3, *A Living Trust as Part of Your Estate Plan*, Section F.)

2. The Successor Trustee's Duties After Your Death

After your death, the successor trustee takes over as trustee. His or her primary responsibility is to distribute trust property to the beneficiaries named in your Declaration of Trust. That is usually a straightforward process that can be completed in a few weeks. An outline of the steps the successor

---

[1]Incapacity is the inability to manage your affairs. The trust document created by *Nolo's Living Trust* defines incapacity and requires that incapacity must be documented in writing by a physician before the successor trustee can take over management of the trust property.

trustee needs to take to transfer certain common kinds of property is in Chapter 10, *After a Grantor Dies*.

The successor trustee may, however, have long-term duties if the trust document creates a child's subtrust for trust property inherited by a young beneficiary (this is explained in Part 7, below).

3. Choosing a Successor Trustee

The person or institution you choose as successor trustee will have a crucial role: to manage your trust property (if you become incapacitated) or distribute it to your beneficiaries (after your death).

If the successor trustee is in charge of managing property over the long term, the trust document produced by *Nolo's Living Trust* gives him or her very broad authority, so that the trustee will be able to do whatever is necessary to respond to the demands of the circumstances. For example, the trustee has the power to invest trust funds in accounts, such as money market accounts, that are not federally insured. The trustee is also free to spend trust income or property for the health and welfare of the incapacitated spouses or beneficiary of a child's subtrust.

Obviously, when you are giving someone this much power and discretion, you should choose someone with good common sense whom you trust completely, such as an adult son or daughter, other relative or close friend. If you don't know anyone who fits this description, think twice about establishing a living trust.

In most situations, the successor trustee will not need extensive experience in financial management; common sense, dependability and complete honesty are usually enough. A successor trustee who may have long-term responsibility over a young beneficiary's trust property needs more management and financial skills than a successor trustee whose only job is to distribute trust property. The successor trustee does have authority, under the terms of the trust document, to get any reasonably necessary professional help—from an accountant, lawyer or tax preparer, perhaps—and pay for it out of trust assets.

Usually, it makes sense to name just one person as successor trustee, to avoid any possibility of conflicts. But it's legal and may be desirable to name more than one person. For example, you might name two or more of your children, if you don't expect any disagreements between them and you think one of them might feel hurt and left out if not named.

Carefully consider the issue of conflicts, however. If you name more than one person as successor trustee, all of them must agree before they can act on behalf of the trust. If they can't agree, it could hold up the distribution of trust property to your beneficiaries. In extreme situations, the other trustees might even have to go to court to get the recalcitrant trustee removed, so that your instructions can be carried out. The result might be more bad feeling than if you had just picked one person to be trustee in the first place.

Having more than one successor trustee is especially likely to cause serious problems if the successor trustees are in charge of the property you have left to a young beneficiary in a child's subtrust. The trustees may have to manage a young beneficiary's property for many years, and will have many decisions to make about how to spend the money—greatly increasing the potential for conflict. (Children's subtrusts are discussed in Part 7, below.)

If you name more than one successor trustee, and one of them can't serve, the others will serve. If none of them can serve, the alternate you name (in the next Section of the program) will take over.

It's perfectly legal to name a beneficiary of the trust (someone who will receive trust property after your death) as successor trustee. In fact, it's common.

EXAMPLE Mildred names her only child, Allison, as both sole beneficiary of her living trust and successor trustee of the living trust. When Mildred dies, Allison uses her authority as trustee to transfer the trust property to herself.

The successor trustee does not have to live in the same state as you do. But if you are choosing between someone local and someone far away, think about how convenient it will be for the person you choose to distribute the living trust property after your death. Someone close by will probably have an easier job, especially with real estate transfers. But for transfers of property such as securities and bank accounts, it usually won't make much difference where the successor trustee lives.

Institutions as Successor Trustees

Normally, your first choice as successor trustee should be a flesh-and-blood person, not the trust department of a bank or other institution. Institutional trustees charge hefty fees, which come out of the trust property and leave less for your family and friends. And they probably won't even be interested in "small" living trusts—ones that contain less than several hundred thousand dollars worth of property.

But if there's no close relative or friend you think is capable of serving as your successor trustee, probably your best bet is to consider naming a private trust services company as successor trustee. Typically, their fees are pricey, but as a rule they charge less than a bank, and your affairs will probably receive more personal attention.

For a very large living trust, another possibility is to name a person and an institution as co-successor trustees. The bank or trust services company can do most of the paperwork, and the person can keep an eye on things and approve all transactions.

Obviously, before you finalize your living trust, you must check with the person or institution you've chosen to be your successor trustee. You want to be sure your choice is willing to serve.

If you don't, you may well create problems down the line. The person you've chosen may not want to serve, for a variety of reasons. And even if the person would be willing, if he or she doesn't know of his or her responsibilities, transfer of trust property after your death could be delayed.

If you choose an institution, you must check out the minimum size of trust it will accept and the fees it charges for management, and make arrangements for how the institution will take over as trustee at your death.

AVOIDING CONFLICTS WITH YOUR WILL AND OTHER DOCUMENTS

Your living trust gives your successor trustee the authority to manage trust property if you become incapacitated. To avoid conflicts, it's a good idea to name the person you choose as successor trustee in your will and Durable Power of Attorney for Finances, too.

- In your will, appoint your successor trustee to be executor, to be responsible for distributing your property (except living trust property) after your death.

- In your Durable Power of Attorney for Finances, appoint your successor trustee to be your "attorney in fact," to have authority to make financial and property management decisions for property (except property owned in the name of the living trust) if you become incapacitated.

---

4.   Payment of the Successor Trustee

Typically, the successor trustee of a simple probate-avoidance living trust isn't paid. This is because in most cases, the successor trustee's only job is to distribute the trust property to beneficiaries soon after the grantor's death. Often, the successor trustee inherits most of the trust property.

An exception is a successor trustee who manages the property in a child's subtrust. In that case, the successor trustee is entitled, under the terms of the trust document, to "reasonable compensation." The successor trustee decides what is reasonable and takes it from the trust property left to the young beneficiary.

Allowing the successor trustee to set the amount of the payment can work well, as long as your successor trustee is completely trustworthy. If the young beneficiary feels the trustee's fees are much too high, he or she will have to go to court to challenge them. If you want to restrict the successor trustee's freedom to decide on payment, see a lawyer.

The trust document created by *Nolo's Living Trust* does not require the successor trustee to post a bond (a kind of insurance policy) to guarantee conscientious fulfillment of his or her duties.

5. Naming an Alternate Successor Trustee

Nolo's Living Trust asks you to name an alternate, in case your first choice as successor trustee is unable to serve.

If you named more than one successor trustee, the alternate won't become trustee unless none of your original choices can serve.

EXAMPLE   Caroline names her two children, Eugene and Vanessa, as successor trustees. She names a close friend, Nicole, as alternate successor trustee. Because Vanessa is ill and can't serve as trustee, Eugene acts as sole successor trustee. If he becomes unable to serve, Nicole would take over.

If no one you named in the trust document can serve, the last trustee to serve has the power to appoint, in writing, another successor trustee. (See Chapter 10, *After a Grantor Dies.*)

EXAMPLE   To continue the previous example, if Nicole were ill and didn't have the energy to serve as successor trustee, she could appoint someone else to serve as trustee.

PART 4. PROPERTY TO BE PUT IN TRUST

Now you're getting to the heart of the program. In this part, you must list each item of property you want to transfer to your living trust. It will take some thought to decide what property to include and how to list it in the trust document. (Later in the program, you will name beneficiaries to receive each item of trust property at your death.)

This is a crucial step: Any property you don't list will not go into your living trust and will not pass under the terms of the trust. It may instead have to go through probate.

Adding property to the trust later. If you mistakenly leave something out or acquire more valuable property after you create your trust, you will be able to add it to your living trust. Chapter 9, *Living With Your Living Trust*, explains how.

A. Inventory Your Valuable Property

The first step is to take inventory—write down the valuable items of property you own. The categories listed below should jog your memory.

Even if you plan to leave everything to your spouse or children, you must make a list. That's because every item (or group of items, in some circumstances) must be specifically described and listed in the trust document.

When you list your property in the program, you can group items, if you're leaving them all to one beneficiary. For example, if you want to leave all your books to your best friend, there's no need to describe each one individually—unless your collection includes some particularly valuable or important books that you want to make extra sure get to the beneficiary.

After you've made an inventory, the next section will help you decide which items you want to transfer to your living trust so they don't have to go through probate after your death.

Getting Organized

While you're taking stock of all your valuable property, it might be a good time to go a step further and gather the information your family will need at your death.

You can use your computer to get organized by using Nolo's *For the Record* database program. It can keep track of all the important information in your family's life, including securities data, investments, real estate records, medical information, insurance records, credit card information and more.

(Ordering information is in the back of the manual.)

VALUABLE PROPERTY

Animals
Antiques
Appliances
Art
Books
Business interests
    Sole proprietorship
    Partnership
    Corporation
Business property
(if you own a sole proprietorship)
Cameras & photographic equipment
Cash accounts
    Certificates of deposit
    Checking
    Money market funds
    Savings
China, crystal, silver
Coins, stamps
Collectibles
Computers
Copyrights, patents, trademarks
Electronic equipment
Furniture
Furs
Jewelry
Limited partnership
Precious metals

Real estate
    Agricultural land
    Boat/Marina dock space
    Co-op
    Condo
    Duplex
    House
    Mobile home
    Rental property
    Time-share
    Undeveloped land
    Vacation house
Retirement accounts
    IRAs
    401(k) plans
    Keogh plans
Royalties
Securities
    Bonds
    Commodities
    Mutual funds
    Stocks
U.S. bills, notes and bonds
Tools
Vehicles
    Cars
    Motorcycles
    Bicycles
    Boats
    Motor homes/RVs
    Planes

 If you're married. If you are married but are making an individual trust, remember that you can transfer to the trust only the property you own. To be sure you understand what you own and what your spouse owns, see Chapter 6, *Creating a Shared Marital Trust*, Part 4.

B. Decide What Property To Put in Your Living Trust

Now that you've got a list of what you own, you're ready to decide what items you want to transfer to your living trust. You're creating a revocable living trust primarily to avoid probate fees. As a general rule, the more an item is worth, the more it will cost to probate it. That means you should transfer at least your most valuable property items to your living trust (or use some other probate-avoidance device to leave them at your death). Think about including:

- houses and other real estate
- jewelry, antiques, furs and valuable furniture
- stock in a closely-held corporation
- stock, bond and other security accounts held by brokerages
- small business interests
- money market and bank accounts
- other financial accounts
- patents and copyrights
- precious metals
- valuable works of art
- valuable collections of stamps, coins or other objects

Adding Property to Your Living Trust

You will be able to add property to your living trust at any time. As trustee, you can always sell or give away property in the trust. You can also take it out of the living trust and put it back in your name as an individual. Chapter 9, *Living With Your Living Trust*, explains how to make these changes.

You don't need to put everything you own into a living trust to save money on probate. For some assets, you may decide to use other probate-avoidance devices instead of a living trust. Property that is of relatively low value (the amount depends on state law) may be exempt from probate or qualify for a streamlined probate procedure that's relatively fast and cheap. (See Chapter 3, *A Living Trust as Part of Your Estate Plan*.)

Even if the non-trust property does have to go through regular probate, attorney and appraisal fees are generally based on the value of the probated property, so they'll be relatively low.

This section discusses how to decide whether or not to transfer various kinds of property to your living trust.

1. Real Estate

The most valuable thing most people own is their real estate: their house, condominium or land. Many people create a living trust just to make sure a house doesn't go through probate. You can probably save your family substantial probate costs by transferring your real estate through a living trust.

If you own the property with someone else, however, you may not want to transfer your real estate to an individual living trust. (See Section 8, Co-Owned Property, below.)

Co-op apartments. If you own shares in a co-op corporation that owns your apartment, you'll have to transfer your shares to your living trust. You may run into difficulties with the corporation; some are reluctant to let a trust, even a revocable trust completely controlled by the grantor, own shares. Check the co-op corporation's rules to see if the transfer is allowed.

2. Small Business Interests

The delay, expense and court intrusion of probate can be especially detrimental to an ongoing small business. Using your living trust to transfer business interests to beneficiaries quickly after your death is almost essential if you want the beneficiaries to be able to keep the business running.

If you want to control the long-term management of your business, however, a revocable living trust is not the right vehicle. See an estate planning lawyer to draft a different kind of trust, with provisions tailored to your situation.

Different kinds of business organizations present different issues when you want to transfer your interest to your living trust:

Sole proprietorships. If you operate your business as a sole proprietorship, with all business assets held in your own name, you can simply transfer your business property to your living trust like you would any other property. You should also transfer the business's name itself: that transfers the customer goodwill associated with the name.

Partnership interests. If you operate your business as a partnership with other people, you can probably transfer your partnership share to your living trust. If there is a partnership certificate, it must be changed to include the trust as owner of your share.

Some partnership agreements require the people who inherit a deceased partner's share of the business to offer that share to the other partners before taking it. But that happens after death, so it shouldn't affect your ability to transfer the property through a living trust.

It's not common, but a partnership agreement may limit or forbid transfers to a living trust. If yours does, you and your partners may want to see a lawyer before you make any changes.

Solely-owned corporations. If you own all the stock of a corporation, you should have no difficulty transferring it to your living trust.

Closely-held corporations. A closely-held corporation is a corporation that doesn't sell shares to the public. All its shares are owned by a few people who are usually actively involved in running the business. Normally, you can use a living trust to transfer shares in a closely-held corporation by listing the stock in the trust document and then having the stock certificates reissued in the trust's name.

You'll want to check the corporation's bylaws and articles of incorporation to be sure that if you transfer the shares to a living trust, you will still have voting rights in your capacity as trustee of the living trust; usually, this is not a problem. If it is, you and the other shareholders should be able to amend the corporation's bylaws to allow it.

There may, however, be legal restrictions on your freedom to transfer your shares to a living trust. Check the corporation's bylaws and articles of incorporation, as well as any separate shareholders' agreements.

One fairly common rule is that surviving shareholders (or the corporation itself) have the right to buy the shares of a deceased shareholder. In that case, you can still use a living trust to transfer the shares, but the people who inherit them may have to sell them to the other shareholders.

3. Bank and Retirement Accounts

It's not difficult to transfer bank or retirement accounts (IRAs, or Keogh or 401k accounts) to your living trust. But you may well decide that you don't need to.

You can directly designate a beneficiary for the funds in a bank or retirement account. If you name a beneficiary to receive whatever is in your account at your death, you don't need to transfer those accounts to a living trust just to avoid probate. Their contents won't need to go through probate in the first place.

This option can be especially useful for personal checking accounts, which you may not want to transfer to your living trust—it can be difficult to cash checks that say the account is owned by a revocable living trust.

A living trust, however, offers one advantage that most pay-on-death arrangements do not: If you transfer an account to a living trust, you can always name an alternate beneficiary to receive the account if your first choice as beneficiary isn't alive at the time of your death. The lack of an alternate may not be a problem if you use a pay-on-death account and name more than one beneficiary to inherit the funds, however; if one of the beneficiaries isn't alive, the other(s) will inherit the money.

Pay-on-death accounts are discussed in Chapter 3, *A Living Trust as Part of Your Estate Plan.*

4. Cars and Property That Is Often Sold

Some kinds of property are cumbersome to keep in a living trust. It's not a legal problem, just a practical one. Two common examples are:

- Cars or other vehicles you use. Having registration and insurance in the trust's name could be confusing, and some insurance companies balk at insuring cars that technically are owned by living trusts. If you have valuable antique autos, or a mobile home that is permanently attached to land and considered real estate under your state's law, however, you may want to go ahead and transfer ownership to your living trust. You should be able to find an insurance company that will cooperate.

- Property you buy or sell frequently. If you don't expect to own the property at your death, there's no compelling reason to transfer it to your living trust. (Remember, the probate process you want to avoid doesn't happen until after your death.) On the other hand, if you're buying property, it's no more trouble to acquire it in the name of the trust.

 Other arrangements for property not in your living trust. If you choose not to put valuable items in your living trust, you may want to make arrangements to have them avoid probate in some other way. If you don't, they will pass to the residuary beneficiary of your back-up will. (See Chapter 3, *A Living Trust as Part of Your Estate Plan.*)

5. Life Insurance

If you own a life insurance policy at your death, the proceeds given to the named beneficiary do not go through probate. (They are, however, considered part of your estate for federal estate tax purposes.)

If you have named a minor or young adult as the beneficiary of an insurance policy, however, you may want to name your living trust as the beneficiary of the policy. Then, in the trust document, you name the child as beneficiary of any insurance proceeds paid to the trust and arrange for an adult to manage the policy proceeds if the beneficiary is still young when you die. If you don't arrange for management of the money, and the beneficiary is still a minor (under 18) when you die, a court will have to appoint a financial guardian after your death. (Young beneficiaries are discussed in Part 7, below.)

Passing the proceeds of a life insurance policy through your living trust is a bit more complicated than leaving other property this way. You must take two steps:

1. Name the living trust as the beneficiary of your life insurance policy. (Your insurance agent will have a form that lets you change the beneficiary of the policy.)

2. When you list property items in the living trust document, list the proceeds of the policy, not the policy itself. (Section C, below, contains sample descriptions.)

6. Securities

If you buy and sell stocks regularly, you may not want to go to the trouble of acquiring them in the living trust's name and selling them using your authority as trustee of the trust.

Fortunately, there's an easier way to do it: hold your stocks in a brokerage account that is owned in the living trust's name. All securities in the account are then owned by your living trust, which means that you can use your living trust to leave all the contents of the account to a specific beneficiary. If you want to leave stock to different beneficiaries, you can either establish more than one brokerage account or leave one account to more than one beneficiary to own together.

An Alternative: Pay-on-Death Registration

Two states, Colorado and Wisconsin, allow ownership of securities to be registered in a "transfer-on-death" form.[2] In those states, you can designate someone to receive the securities, including mutual funds and brokerage accounts, after your death. No probate will be necessary. Ask your broker about the forms you need to fill out to name a beneficiary for your securities.

Stock in closely-held corporations. See Section 2, Small Business Interests, above.

7. Cash

It's common for people to want to leave cash to beneficiaries—for example, to leave $5,000 to a relative, friend or charity. Don't, however, just type in "$5,000 cash" when you list the property you want to transfer to the living trust. There's no way to transfer cash to a living trust.

You can, however, easily accomplish the same goal by transferring ownership of a cash account—savings account, money market account or certificate of deposit, for example—to your living trust. You can then name a beneficiary to receive the contents of the account. So if you want to leave

---

[2]These states have adopted the Uniform Transfer-on-Death Security Registration Act.

$5,000 to cousin Fred, all you have to do is put the money in a bank or money market account, transfer it to your living trust and name Fred, in the trust document, as the beneficiary.

If you don't want to set up a separate account to leave a modest amount of cash to a beneficiary, think about buying a savings bond and leaving it to the beneficiary, or leaving one larger account to several beneficiaries.

EXAMPLE Michael would like to leave some modest cash gifts to his two grown nephews, Warren and Brian, whom he's always been fond of. He puts $5,000 into a money market account and then transfers the account into his living trust. In his trust document, he names Warren and Brian as beneficiaries of the account. After Michael's death, the two nephews will inherit the account together, and each will be entitled to half of the funds.

8. Co-Owned Property

If you co-own property with someone, you can transfer your share of the property to your living trust. But whether or not you will want to depends on how you hold title to the property.

IF YOU'RE NOT SURE HOW YOU HOLD TITLE

If you own real estate with someone else but aren't sure how the title is held, look at the deed. It should say how title is held: in joint tenancy, tenancy in common, community property (in community property states) or tenancy by the entirety. In a community property state, if the deed says the property is owned "as husband and wife," that means community property.

If you do decide to transfer just your interest in co-owned property to your living trust, you don't need to specify that your share is one half or some other fraction. For example, if you and your sister own a house together, you need only list "the house at 7989 Lafayette Court, Boston, MA." Your trust document will simply state that you have transferred all your interest in that property to the trust.

If you are married and want to transfer only your share of property you own together with your spouse, see Chapter 6, Part 4.

a. Property Held in Joint Tenancy

Property owned in joint tenancy does not go through probate. When one co-owner (joint tenant) dies, his or her share goes directly to the surviving co-owners, without probate. So if avoiding probate is your only concern, you don't need to transfer joint tenancy property to your living trust.

A living trust does, however, offer more flexibility than joint tenancy.

Beneficiaries. If you do transfer your share of joint tenancy property to a living trust, the joint tenancy is destroyed, and you can leave your share of the property to anyone you choose—it won't automatically go to the surviving co-owners.

Simultaneous death. Joint tenancy doesn't avoid probate if the joint owners die simultaneously. If that happens, each co-owner's half-interest in the property is passed to the beneficiaries named in the residuary clauses of their wills. If there's no will, the property passes to the closest relatives under the state "intestate succession" law.

If you transfer the property to your living trust, you can name an alternate beneficiary to receive your share of the property. It's a bit more paperwork, but you're assured that probate will be avoided even in the (statistically very unlikely) event of simultaneous death.

b. Property Held in Tenancy by the Entirety

"Tenancy by the entirety" is, basically, a kind of joint tenancy that's only for married couples. It is available only in the states listed below.

Alaska*	Maryland	Ohio
Arkansas	Massachusetts	Oklahoma
Delaware	Michigan*	Oregon*
District of Columbia	Mississippi	Pennsylvania
Florida	Missouri	Tennessee
Hawaii	New Jersey*	Vermont
Indiana*	New York*	Virginia*
Kentucky	North Carolina*	Wyoming*

*allowed only for real estate

If you own property with your spouse in tenancy by the entirety, you cannot transfer your half-interest in the property to an individual living trust. Neither spouse can transfer his or her half of the property alone, either while alive or by will or trust. It must go to the surviving spouse. (This is different from joint tenancy; a joint tenant is free to transfer his or her share to someone else during his life.)

c. Community Property

Arizona	Louisiana	Texas
California	Nevada	Washington
Idaho	New Mexico	Wisconsin

Community property is another form of ownership that's only for married couples, in the states listed above. If you and your spouse together own community property, you should probably create a shared living trust. See Chapter 4, *What Kind of Living Trust Do You Need?*

For more about putting community property into a living trust, see Chapter 6, *Creating a Shared Marital Trust*, Part 4.

C. How to Describe Trust Property

When *Nolo's Living Trust* asks you to list the property you want to put in your trust, describe each item clearly enough so that the successor trustee can identify the property and transfer it to the right person. No magic legal words are required.

Think about whom the property will ultimately go to. If you're leaving everything to one person, or a few major items will be divided among a few people, there's less need to go into great detail. But if there will be a number of trust beneficiaries, and objects could be confused, be more specific about each one. When in doubt, err on the side of including more information.

RULES FOR ENTERING DESCRIPTIONS OF TRUST PROPERTY

- Don't use "my" or "our" in a description. Don't, for example, enter "my books" or "my stereo system." That's because once the property is in the living trust, technically it doesn't belong to you anymore—it belongs to the living trust.

- Don't begin a description with a capital letter (unless it must begin with a proper name, like "Steinway"). That's because the descriptions will be inserted into a sentence in the trust document, and it would look odd to see a capital letter in the middle of a sentence.

- Don't end a description with a period. Again, this is because the descriptions will be inserted into a sentence in the trust document.

You may want to identify some items by their location—for example, "the books kept at 335 Forest Way, Denver, CO." But if the property you're describing is valuable—expensive jewelry or artworks, for example—be more specific. Describe the item in detail, in much the same way you would describe it if you were listing it on an insurance policy.

Here are some sample descriptions:

Real estate

- "the house at 321 Glen St., Omaha, NE"

- "the house at 4444 Casey Road, Fandon, Illinois and the 20-acre parcel on which it is located."

Usually, the street address is enough. It's not necessary to use the "legal description" found on the deed, which gives a subdivision plat number or a metes-and-bounds description. If the property has no street address—for example, if it is undeveloped land out in the country—you will need to carefully copy the full legal description, word for word, from the deed.

If you own a house and several adjacent lots, it's a good idea to indicate that you are transferring the entire parcel to your living trust by describing the land as well as the house.

If you own the property with someone else and are transferring only your share, you don't need to specify the share you own. Just describe the property. The trust document will show that you are transferring all your interest in the property, whatever share that is, to the living trust.

Bank and retirement accounts

- "Savings Account No. 9384-387, Arlington Bank, Arlington, MN"

- "Money Market Account 47-223 at Charles Schwab & Co., Inc., San Francisco, CA"

- "IRA Account No. 990-66-221, Working Assets Money Fund, San Francisco, CA"

Household items

- "all the furniture normally kept in the house at 44123 Derby Ave., Ross, KY"

- "the antique brass bed in the master bedroom in the house at 33 Walker Ave., Fort Lee, New Jersey"

- "all furniture and household items normally kept in the house at 869 Hopkins St., Great Falls, Montana"

Sole proprietorship business property

- "Mulligan's Fish Market"

- "Fourth Street Records and CDs"

- "all accounts receivable of the business known as Garcia's Restaurant, 988 17th St., Atlanta, GA"

- "all food preparation and storage equipment, including refrigerator, freezer, hand mixers and slicer used at Garcia's Restaurant, 988 17th St., Atlanta, GA"

As explained in Section B, above, you should both list the name of the business and separately list items of business property.

Partnership interest

- "all interest in the Don and Dan's Bait Shop Partnership owned by the grantor before being transferred to this living trust"

Because a partnership is a legal entity that can own property, you don't need to list items of property owned by the partnership.

Shares in a closely-held corporation

- "The stock of ABC Hardware, Inc."

Shares in a solely owned corporation

- "all shares in the XYZ Corporation"

- "all stock in Fern's Olde Antique Shoppe, Inc., 23 Turnbridge Court, Danbury, Connecticut"

Securities

- "all securities in account No. 3999-34-33 at Smith Brokerage, 33 Lowell Place, New York, NY"

- "200 shares of General Industries, Inc. stock"

- "Good Investment Co. mutual fund account No. 888-09-09"

Life insurance proceeds

- "the proceeds of Acme Co. Life Insurance Policy #9992A"

Miscellaneous items

- "the Macintosh SE30 computer (serial number 129311) with keyboard (serial number 165895)"

- "the medical textbooks in the office at 1702 Parker Towers, San Francisco, CA"

- "the stamp collection usually kept at 321 Glen St., Omaha, NE"

- "the collection of European stamps, including [describe particularly valuable stamps], usually kept at 440 Loma Prieta Blvd., #450, San Jose, CA"

- "the Martin D-35 acoustic guitar, serial number 477597"

- "the signed 1960 Ernie Banks baseball card kept in safe deposit box 234, First National Bank of Augusta, Augusta, IL"

- "the Baldwin upright piano kept at 985 Dawson Court, South Brenly, Massachusetts"

IMPORTANT REMINDER: TRANSFERRING PROPERTY TO THE TRUST

If an item has a title (ownership) document, such as a deed or title slip, its ownership is not transferred to the trust just by listing it in the program. You *must* also change the title document to show the living trust as the legal owner of the property.

YOU SHOULD TRANSFER OWNERSHIP AS SOON AS POSSIBLE AFTER YOU PRINT OUT AND SIGN YOUR DECLARATION OF TRUST.

Instructions are in Chapter 8, *Transferring Property to the Trust.*

PART 5. BENEFICIARIES OF TRUST PROPERTY

Once you've entered a list of the property you're transferring to your living trust, the next step is to say who you want to inherit that property. *Nolo's Living Trust* lets you name a beneficiary for each item of trust property separately, or name one beneficiary to receive all the trust property.

The beneficiaries you name in your trust document are not entitled to anything while you are alive. Just as with a will, you can amend your trust document and change the beneficiaries any time you wish.

Disinheriting a Spouse or Child

If you are married and don't plan to leave at least half of what you own to your spouse, consult a lawyer experienced in estate planning. State law may entitle your spouse to some of your estate, including the property in your living trust.

In most circumstances, you don't have to leave anything to your children. But if you want to disinherit a child, you should make a back-up will and specifically mention the child in it.

See Chapter 2, *About Living Trusts*.

A. How Do You Want Your Property Distributed?

Nolo's Living Trust asks you first whether you want to leave all your trust property to one beneficiary (or more than one, to share it all) or leave different items to different beneficiaries.

The simplest approach is to leave all your trust property to one person, or to one or more person to share. If you choose that option, all you have to do is name each beneficiary and then name an alternate beneficiary for each, who will inherit the trust property if a primary beneficary does not survive you by five days. (Alternates are discussed in Section C, below.)

If you choose to leave different items to different beneficiaries, you will be taken to a screen that displays a list of all the property items you listed earlier. You can choose any number of the items and name beneficiaries for them.

1. Minors or Young Adults

If a beneficiary you name is a minor or a young adult who can't yet manage property without adult help, you can arrange for an adult to manage the trust property for the beneficiary. *Nolo's Living Trust* lets you do this after you have named all your beneficiaries. (See Part 7, below.)

2. Your Successor Trustee

It's very common and perfectly legal to make the person you named to be successor trustee (the person who will distribute trust property after your death) a beneficiary as well.

EXAMPLE Nora names her son Liam as successor trustee of her living trust. She also names him as sole beneficiary of her trust property. When Nora dies, Liam, acting as trustee, will transfer ownership of the trust property from the trust to himself.

3. Co-Beneficiaries

You can name more than one beneficiary to share any item of trust property. Simply list their names in the box provided on the screen. Type the names one per line; don't join the names with an "and." (See the User's Manual for examples.)

Always use the beneficiaries' actual names; don't use collective terms such as "my children." It's not always clear who is included in such descriptions. And there can be serious confusion if one of the people originally included as a beneficiary dies before you do.

Obviously, if you name co-beneficiaries for a piece of property that can't be physically divided—a cabin, for example—give some thought to whether or not the beneficiaries are likely to get along. If they are incompatible, disagreements could arise over taking care of property or deciding whether or not to sell it. If they can't settle their differences, any co-owner could go to court and demand a partition—a court-ordered division and sale—of the property.

Co-beneficiaries will share the property equally unless you state otherwise. You will be asked, after you enter the names, whether or not you want this item of trust property to be shared equally among the beneficiaries.

EXAMPLE   Georgia wants to leave her house to her two children, Ross and Ryan, but wants Ross to have a 75% share of it. She enters their names and then, on a later screen, enters their interests, in fractions: 3/4 for Ross and 1/4 for Ryan.

When the children inherit the property, they own it together. But Ross will be liable for 75% of the taxes and upkeep cost, and entitled to 75% of any income the house produces. If they sell it, Ross will be entitled to 75% of the proceeds.

4. Beneficiaries for Your Share of Co-Owned Trust Property

If you own property together with someone else, you will name beneficiaries for your share of the property. At your death, only your interest in the property will go to the beneficiary you name.

As with naming co-beneficiaries (Section 3, above), pay attention to who will end up as co-owners of the property after your death. If, for example, you and your brother own a house together, and you leave your share to your daughter—who detests her uncle—problems are likely.

B. Entering Beneficiaries' Names

When you enter a beneficiary's name, use the name by which the beneficiary is known for purposes such as a bank account or driver's license. Generally, if the name you use clearly and unambiguously identifies the person, it is sufficient.

The name you use doesn't have to be the one that appears on the person's birth certificate. And you don't need to include all the nicknames ("Chuck" for someone whose real name is Charles, for example) a beneficiary is known by.

If you name an institution (charitable or not) to inherit the property in your trust, enter its complete name. It may be commonly known by a shortened version, which could cause confusion if there are similarly named organizations. Call to ask if you're unsure. (An institution that stands to inherit some of your money will be more than happy to help you.) Also be sure to specify if you want a specific branch or part of a national organization to receive your gift—for example, a local chapter of the Sierra Club.

C. Alternate Beneficiaries

Nolo's Living Trust allows you to name an alternate for every person you name as a primary beneficiary. The alternate will get the property left to the primary beneficiary if your first choice does not live for more than 120 hours (five days) after your death. This "survivorship" period ensures that if you and a primary beneficiary die simultaneously or almost so, the property will go to the alternate beneficiary you chose, not to the primary beneficiary's heirs.

EXAMPLE Laura leaves all her trust property to her sister Jean, and names her daughter as alternate beneficiary. Laura and Jean are seriously injured in a car accident; Jean dies a day after Laura does. Because Jean did not survive Laura by at least five days, the trust property she would have inherited from Laura goes to Laura's daughter instead.

If there had been no survivorship requirement, the trust property would have gone to Jean; when she died a day later, it would have gone to the beneficiaries she had named (or, if she had made no will, to the heirs according to state law).

You don't have to name an alternate for a charitable (or other) institution you name as a beneficiary. If the institution is well established, it is probably safe to assume that it will still exist at your death.

With other beneficiaries, however, there is always the chance that the primary beneficiary may not survive you. If you don't name an alternate, the property that beneficiary would have received will be distributed to the person or institution you name, in the next part of the program, as your "residuary beneficiary." (See Part 6, below.)

You can name more than one person or institution as alternate beneficiaries. If you do, these "co-alternate beneficiaries" will share the property equally.

EXAMPLE   Sherry transfers her half-interest in a house to her living trust. She names her brother, the co-owner, as beneficiary. As alternate beneficiaries, she names her three children, Sean, Colleen and Tim.

Sherry's brother dies shortly before she does, leaving his half of the house to Sherry. She transfers her new half-interest in the house to the trust. At Sherry's death, the house goes to the three children equally. All three own equal shares in all of it. If they sell the property, each will be entitled to a third of the proceeds.

PART 6. RESIDUARY BENEFICIARY

You must name a residuary beneficiary for your living trust. The residuary beneficiary of your living trust is the person or organization who will receive:

- any trust property for which both the primary and alternate beneficiaries you named die before you do

- any trust property that you didn't leave to a named beneficiary (this could include property you transferred to the trust later but didn't name a beneficiary for)

- any property you leave to your living trust through your will. (Because property left through a pour-over will doesn't avoid probate, there's usually no reason to use one. See Chapter 3, *A Living Trust as Part of Your Estate Plan.*)

- any property that you actually transferred to your living trust but didn't list in the trust document

Often, the residuary beneficiary of a living trust doesn't inherit anything from the trust. Usually, naming a residuary beneficiary is just a back-up measure, to guard against the extremely small chance that both a primary and alternate trust beneficiary do not survive you.

You may, however, deliberately leave the residuary beneficiary trust property by:

- Adding property to the trust later and not naming a specific beneficiary to receive it after your death.

- Using a pour-over will to leave property to your living trust.

If you name more than one person or institution as residuary beneficiary, they will each get an equal share of any trust property they receive.

EXAMPLE You name your two children, Anne and Alice, as your residuary beneficiaries. If they end up receiving trust property, they will own it together, and both will own an equal share of it.

PART 7. PROPERTY MANAGEMENT FOR YOUNG BENEFICIARIES

If any of your beneficiaries (including alternate and residuary beneficiaries) might inherit trust property before they are ready to manage it without an adult's help, you should arrange for someone else to manage it for them for a while. There are several ways to go about it:

- **Leave the property to an adult to use for the child.** Many people don't leave property directly to a child. Instead, they leave it to the child's parent or to the person they expect to have care and custody of the child if neither parent is available. There's no formal legal arrangement, but they trust the adult to use the property for the child's benefit.

- **Create a child's subtrust.** You can use *Nolo's Living Trust* to establish a "child's subtrust" in your living trust. If you do, your successor trustee will manage the property you left the child and dole it out for education, health and other needs. The subtrust ends at whatever age you designate (up to 35), and any remaining property is turned over to the child outright.

- **Name a custodian under the Uniform Transfers to Minors Act (UTMA).** In many states, you can name a "custodian" to manage property you leave a child until the child reaches 18 or 21, depending on state law (up to 25 in Alaska or California). If you don't need management to last beyond that age, a custodianship is probably preferable.

Subtrusts and custodianships are explained below.

 Children with special needs. These property management options are not designed to provide long-term property management for a child with serious disabilities. You should see a lawyer and make arrangements geared to your particular situation.

A. Should You Arrange for Management?

It's up to you whether or not to make arrangements, in the trust document, to have someone manage trust property if it is inherited by young beneficiaries.

The consequences of forgoing management for trust property inherited by a young beneficiary depend on whether the beneficiary is over or under age 18 at your death.

1. Children Under 18 Years Old

Minors—children under 18—cannot, legally, own or manage significant amounts of property. An adult must be in charge if the minor acquires more than a few thousand dollars' worth of property. (The exact amount depends on state law.)

If your minor beneficiaries won't inherit anything of great value—if you're leaving them objects that have more sentimental than monetary value—you don't need to arrange for an adult to manage the property.

But if a beneficiary inherits valuable trust property while still a minor, and you have not arranged for the property to be managed by an adult, the beneficiary will have to have a court-appointed guardian to manage the property. Contrary to what you might expect, a child's parent does not automatically have legal authority to manage any property the child inherits. So even if one or both of the beneficiary's parents are alive, they will not automatically have authority to manage the property. They will have to ask the court to grant them that authority, and will be subject to the court's supervision. If neither of the beneficiary's parents are alive, there may be no obvious person for the court to appoint as property guardian. In that case, it may be even more important for you to name someone in your living trust.

2. Young Adults 18 to 35 Years Old

If a living trust beneficiary is over 18 when he or she inherits trust property, you do not need, legally, to have anyone manage the property on the beneficiary's behalf. And if you don't make any arrangements, the beneficiary will get the property with no strings attached. But you can arrange for property management to last until a beneficiary turns any age up to 35.

There is no legal requirement that management for a trust beneficiary's property must end at 35, but we think 35 is a reasonable cutoff. If you don't want to let a beneficiary get his or her hands on trust property by the time he or she reaches 35, you probably need to see a lawyer and tailor a plan to the beneficiary's needs.

B. Which Method Is Best: Subtrust or Custodianship?

Using *Nolo's Living Trust*, you can create either a child's subtrust or a custodianship under the Uniform Transfer to Minors Act (if it's available in your state). Both are safe, efficient ways of managing trust property that a young person inherits. Under either system, the person in charge of the young beneficiary's property has the same responsibility to use the property for the beneficiary's support, education and health.

The most significant difference is that a child's subtrust can last longer than a custodianship, which must end at age 18 to 21 (up to 25 in Alaska and California) in most states. For that reason, a child's subtrust is a good choice when a child could conceivably inherit a large amount of property.

Because an UTMA custodianship is easier to administer, it is usually preferable if the beneficiary will inherit no more than about $50,000 worth of trust property ($100,000 or more if the child is quite young). That amount is likely to be used up for living and education expenses by the time the beneficiary is 18 to 21, so there's no need to create a child's subtrust that can continue beyond that age.

A custodianship has other advantages as well:

- Handling a beneficiary's property can be easier with a custodianship than with a trust. A custodian's powers are written into state law, and most institutions, such as banks and insurance companies, are familiar with the rules. Trusts, on the other hand, vary in their terms. So before a bank lets a trustee act on behalf of a beneficiary, it may demand to see and analyze a copy of the Declaration of Trust.

- You can name whomever you wish to be a custodian, and you can name different custodians for different beneficiaries. So if you want to arrange custodianships for grandchildren, for example, you could name each child's parent as custodian. A child's subtrust is not quite so flexible: the successor trustee will be the trustee of all children's subtrusts created for your young beneficiaries.

STATES THAT HAVE ADOPTED THE UNIFORM TRANSFERS TO MINORS ACT

State	Age at which minor gets property
Alabama	21
Alaska	18-25
Arizona	21
Arkansas	18-21
California	18-25
Colorado	21
District of Columbia	18
Florida	21
Georgia	21
Hawaii	21
Idaho	21
Illinois	21
Iowa	21
Kansas	21
Kentucky	18
Maine	18-21
Maryland	21
Massachusetts	21
Minnesota	21
Missouri	21
Montana	21
Nevada	18
New Hampshire	21
New Jersey	18-21
New Mexico	21
North Carolina	18-21
North Dakota	21
Ohio	21
Oklahoma	18
Oregon	21
Rhode Island	18
South Dakota	18
Utah	21
Virginia	18-21
Washington	21
West Virginia	21
Wyoming	21

C. Children's Subtrusts

Nolo's Living Trust allows you to set up a separate "child's subtrust" for each young beneficiary.

1. How a Child's Subtrust Works

In your trust document, you state the age at which the beneficiary should receive trust property outright. If at your death the beneficiary is younger than the age you specified, a subtrust will be created for that beneficiary. (If the beneficiary is older, he or she gets the trust property with no strings attached, and no subtrust is created.) Each beneficiary gets a separate child's subtrust.

Nolo's Living Trust is set up so that the successor trustee will serve as trustee of any children's subtrusts. If you want different people to manage property inherited by different beneficiaries, you may want to use a custodianship instead of a child's subtrust. (To appoint someone else to be trustee of a child's subtrust, the trust document would have to be changed significantly; see a lawyer.)

Whatever trust property the beneficiary is entitled to receive upon your death will go into the child's subtrust, if the child is still under the age set for termination of the subtrust. The trustee will manage the subtrust property and use it as necessary for the beneficiary's health, education and support. After your death, the subtrust cannot be revoked or amended. (Until then, you are free to change your mind about having a subtrust set up for a particular beneficiary.)

The child's subtrust will end when the beneficiary reaches the age you designated in your Declaration of Trust. This can be any age up to and including 35. The trustee will then give the beneficiary what remains of the subtrust property.

How a Child's Subtrust Works

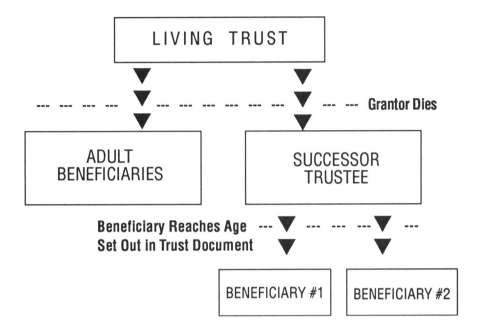

EXAMPLE 1. In his trust document, Stanley names his 14-year-old son Michael as beneficiary of $25,000 worth of stock. He specifies that any stock Michael becomes entitled to when Stanley dies should be kept in a subtrust until Michael is 25, subject to the trustee's right to spend it on Michael's behalf.

Stanley dies when Michael is 19. The stock goes into a subtrust for him, managed by the successor trustee of Stanley's living trust. The trustee is free to use the stock (or the income it produces) to pay for Michael's education and support. Michael will receive what's left of the stock when he turns 25.

EXAMPLE 2. Victoria creates a living trust and leaves her trust property to her daughters, who are 22 and 25. She specifies that any trust property they inherit should stay in children's subtrusts until each daughter reaches 30. Victoria names her sister, Antoinette, as successor trustee.

Victoria dies in a car accident when one daughter is 28 and the other is 31. The 28-year-old's half of the trust property stays in a subtrust, managed by Antoinette, until she turns 30. The 31-year-old gets her half outright; no subtrust is created for her.

2. The Trustee's Duties

The subtrust trustee must:

- Manage subtrust property until the beneficiary reaches the age set out in the trust document—which can take years.

- Use subtrust property or income to pay for expenses such as the beneficiary's support, education and health care.

- Keep separate records of subtrust transactions and file income tax returns for the subtrust.

The trustee's powers and responsibilities are spelled out in the trust document. If the subtrust trustee needs to hire an accountant, tax lawyer or other expert, he or she can use subtrust assets to pay a reasonable amount for the help.

The trust document also provides that the trustee of a subtrust is entitled to reasonable compensation for his or her work as trustee. The trustee decides what is a reasonable amount; the compensation is paid from the subtrust assets.

For more on the trustee's responsibilities, see Chapter 10, *After a Grantor Dies*.

D. Custodianships

A custodianship is the preferable alternative for many people. Here's how it works.

1. How a Custodianship Works

In the trust document, the grantor names someone to serve as custodian for a particular beneficiary. That person manages any trust property the young beneficiary inherits until the beneficiary reaches the age at which state law says the custodianship must end. (See table in Section B, above.)

How a Custodianship Works

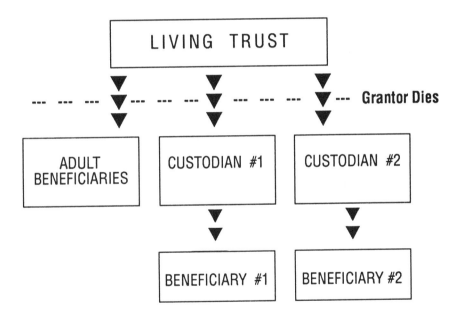

EXAMPLE.   In her living trust, Sandra leaves 100 shares of General Motors stock to her niece, Jennifer. She names Hazel, Jennifer's mother, as custodian under the Illinois Uniform Transfers to Minors Act.

After Sandra's death, her successor trustee gives the stock to the custodian, Hazel. She will manage it for Jennifer until Jennifer turns 21, the age Illinois law says she must be given the property outright.

In some states, you can specify—within limits—at what age the custodian-ship will end. If your state allows this, the program will ask you to enter an age at which you want the custodianship to end.

EXAMPLE. Jonathan, a divorced father who lives in New Jersey, makes a living trust. He leaves a substantial amount of trust property to his young children, Ian and Noel. He specifies, in the trust document, that any trust property the children inherit should be managed by his ex-wife, Elizabeth, as custodian under the New Jersey Uniform Transfers to Minors Act, until the boys turn 21.

When Jonathan dies, Elizabeth takes over management of the trust property for her children. When each boy turns 21, he will receive whatever of the property hasn't been used for his support or education.

2. The Custodian's Responsibilities

A custodian has roughly the same responsibility as the trustee of a child's subtrust: to manage the beneficiary's property wisely and honestly. The custodian's authority and duties are clearly set out by state law (the Uniform Transfers to Minors Act, as enacted by your state[3]). No court directly supervises the custodian.

The custodian must:

- Manage the property until the beneficiary reaches the age at which, by law, he or she gets the property outright. If the child is a minor at your death, this can be a number of years.

- Use the property or income to pay for expenses such as the young bene-ficiary's support, education and health care.

- Keep the property separate from his or her own property.

- Keep separate records of trust transactions. The custodian does not have to file a separate income tax return; income from the property can be reported on the young beneficiary's return. (By comparison, the trustee of a child's subtrust must file a separate tax return for the subtrust.)

---

[3]The UTMA is a model law written by a national panel of experts, but legislatures may make minor modifications in it when they adopt it for their states.

A custodian who needs to hire an accountant, tax lawyer or other expert can use the property to pay a reasonable amount for the help.

If state law allows it, the custodian is entitled to reasonable compensation and reimbursement for reasonable expenses. The payment, if any is taken, comes from the property the custodian manages for the beneficiary.

3. Choosing a Custodian

You can name a different custodian for each young beneficiary, if you wish.

In most cases, you should name the person who will have physical custody of the minor child. That's almost always one of the child's parents. If the beneficiary is your child, name the child's other parent unless you have serious reservations about that person's ability to handle the property for the child.

Only one person can be named as custodian for one beneficiary. You can, however, name an alternate custodian to take over if your first choice is unable to serve.

SAMPLE INDIVIDUAL TRUST

Signing, Storing and Registering the Trust Document

Before You Sign

Before you sign the trust document, make sure it says exactly what you want it to say and that you understand it all. If you want to make changes, use the program and print out another trust document. (If you need help, see the User's Guide) Don't write any changes on the document.

Get Your Signature Notarized

Sign your living trust document in front of a notary public for your state.

Making Copies

If you need copies of the trust document, use a photocopy of the original trust document—the one you signed and had notarized. Do not just print out and sign another copy.

Registering the Trust

Some states (Alaska, Colorado, Florida, Hawaii, Idaho, Maine, Michigan, Nebraska, New Mexico, North Dakota and Tennessee) require that you register your living trust document with the local court. But there are no legal consequences or penalties if you don't. See Chapter 7 for instructions on how to register.

Storing the Trust Document

Store your living trust document and the *Nolo's Living Trust* disk where you keep important papers. Make sure your successor trustee knows where the original trust document is and can get hold of it soon after your death.

Declaration of Trust

Part 1. Trust Name

This revocable living trust shall be known as The Judith M. Avery Revocable Living Trust.

Part 2. Declaration of Trust

Judith M. Avery, called the grantor, declares that she has transferred and delivered to the trustee all her interest in the property described in Schedule A attached to this Declaration of Trust. All of that property is called the "trust property." The trustee hereby acknowledges receipt of the trust property and agrees to hold the trust property in trust, according to this Declaration of Trust.

The grantor may add property to the trust.

Part 3. General Administrative Provisions

A. Controlling Law

The validity of this trust shall be governed by the laws of Illinois.

B. Severability of Clauses

If any provision of this Declaration of Trust is ruled unenforceable, the remaining provisions shall stay in effect.

C. Amendments

The term "this Declaration of Trust" includes any provisions added by valid amendment.

Part 4. Amendment and Revocation

A. Amendment or Revocation by Grantor

The grantor may amend or revoke this trust at any time, without notifying any beneficiary. An amendment must be made in writing and signed by the grantor. Revocation may be in writing or any manner allowed by law.

B. Amendment or Revocation by Other Person

The power to revoke or amend this trust is personal to the grantor. A conservator, guardian or other person shall not exercise it on behalf of the grantor, unless the grantor specifically grants a power to revoke or amend this trust in a Durable Power of Attorney.

Part 5. Payments from Trust During Grantor's Lifetime

The trustee shall pay to or use for the benefit of the grantor as much of the net income and principal of the trust property as the grantor requests. Income not paid to or used for the benefit of the grantor shall be accumulated and added to principal.

Part 6. Trustees

A. Trustees

Judith M. Avery shall be trustee of this trust.

B. Trustee's Responsibility

The trustee in office shall serve as trustee of all trusts created under this Declaration of Trust, including children's subtrusts.

C. Terminology

In this Declaration of Trust, the term "trustee" includes successor trustees or alternate successor trustees serving as trustee of this trust. The singular "trustee" also includes the plural.

D. Successor Trustee

Upon the death or incapacity of Judith M. Avery, the trustee of this trust and of any children's subtrusts created by it shall be Robert S. Avery and Anne Avery Puckett. If Robert S. Avery and Anne Avery Puckett are both unable or unwilling to serve as successor trustee, David R. Puckett shall be the trustee.

E. Resignation of Trustee

Any trustee in office may resign at any time by signing a notice of resignation. The resignation must be delivered to the person or institution who is either named in this Declaration of Trust, or appointed by the trustee under Part 6, Section F, to next serve as the trustee.

F. Power to Appoint Successor Trustee

If no one named in this Declaration of Trust as a successor trustee or alternate successor trustee is willing or able to serve as trustee, the last acting trustee may appoint a successor trustee and may require the posting of a reasonable bond, to be paid from the trust property. The appointment must be made in writing, signed by the trustee and notarized.

G. Bond

No bond shall be required for any trustee named in this Declaration of Trust.

H. Compensation

No trustee shall receive any compensation for serving as trustee, unless the trustee serves as a trustee of a child's subtrust created by this Declaration of Trust.

I. Liability of Trustee

With respect to the exercise or non-exercise of discretionary powers granted by this Declaration of Trust, the trustee shall not be liable for actions taken in good faith. Such actions shall be binding on all persons interested in the trust property.

Part 7. Trustee's Management Powers and Duties

A. Powers Under State Law

The trustee shall have all authority and powers allowed or conferred on a trustee under Illinois law, subject to the trustee's fiduciary duty to the grantor and the beneficiaries.

B. Other Powers

The trustee's powers shall also include:

1. The power to borrow money and to encumber trust property, including trust real estate, by mortgage, deed of trust or other method.

2. The power to manage trust real estate as if the trustee were the absolute owner of it, including the power to lease (even if the lease term may extend beyond the period of any trust) or grant options to lease the property, to make repairs or alterations and to insure against loss.

3. The power to sell or grant options for the sale or exchange of any trust property, including stocks, bonds, debentures and any other form of security or security account, at public or private sale for cash or on credit.

4. The power to invest trust property in property of any kind, including but not limited to bonds, debentures, notes, mortgages and stocks.

5. The power to receive additional property from any source and add to any trust created by this Declaration of Trust.

6. The power to employ and pay reasonable fees to accountants, lawyers or investment experts for information or advice relating to the trust.

7. The power to deposit and hold trust funds in both interest-bearing and non-interest-bearing accounts.

8. The power to deposit funds in bank or other accounts uninsured by FDIC coverage.

9. The power to enter into electronic fund transfer or safe deposit arrangements with financial institutions.

Part 8. Incapacity of Grantor

If the grantor becomes physically or mentally incapacitated, whether or not a court has declared the grantor incompetent or in need of a conservator, the successor trustee named in Part 6 shall be trustee. Incapacity must be certified in writing by a licensed physician.

In that event, the trustee shall manage the trust property. The trustee shall use any amount of trust income or trust property necessary for the grantor's proper health care, support, maintenance, comfort and welfare, in accordance with the grantor's accustomed manner of living. Any income not spent for the benefit of the grantor shall be accumulated and added to the trust property.

The successor trustee shall manage the trust until a licensed physician certifies in writing that the grantor is no longer physically or mentally incompetent.

Part 9. Death of Grantor

When the grantor dies, this trust shall become irrevocable. It may not be amended or altered except as provided for by this Declaration of Trust. It may be terminated only by the distributions authorized by this Declaration of Trust.

The trustee shall pay out of trust property such amounts as necessary for payment of debts, estate taxes and expenses of the last illness and funeral.

Part 10. Beneficiaries

At the death of the grantor, the trustee shall distribute the trust property as follows, subject to provisions in this Declaration of Trust that create children's subtrusts or create custodianships under the Uniform Transfers to Minors Act:

1. Anne Avery Puckett and Robert S. Avery shall be given all the grantor's interest in all household furnishings in the house at 88823 Lakeview Dr., Crystal Lake, Illinois and the house at 88823 Lakeview Dr., Crystal Lake, Illinois in equal shares. If Anne Avery Puckett fails to survive the grantor by 120 hours, his or her interest in this property shall be given to David R. Puckett. If Robert S. Avery fails to survive the grantor by 120 hours, his or her interest in this property shall be given to Cheryl Avery.

2. David R. Puckett shall be given all the grantor's interest in the two $100 United States Saving Bonds kept in safe deposit box 3351 at Crystal Lake Savings and Loan, Crystal Lake, Illinois.

3. Anne Avery Puckett shall be given all the grantor's interest in account No. 3999-34-3 at Smith Brokerage, 33 Lowell Place, New York, NY. If Anne Avery Puckett does not survive the grantor by 120 hours, that property shall be given to David R. Puckett.

4. Robert S. Avery shall be given all the grantor's interest in 200 shares of General Industries stock. If Robert S. Avery does not survive the grantor by 120 hours, that property shall be given to Cheryl Avery.

5. Robert S. Avery and Anne Avery Puckett shall be given all trust property not otherwise specifically and validly disposed of by this Part.

Part 11. Custodianships Under the Uniform Transfers to Minors Act

1. Any property David R. Puckett becomes entitled to under Part 10 of this Declaration of Trust shall be given to Anne Avery Puckett, as custodian for David R. Puckett under the Illinois Uniform Transfers to Minors Act, until David R. Puckett reaches the age of 21. If Anne Avery Puckett is unable or ceases to serve as custodian, Anthony B. Puckett shall serve as custodian.

I certify that I have read this Declaration of Trust and that it correctly states the terms and conditions under which the trust property is to be held, managed, and disposed of by the trustees, and I approve the Declaration of Trust.

Dated: _____

_____

Judith M. Avery, Grantor and Trustee

State of _____

County of _____

On _____, 19___, before me, a notary public for the State of Illinois, personally appeared Judith M. Avery, known to me to be the grantor and trustee of the trust created by the above Declaration of Trust, and to be the person whose name is subscribed to the Declaration of Trust, and acknowledged and executed the same as grantor and trustee.

IN WITNESS WHEREOF, I have set my hand and affixed by official seal.

_____

NOTARY PUBLIC for

the State of Illinois

My commission expires _____, 19___.

Schedule A

1. 200 shares of General Industries stock.

2. Account No. 3999-34-3 at Smith Brokerage, 33 Lowell Place, New York, NY.

3. All household furnishings in the house at 88823 Lakeview Dr., Crystal Lake, Illinois.

4. The house at 88823 Lakeview Dr., Crystal Lake, Illinois.

5. The two $100 United States Saving Bonds kept in safe deposit box 3351 at Crystal Lake Savings and Loan, Crystal Lake, Illinois.

6 Creating a Shared Marital Trust

When you create your living trust document with *Nolo's Living Trust*, you have only a few choices to make. Basically, you must decide five things:

- Whether to make an individual living trust or a shared living trust with your spouse.

- What property you want to put in your living trust.

- Who you want to receive trust property at your death. These people or organizations are the beneficiaries of your living trust.

- Who is to be the successor trustee—the person or institution who, after both spouses have died, will distribute the surviving spouse's trust property.

- How you should arrange for someone to manage trust property inherited by beneficiaries who are too young to handle it without supervision.

You may already have a good idea of how you want to decide these issues. This chapter discusses the factors you should think about as you make each decision. It is organized the same way as the program is (Parts 1 through 7), so that you can easily refer to it while you're actually running *Nolo's Living Trust*. It's a good idea, though, to read through this chapter before you sit down at the computer—it will make the whole process clearer and easier.

CHECKLIST FOR CREATING A VALID LIVING TRUST

√ Prepare the trust document with *Nolo's Living Trust*.

√ Print out the trust document and sign it in front of a notary public.

√ Transfer ownership of the property listed in the trust document into the name of the trust.

√ Update your trust document when needed.

AN OVERVIEW: HOW A SHARED MARITAL TRUST WORKS

Here, in brief, are the important points about how a shared trust works:

Control of trust property. You and your spouse will both be trustees of your living trust, so you'll both have control over the property in the trust. Either spouse can act on behalf of the trust—sell or give away trust property, for example. (As a practical matter, the consent of both spouses may be necessary—see Part 3, below.)

Amendments or revocation. Either spouse can revoke the trust or add separately owned property to it at any time. Both spouses, however, must consent to change any terms of the trust document—who gets what property, or who is named as successor trustee, for example.

This way either spouse can, by revoking the trust, return the situation to exactly what it was before the trust was formed. (Co-owned property is returned to both spouses, and separately owned property to the owner-spouse.) But while both spouses are living, neither can alone change what they've decided on in the trust—who should get what property when each spouse dies.

Death of the first spouse. When the first spouse dies, the shared living trust is automatically split into two trusts.

- Trust #1 contains the deceased spouse's share of trust property, except any trust property left to the surviving spouse.

- Trust #2 contains the surviving spouse's share, including any trust property left by the deceased spouse to the survivor.

The surviving spouse is sole trustee of both trusts. The survivor must distribute the deceased spouse's property (what's in Trust #1) exactly as he or she instructed in the trust document, with no modifications. The surviving spouse is also responsible for managing any Trust #1 property left to a young beneficiary in a child's subtrust (explained later in the chapter). When all the property in Trust #1 is distributed to the beneficiaries, Trust #1 ceases to exist.

How a Marital Living Trust Works

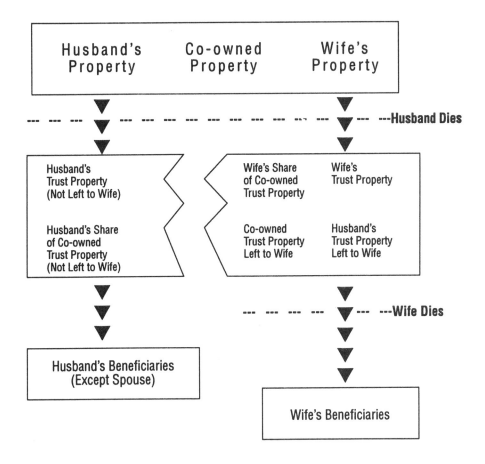

Continuation of the living trust. Trust #2 (the survivor's) goes on as before, with the addition of any trust property the survivor inherited from the deceased spouse. The surviving spouse is free to change the trust document as he or she wishes. For example, the surviving spouse might name someone else as successor trustee, or name a new beneficiary for property that was to have gone to the deceased spouse.

Death of the second spouse. When the second spouse dies, the person named in the trust document as successor trustee takes over. He or she is responsible for distributing trust property to the beneficiaries and managing any trust property left to a young beneficiary in a child's subtrust (explained later).

To see how a shared living trust works, read the example below. You may want to refer it later as you're using the program.

EXAMPLE Harry and Maude, a married couple, set up a shared revocable living trust to avoid probate. In the trust document, they make themselves co-trustees, and appoint their niece Emily as successor trustee, to take over as trustee after they have both died. They transfer much of their co-owned property—their house, savings accounts and stocks—to the living trust. Maude also puts some of her family heirlooms, which are her separate property, in the trust.

The trust document states that Maude's brother is to receive the heirlooms when she dies; everything else goes to Harry. Harry leaves all his trust property to Maude.

Maude dies first. The trust splits into Trust #1, which contains Maude's heirlooms, and Trust #2, which contains everything else—Harry's trust property and the trust property he inherits from Maude. Harry becomes the sole trustee of both trusts.

Following the terms of the trust document, Harry distributes Maude's heirlooms (Trust #1) to her brother, without probate. When the property is distributed, Trust #1 ceases to exist. Harry doesn't have to do anything with the trust property Maude left him; it's already in Trust #2.

After Maude's death, Harry decides to make a couple of changes in his living trust document. He names his nephew, Burt, as successor trustee. And he names his 12-year-old granddaughter, Cecile, to receive some trust property. In the trust document, he provides that if Cecile is not yet 25 when he dies, the trust property she inherits will stay in a child's subtrust, managed by the successor trustee, Burt.

When Harry dies, Burt becomes trustee and distributes the trust property following Harry's instructions in the trust document. He also manages the property inherited by Cecile, who is 21 at Harry's death, until her 25th birthday. When all the property is given to Harry's beneficiaries, the trust ends.

PART 1. YOUR STATE

In this part of the program, you choose the state that is your legal residence, also called your "domicile." That's the state where you and your spouse live now and intend to keep living.

Your choice affects many aspects of your living trust, including the ways you can set up management for any trust property young beneficiaries may inherit and what property belongs to each spouse.

(You may notice that the list of states on the screen doesn't include Louisiana. We didn't forget it—but because Louisiana law is different from all other states, you can't use this program if you live there.)

A. If You Live in More Than One State

If during the course of a year you live in more than one state, your residence is the state with which you have the most significant contacts—where you vote, register vehicles, own valuable property, have bank accounts or run a business.

If you might be justified in claiming more than one state as your legal residence, you may want to arrange your affairs so that your legal residence is in the state with the most advantageous state estate tax laws. Some states (such as New York) impose stiff inheritance taxes; others (California and Florida, for example) have essentially no inheritance tax. If you have significant contacts with more than one state and a substantial estate, it may pay to have a lawyer with tax and estate planning experience advise you.

EXAMPLE Ben and Geraldine, a couple in their 60s, spend about half the year in Florida and the other half in New York. They have bank accounts and other real estate in both states.

To take advantage of Florida's lack of a state inheritance tax, they register their car in Florida, vote there and move their bank accounts there. This leaves them owning nothing in New York but a condominium near where their son lives. They decide to sell him the condo and lease it back six months of every year, severing their last important property ownership contact with New York.

B. If You Live Outside the United States

If you are living outside the U.S., your residence is the state you still have contacts with and expect to return to. If you don't maintain ties with a particular state and have a large estate, see a lawyer to discuss what state you should declare as your residence.

If you are in the Armed Forces and living out of the country temporarily, your legal residence is the state you declared as your Home of Record—the state you lived in before going overseas, or where your spouse or parents live.

PART 2. YOUR NAMES

The first information the program asks you for is easy: your names. The names you enter in this part of the program will form part of the name of your trust. For example, if you enter "William S. Jorgensen" and "Helga M. Jorgensen," your trust will be named "The William S. Jorgensen and Helga M. Jorgensen Revocable Living Trust." Your names will also appear as the original trustees of your living trust (see Part 3, below).

Enter your name the way it appears on other formal business documents, such as your driver's license or bank accounts. This may or may not be the name on your birth certificate.

Use only one name per person; don't enter various versions of your name joined by "aka" (also known as).

If you go by more than one name, be sure that the name you use for your living trust is the one that appears on the ownership documents for property you plan to transfer to the trust. If it isn't, it could cause confusion later, and you should change the name on your ownership documents before you transfer the property to the trust.

EXAMPLE   You use the name William Dix for your trust, but own real estate in your former name of William Geicherwitz. You should prepare and sign a new deed, changing the name of the owner to William Dix, before you prepare another deed to transfer the property to your living trust.

PART 3. TRUSTEES

To be legally valid, every living trust must have a trustee—someone to manage the property owned by the trust. When you create a revocable living trust with this program, you and your spouse are the trustees while you are alive. Someone else, who you named in the trust document to be the successor trustee, takes over after both you and your spouse have died.

A. The Original Trustees

You and your spouse will be the original trustees of your living trust. As trustees, both of you will have complete control over the property that will technically be owned by the trust.

As a day-to-day, practical matter, it makes little difference that your property is now owned by your living trust. You won't have any special duties as trustees of your trust. You do not even need to file a separate income tax return for the living trust. Any income the property generates must be reported on your personal income tax return, as if the trust did not exist.

You have the same freedom to sell, give away or mortgage trust property as you did before you put the property into the living trust. The only difference is that you must now sign documents in your capacity as trustee. It's that easy.

EXAMPLE Celeste and Robert want to sell a piece of land that is owned in the name of their living trust. They prepare a deed transferring ownership of the land from the trust to the new owner, and sign the deed as "Celeste Tornetti and Robert Tornetti, trustees of the Celeste Tornetti and Robert Tornetti Revocable Living Trust dated February 4, 1991."

It's important to realize that once the property belongs to the trust, either trustee (spouse) has authority over it. That means that either spouse can sell or give away any of the trust property—including the property that was co-owned or was the separate property of the other spouse before it was transferred to the trust. In practice, however, both spouses will probably have to consent to transfer real estate out of the living trust. Especially in community property states, buyers and title insurance companies usually insist on both spouses' signatures on transfer documents.

If you don't want to give your spouse legal authority over your separately owned property, it's best to make separate living trusts. (See Chapter 4, *What Kind of Living Trust Do You Need?*)

 Naming someone else as trustee. In the unlikely event you and your spouse don't want to be the trustees, or want only one of you to be trustee, you cannot use *Nolo's Living Trust*; you need to see an estate planning lawyer to draw up a more specialized living trust. If only one spouse is a trustee, the other loses legal control over his or her trust property. And if you name someone else as trustee, there are important tax consequences.

B. The Trustee After One Spouse's Death or Incapacity

When one spouse dies or becomes incapacitated and unable to manage his or her affairs, the other becomes sole trustee.

A spouse's physical or mental incapacity must be certified in writing by a physician. The other spouse, as sole trustee, takes over management of trust property. That's the extent of his or her authority; he or she has no power over property not owned by the living trust, and no authority to make health care decisions for the incapacitated spouse. For this reason, it's also wise for each spouse to create documents called Durable Powers of Attorney, giving the other spouse authority to manage property not owned in the name of the trust and to make health care decisions. (See Chapter 3, *A Living Trust as Part of Your Estate Plan*, Section F.)

After one spouse's death, the surviving spouse, as trustee, is responsible for distributing trust property of the deceased spouse that is not left to the surviving spouse. The surviving spouse must follow the deceased spouse's wishes as they are set out in the trust document. The surviving spouse has no legal power to modify the deceased spouse's intentions in any way. (See Chapter 10, *After a Grantor Dies.*)

Usually, the process takes only a few weeks. The surviving spouse may, however, have long-term duties if the trust document creates a child's subtrust for trust property inherited by a young beneficiary. It falls to the surviving spouse to manage trust property left to a young beneficiary in this way, possibly for many years (this is explained in Part 7, below).

C. The Successor Trustee

You and your spouse must also choose a successor trustee—someone to act as trustee after both of you have died or become incapacitated.[1] The successor trustee has no power or responsibility if at least one spouse is alive and capable of managing your affairs.

1. The Successor Trustee's Duties After Both Spouses' Deaths

After both spouses have died, the successor trustee named in the trust document takes over as trustee. The successor trustee's primary responsibility is to distribute trust property to the beneficiaries named in the trust document. That is usually a straightforward process that can be completed in a few weeks. (How to transfer certain common kinds of property is explained in Chapter 10, *After a Grantor Dies.*)

---

[1]Incapacity is the inability to manage your affairs. The trust document created by *Nolo's Living Trust* requires that incapacity be documented in writing by a physician before your spouse or the successor trustee can take over management of the trust property.

The successor trustee may, however, have long-term duties if the trust document creates a "child's subtrust" for trust property inherited by a young beneficiary (this is explained in Part 7, below).

2. The Successor Trustee's Duties if You or Your Spouse Is Incapacitated

The successor trustee will take over as trustee before both spouses have died if neither spouse is able to manage his or her affairs. A spouse's incapacity must be documented in writing by a physician. In this situation, the successor trustee has broad authority to manage the property in the living trust and use it for both spouses' health care, support and welfare. The law requires him or her to act honestly and prudently in managing the property. And because the grantors are no longer the trustees, the new trustee must file an income tax return for the trust.

3. Choosing a Successor Trustee

The person or institution you choose as successor trustee will have a crucial role: to manage trust property (if you and your spouse become incapacitated, or if the successor trustee must manage a child's subtrust) or distribute it to your beneficiaries (after you and your spouse have died).

If the successor trustee is in charge of managing property over the long term, the trust document produced by *Nolo's Living Trust* gives him or her very broad authority, so that the trustee will be able to do whatever is necessary to respond to the demands of the circumstances. For example, the trustee has the power to invest trust funds in accounts, such as money market accounts, that are not federally insured. The trustee is also free to spend trust income or property for the health and welfare of the incapacitated spouses or beneficiary of a child's subtrust.

Obviously, when you are giving someone this much power and discretion, you should choose someone with good common sense whom you trust completely, such as an adult son or daughter, other relative or close friend. If you don't know anyone who fits this description, think twice about establishing a living trust.

Keep in mind that the successor trustee does not take over until both spouses have died (or become incapacitated). That means that after one spouse's death, the surviving spouse will probably have plenty of time to amend the trust document and name a different successor trustee if he or she wishes.

In most situations, the successor trustee will not need extensive experience in financial management; common sense, dependability and complete honesty are usually enough. A successor trustee who may have long-term responsibility over a young beneficiary's trust property needs more management and financial skills than a successor trustee whose only job is to distribute trust property. The successor trustee does have authority, under the terms of the trust document, to get any reasonably necessary professional help—from an accountant, lawyer or tax preparer, perhaps—and pay for it out of trust assets.

Usually, it makes sense to name just one person as successor trustee, to avoid any possibility of conflicts. But it's legal and may be desirable to name more than one person. For example, you might name two or more of your children, if you don't expect any disagreements between them and you think one of them might feel hurt and left out if not named.

Carefully consider the issue of conflicts, however. If you name more than one person as successor trustee, all of them must agree before they can act on behalf of the trust. If they can't agree, it could hold up the distribution of trust property to your beneficiaries. In extreme situations, the other trustees might even have to go to court to get the recalcitrant trustee removed, so that your instructions can be carried out. The result might be more bad feeling than if you had just picked one person to be trustee in the first place.

Having more than one successor trustee is especially likely to cause serious problems if the successor trustees are in charge of the property you have left to a young beneficiary in a child's subtrust. The trustees may have to manage a young beneficiary's property for many years, and will have many decisions to make about how to spend the money—greatly increasing the potential for conflict. (Children's subtrusts are discussed in Part 7, below.)

If you name more than one successor trustee, and one of them can't serve, the others will serve. If none of them can serve, the alternate you name (in the next section of the program) will take over.

It's perfectly legal to name a beneficiary of the trust (someone who will receive trust property after your death) as successor trustee. In fact, it's common.

EXAMPLE Mildred and James name their only child, Allison, to be successor trustee of their living trust. They name each other as trust beneficiaries, and Allison as alternate beneficiary. When James dies, his share of the trust property goes to Mildred. When Mildred dies, Allison uses her authority as trustee to transfer the remaining trust property to herself, the beneficiary.

The successor trustee does not have to live in the same state as you do. But if you are choosing between someone local and someone far away, think about how convenient it will be for the person you choose to distribute the living trust property after your death. Someone close by will probably have an easier job, especially with real estate transfers. But for transfers of property such as securities and bank accounts, it usually won't make much difference where the successor trustee lives.

Institutions as Successor Trustees

Normally, your first choice as successor trustee should be a flesh-and-blood person, not the trust department of a bank or other institution. Institutional trustees charge hefty fees, which come out of the trust property and leave less for your family and friends. And they probably won't even be interested in "small" living trusts—ones that contain less than several hundred thousand dollars worth of property.

But if there's no close relative or friend you think is capable of serving as your successor trustee, probably your best bet is to consider naming a private trust services company as successor trustee. Typically, their fees are pricey, but as a rule they charge less than a bank, and your affairs will probably receive more personal attention.

For a very large living trust, another possibility is to name a person and an institution as co-successor trustees. The bank or trust services company can do most of the paperwork, and the person can keep an eye on things and approve all transactions.

Obviously, before you and your spouse finalize your living trust, you must check with the person you've chosen to be your successor trustee. You want to be sure your choice is willing to serve. If you don't, you may well create problems down the line. The person you've chosen may not want to serve, for a variety of reasons. And even if the person would be willing, if he or she doesn't know of his or her responsibilities, transfer of trust property after your death could be delayed.

If you choose an institution, you must check out the minimum size of trust it will accept and the fees it charges for management, and make arrangements for how the institution will take over as trustee at the second spouse's death.

AVOIDING CONFLICTS WITH YOUR WILL AND OTHER DOCUMENTS

Your living trust gives your spouse the authority to manage trust property if you become incapacitated. To avoid conflicts, you should also give your spouse authority to make other decisions if you can't:

- In your will, appoint your spouse to be executor, to be responsible for distributing your property (except living trust property) after your death.

- In your Durable Power of Attorney for Finances, appoint your spouse to be your "attorney-in-fact," to have authority to make financial and management decisions for property (except property owned in the name of the living trust) if you become incapacitated.

If you do choose different people to be your attorney-in-fact and successor trustee, each will have a role after your death or incapacity. The successor trustee will be in charge of all trust property, and the attorney-in-fact will have authority, granted in the Power of Attorney, to control property not owned by the living trust.

---

4. Payment of the Successor Trustee

Typically, the successor trustee of a simple probate-avoidance living trust isn't paid. This is because in most cases, the successor trustee's only job is to distribute the trust property to beneficiaries soon after the grantor's death—and often, the successor trustee inherits most of the trust property anyway.

An exception is a successor trustee who manages the property in a child's subtrust. In that case, the successor trustee is entitled, under the terms of the trust document, to "reasonable compensation." The successor trustee decides what is reasonable and takes it from the trust property left to the young beneficiary.

Allowing the successor trustee to set the amount of the payment can work well, as long as your successor trustee is completely trustworthy. If the young beneficiary feels the trustee's fees are much too high, he or she will have to go to court to challenge them. If you want to restrict the successor trustee's freedom to decide on payment, see a lawyer.

The trust document created by *Nolo's Living Trust* does not require the successor trustee to post a bond (a kind of insurance policy) to guarantee conscientious fulfillment of his or her duties.

5. Naming an Alternate Successor Trustee

Nolo's Living Trust asks you to name an alternate successor trustee, in case your first choice is unable to serve.

If you named two or more successor trustees, the alternate won't become trustee unless none of your original choices can serve.

EXAMPLE Caroline and Oscar name their two grown children, Eugene and Vanessa, as successor trustees. They name a close friend, Nicole, as alternate successor trustee. After Caroline and Oscar have died, Vanessa is ill and can't serve as trustee. Eugene acts as sole successor trustee. If he were unable to serve or had died, Nicole would take over.

If no one you named in the trust document can serve, the last trustee to serve has the power to appoint, in writing, another successor trustee. (See Chapter 10, *After a Grantor Dies.*)

EXAMPLE To continue the previous example, if Nicole were ill and didn't have the energy to serve as successor trustee, she could appoint someone else to serve as trustee.

PART 4. PROPERTY TO BE PUT IN TRUST

Now you're getting to the heart of the program. In this part, you and your spouse must list each item of property—both jointly owned and separately owned—you want to transfer to your living trust. It will take some thought to decide what property to include and how to list it in the trust document. (Later in the program, you will name beneficiaries to receive each item of trust property at your death.)

This is a crucial step. Any property you don't list will not go into your living trust and will not pass under the terms of the trust. It may instead have to go through probate.

Adding property to the trust later. If you mistakenly leave something out or acquire more valuable property after you create your trust, you will be able to add it to your living trust. Chapter 9, *Living With Your Living Trust*, explains how.

A. Inventory Your Valuable Property

Before you begin to list your property in the program, sort out what you have and who owns it—you, your spouse, or both of you. You need to label each item this way because each spouse names beneficiaries for his or her share of the trust property separately.

After you've made an inventory, the next section will help you decide which items you want to transfer to your living trust so they don't have to go through probate after your death.

1. Take Inventory

First, get out a pencil or your word processor and make a list all the valuable items of property you own. The categories below should jog your memory.

Even if you plan to leave everything to your spouse or children, you must make a list. That's because every item (or group of items, in some circumstances) must be specifically described and listed in the trust document.

When you list your property in the program, you can group items, if you're leaving them all to one beneficiary. For example, if you want to leave all your books to your daughter, there's no need to describe each one individually—unless your collection includes some particularly valuable or important books that you want to make extra sure get to the beneficiary.

Getting Organized

While you're taking stock of all your valuable property, it might be a good time to go a step further and gather the information your family will need at your death.

You can use your computer to get organized by using Nolo's *For the Record* database program. It can keep track of all the important information in your family's life, including securities data, investments, real estate records, medical information, insurance records, credit card information and more.

(Ordering information is in the back of the manual.)

VALUABLE PROPERTY

Animals
Antiques
Appliances
Art
Books
Business interests
    Sole proprietorship
    Partnership
    Corporation
Business property
(if you own a sole proprietorship)
Cameras & photographic equipment
Cash accounts
    Certificates of deposit
    Checking
    Money market funds
    Savings
China, crystal, silver
Coins, stamps
Collectibles
Computers
Copyrights, patents, trademarks
Electronic equipment
Furniture
Furs
Jewelry
Limited partnership
Precious metals

Real estate
    Agricultural land
    Boat/Marina dock space
    Co-op
    Condo
    Duplex
    House
    Mobile home
    Rental property
    Time-share
    Undeveloped land
    Vacation house
Retirement accounts
    IRAs
    401(k) plans
    Keogh plans
Royalties
Securities
    Bonds
    Commodities
    Mutual funds
    Stocks
U.S. bills, notes and bonds
Tools
Vehicles
    Cars
    Motorcycles
    Bicycles
    Boats
    Motor homes/RVs
    Planes

VALUABLE PROPERTY INVENTORY

Item	His	Hers	Ours

2. Who Owns It?

You'll need to label each item as "his, hers or ours" when you enter it in the program. This is because only your share of the trust property is distributed at your death.

For many couples, especially if they've been married a long time, nearly everything is owned together. But if you haven't been married long, or have been married before, you may own a sizeable amount of property separately. If you're unsure about who owns what, this section explains the ownership rules for community property and non-community property states.

a. Community property states

Arizona	Louisiana	Texas
California	Nevada	Washington
Idaho	New Mexico	Wisconsin

If you live in a community property state and you aren't sure who owns what, don't rely on whose name is on the title document. For example, if while you were married you bought a house with money you earned, your spouse legally owns a share of that property—even if only your name is on the deed.

Generally, any property that either spouse earns or acquires during the marriage (before permanent separation) is community property. Both spouses (the "community") own it together. The main exception to this shared ownership rule is that property one spouse acquires by gift or inheritance belongs to that spouse alone. Property acquired before marriage also belongs to each spouse separately.

Even separate property may, however, turn into community property if it is mixed ("commingled") with community property. For example, if you deposit separate property funds into a joint bank account and then make more deposits and withdrawals, making it impossible to tell what part of the account is separate money, it's all considered community property.

In most community property states, there are restrictions on one spouse's freedom to transfer community property. Especially in the case of real estate, the consent of both spouses is necessary for either to sell or give away his or her half-interest in the property. Each spouse can, however, leave his or her half-interest in the property through a will or living trust.

Married couples don't have to accept the property ownership rules established by their states' community property laws. They can sign a written agreement that makes some or all community property the separate property of one spouse, or vice versa. If you and your spouse have such an agreement about who owns what, you may want to prepare individual living trusts. (See Chapter 4, *What Kind of Living Trust Do You Need?*)

What happens to community property put in a living trust

If you live in a community property state and you and your spouse create a living trust together, transferring property to the trust won't change its legal character.

Community property (owned by both spouses equally) transferred to your living trust will stay community property, even though it is technically owned by the living trust. Separately owned property (property of only one spouse) will remain the separate property of the spouse. That means that the community property transferred to a living trust is still eligible for the favorable tax treatment given community property at one spouse's death. (Both halves of community property left to the surviving spouse get a "stepped-up basis" for income tax purposes; see Chapter 3, *A Living Trust as Part of Your Estate Plan.*)

It also means that if either spouse revokes the living trust, ownership of the property will go back to the spouses as it was before the property was transferred to the living trust. Community property goes back to both spouses equally, and separate property goes to the spouse who owned it before ownership was transferred to the trust.

b. Non-community property states

Alabama	Kentucky	North Dakota
Alaska	Maine	Ohio
Arkansas	Maryland	Oklahoma
Colorado	Massachusetts	Oregon
Connecticut	Michigan	Pennsylvania
Delaware	Minnesota	Rhode Island
District of Columbia	Mississippi	South Carolina
Florida	Missouri	South Dakota
Georgia	Montana	Tennessee
Hawaii	Nebraska	Utah
Illinois	New Hampshire	Vermont
Indiana	New Jersey	Virginia
Iowa	New York	West Virginia
Kansas	North Carolina	Wyoming

In these states, it is usually fairly simple to figure out who owns what. If the property has a title document—for example, a deed to real estate or a car title slip—then the spouse whose name is on the title is the owner. If the property doesn't have a title document, it belongs to the spouse who paid for it or received it as a gift.[2]

If the trust is revoked, the property will be returned to each spouse based on the same ownership rights they had before the property was transferred to the trust.

B. Decide What Property To Put in Your Living Trust

Now that you've got a list of what you and your spouse own, you're ready to decide what items you want to transfer to your living trust. You're creating a revocable living trust primarily to avoid probate fees. As a general rule, the more an item is worth, the more it will cost to probate it. That means you should transfer at least your most valuable property items to your living trust (or use some other probate-avoidance device to leave them at your death). Think about including:

- houses and other real estate
- jewelry, antiques, furs and valuable furniture
- stock in a closely-held corporation
- stock, bond and other security accounts held by brokerages
- small business interests
- money market and bank accounts
- other financial accounts
- patents and copyrights
- precious metals
- valuable works of art
- valuable collections of stamps, coins or other objects

---

[2]It's possible, though, that if there were a dispute between spouses, a judge could determine, based on the circumstances, that a spouse whose name is not on the title document might own an interest in the property.

 **Adding Property to Your Living Trust**

You and your spouse will be able to add property to your living trust at any time. As trustees, you can always sell or give away property in the trust. You can also take it out of the living trust and put it back in your name as individuals. Chapter 9, *Living With Your Living Trust*, explains how to make these changes.

You don't need to put everything you own into a living trust to save money on probate. For some assets, you may decide to use other probate-avoidance devices instead of a living trust. Property that is of relatively low value (the amount depends on state law) may be exempt from probate or qualify for a streamlined probate procedure that's relatively fast and cheap. And at least some of the property left to a surviving spouse can probably be transferred without a full-blown probate court proceeding. (See Chapter 3, *A Living Trust as Part of Your Estate Plan.*)

Even if the non-trust property does have to go through regular probate, attorney and appraisal fees are generally based on the value of the probated property, so they'll be relatively low.

This section discusses how to decide whether or not to transfer various kinds of property to your living trust.

1. Real Estate

The most valuable thing most people own is their real estate: their house, condominium or land. You and your spouse can probably save your family substantial probate costs by transferring your real estate through a living trust.

In some situations, however, you and your spouse may not want to transfer your real estate to your living trust. See:

- Section 8, Property Held in Joint Tenancy
- Section 9, Property Held in Tenancy by the Entirety
- Section 10, Community Property

IF YOU'RE NOT SURE HOW YOU HOLD TITLE

If you own real estate with someone else but aren't sure how the title is held, look at the deed. It should say how title is held: in joint tenancy, tenancy in common, community property (in community property states) or tenancy by the entirety. In a community property state, if the deed says the property is owned "as husband and wife," that means community property.

If you or your spouse owns real estate with someone else, you can transfer just your interest in it to your living trust. You won't need to specify that your share is one half or some other fraction. For example, if you and your sister own a house together, you need only list "the house at 7989 Lafayette Court, Boston, MA." Your trust document will state that you have transferred all your interest in that property to the trust. The share of the property owned by your sister, obviously, is not included.

Co-op apartments. If you own shares in a co-op corporation that owns your apartment, you'll have to transfer your shares to your living trust. You may run into difficulties with the corporation; some are reluctant to let a trust, even a revocable trust completely controlled by the grantor, own shares. Check the co-op corporation's rules to see if the transfer is allowed.

---

2. Small Business Interests

The delay, expense and court intrusion of probate can be especially detrimental to an ongoing small business. Using your living trust to transfer business interests to beneficiaries quickly and after your death is almost essential if you want the beneficiaries to be able to keep the business running.

If you want to control the long-term management of your business, however, a revocable living trust is not the right vehicle. See an estate planning lawyer to draft a different kind of trust, with provisions tailored to your situation.

Different kinds of business organizations present different issues when you want to transfer your interest to your living trust:

Sole proprietorships. If you operate your business as a sole proprietorship, with all business assets held in your own name, you can simply transfer your business property to your living trust like you would any other property. You should also transfer the business's name itself: that transfers the customer goodwill associated with the name.

Partnership interests. If you operate your business as a partnership with other people, you can probably transfer your partnership share to your living trust. If there is a partnership certificate, it must be changed to include the trust as owner of your share.

Some partnership agreements require the people who inherit a deceased partner's share of the business to offer that share to the other partners before taking it. But that happens after death, so it shouldn't affect your ability to transfer the property through a living trust.

It's not common, but a partnership agreement may limit or forbid transfers to a living trust. If yours does, you and your partners may want to see a lawyer before you make any changes.

Solely owned corporations. If you own all the stock of a corporation, you should have no difficulty transferring it to your living trust.

Closely-held corporations. A closely-held corporation is a corporation that doesn't sell shares to the public. All its shares are owned by a few people who are usually actively involved in running the business. Normally, you can use a living trust to transfer shares in a closely-held corporation by listing the stock in the trust document and then having the stock certificates reissued in the trust's name.

You'll want to check the corporation's bylaws and articles of incorporation to be sure that if you transfer the shares to a living trust, you will still have voting rights in your capacity as trustee of the living trust; usually, this is not a problem. If it is, you and the other shareholders should be able to amend the corporation's bylaws to allow it.

There may, however, be legal restrictions on your freedom to transfer your shares to a living trust. Check the corporation's bylaws and articles of incorporation, as well as any separate shareholders' agreements.

One fairly common rule is that surviving shareholders (or the corporation itself) have the right to buy the shares of a deceased shareholder. In that case, you can still use a living trust to transfer the shares, but the people who inherit them may have to sell them to the other shareholders.

3. Bank and Retirement Accounts

It's not difficult to transfer bank or retirement accounts (IRAs, or Keogh or 401k accounts) to your living trust. But you may well decide that you don't need to.

You can directly designate a beneficiary for the funds in a bank or retirement account. If you name a beneficiary to receive whatever is in your account at your death, you don't need to transfer those accounts to a living trust just to avoid probate. Their contents won't need to go through probate in the first place.

This option can be especially useful for personal checking accounts, which you may not want to transfer to your living trust—it can be difficult to cash checks that say the account is owned by a revocable living trust.

A living trust, however, offers one advantage that most pay-on-death arrangements do not: If you transfer an account to a living trust, you can always name an alternate beneficiary to receive the account if your first choice as beneficiary isn't alive at your death. The lack of an alternate may not be a problem if you use a pay-on-death account and name more than one beneficiary to inherit the funds, however; if one of the beneficiaries isn't alive, the other(s) will inherit the money.

Pay-on-death accounts are discussed in Chapter 3, *A Living Trust as Part of Your Estate Plan.*

4. Vehicles and Property That Is Often Sold

Some kinds of property are cumbersome to keep in a living trust. It's not a legal problem, just a practical one. Two common examples are:

- Cars or other vehicles you use. Having registration and insurance in the trust's name could be confusing, and some insurance companies balk at insuring cars that technically are owned by living trusts. If you have valuable antique autos, or a mobile home that is permanently attached to land and considered real estate under your state's law, however, you may want to go ahead and transfer ownership to your living trust. You should be able to find an insurance company that will cooperate.

- Property you buy or sell frequently. If you don't expect to own the property at your death, there's no compelling reason to transfer it to your living trust. (Remember, the probate process you want to avoid doesn't happen until after your death.) On the other hand, if you're buying property, it's no more trouble to acquire it in the name of the trust.

 Other arrangements for property not in your living trust. If you choose not to put valuable items in your living trust, you may want to make arrangements to have them avoid probate in some other way. If you don't, they will pass to the residuary beneficiary of your back-up will. (See Chapter 3, *A Living Trust as Part of Your Estate Plan.*)

5. Life Insurance

If you own a life insurance policy at your death, the proceeds given to the named beneficiary do not go through probate. (They are, however, considered part of your estate for federal estate tax purposes.)

If you have named a minor or young adult as the beneficiary of an insurance policy, however, you may want to name your living trust as the beneficiary of the policy. Then, in the trust document, you name the child as beneficiary of any insurance proceeds paid to the trust and arrange for an adult to manage the policy proceeds if the beneficiary is still young when you die. If you don't arrange for management of the money, and the beneficiary is still a minor (under 18) when you die, a court will have to appoint a financial guardian after your death. (Young beneficiaries are discussed in Part 7, below.)

Passing the proceeds of a life insurance policy through your living trust is a bit more complicated than leaving other property this way. You must take two steps:

1. Name the living trust as the beneficiary of your life insurance policy. (Your insurance agent will have a form that lets you change the beneficiary of the policy.)

2. When you list property items in the living trust document, list the proceeds of the policy, not the policy itself. (Section C, below, contains sample descriptions.)

6. Securities

If you buy and sell stocks regularly, you may not want to go to the trouble of acquiring them in the living trust's name and selling them using your authority as trustee of the trust.

Fortunately, there's an easier way to do it: hold your stocks in a brokerage account that is owned in the living trust's name. All securities in the account are then owned by your living trust, which means that you can use your living trust to leave all the contents of the account to a specific beneficiary. If you want to leave stock to different beneficiaries, you can either establish more than one brokerage account or leave one account to more than one beneficiary to own together.

An Alternative: Pay-on-Death Registration

Two states, Colorado and Wisconsin, allow ownership of securities to be registered in a "transfer-on-death" form.[3] In those states, you can designate someone to receive the securities, including mutual funds and brokerage accounts, after your death. No probate will be necessary. Ask your broker about the forms you need to fill out to name a beneficiary for your securities.

Stock in closely-held corporations. See Section 2, Small Business Interests, above.

7. Cash

It's common for people to want to leave cash to beneficiaries—for example, to leave $5,000 to a relative, friend or charity. Don't, however, just type in "$5,000 cash" when you list the property you want to transfer to the living trust. There's no way to transfer cash to a living trust.

You can, however, easily accomplish the same goal by transferring owner-ship of a cash account—savings account, money market account or certificate of deposit, for example—to your living trust. You can then name a beneficiary to receive the contents of the account. So if you want to leave $5,000 to cousin Fred, all you have to do is put the money in a bank or money market account, transfer it to your living trust and name Fred, in the trust document, as the beneficiary.

If you don't want to set up a separate account to leave a modest amount of cash to a beneficiary, think about buying a savings bond and leaving it to the beneficiary, or leaving one larger account to several beneficiaries.

EXAMPLE Michael would like to leave some modest cash gifts to his two grown nephews, Warren and Brian, whom he's always been fond of. He puts $5,000 into a money market account and then transfers the account into his living trust. In his trust document, he names Warren and Brian as beneficiaries of the account. After Michael's death, the two nephews will inherit the account together, and each will be entitled to half of the funds.

---

[3]These states have adopted the Uniform Transfer-on-Death Security Registration Act.

8. Property Held in Joint Tenancy

Property owned in joint tenancy does not go through probate. When one co-owner (joint tenant) dies, his or her share goes directly to the surviving co-owners, without probate. So if avoiding probate is your only concern, you and your spouse don't need to transfer your joint tenancy property to your living trust.

Joint tenancy doesn't avoid probate, however, if the joint owners die simultaneously—there is no survivor to inherit the other's share. If spouses die at the same time, each spouse's half-interest in the joint tenancy property is passed to the beneficiaries named in the residuary clauses of their wills. If a spouse didn't make a will, the property passes to the closest relatives under the state "intestate succession" law.

If you're concerned about what would happen to the property in the (statistically very unlikely) event that you and your spouse died simultaneously, you have two choices.

- You can name a beneficiary, who would inherit the property in the event of simultaneous death, in your back-up will. If the property passes under your will, however, it will probably go through probate.

- You can transfer the property to your living trust, and each spouse can name the other as primary beneficiary and name an alternate beneficiary to receive his or her share of the property in case of simultaneous death. It's a bit more paperwork, but you're assured that probate will be avoided even in the event of simultaneous death.

There's another reason to use a living trust for joint tenancy property: If you want to leave your share of the property to someone besides the other joint tenant(s). Joint tenancy property automatically goes to the surviving co-owners when one co-owner dies. But if you transfer joint tenancy property to a living trust, the joint tenancy is destroyed, and you can leave your share to anyone you please.

9. Property Held in Tenancy by the Entirety

STATES THAT ALLOW TENANCY BY THE ENTIRETY

Alaska*	Maryland	Ohio
Arkansas	Massachusetts	Oklahoma
Delaware	Michigan*	Oregon*
District of Columbia	Mississippi	Pennsylvania
Florida	Missouri	Tennessee
Hawaii	New Jersey*	Vermont
Indiana*	New York*	Virginia*
Kentucky	North Carolina*	Wyoming*

*allowed only for real estate

You and your spouse may hold title to property in "tenancy by the entirety"—basically, a kind of joint tenancy that's only for married couples. Not all states have this form of ownership.

Like joint tenancy, tenancy by the entirety property does not go through probate when one spouse dies; it automatically goes to the surviving spouse. So if avoiding probate is your only concern, you and your spouse don't need to transfer your tenancy by the entirety property to your living trust.

Tenancy by the entirety property doesn't avoid probate, however, if the spouses die simultaneously. If spouses die at the same time, each spouse's half-interest in the property is passed to the beneficiaries named in the residuary clauses of their wills. If a spouse didn't make a will, the property passes to the closest relatives under the state "intestate succession" law.

If you're concerned about what would happen to the property in the (statistically very unlikely) event you and your spouse died simultaneously, you have two choices.

- You can name a beneficiary, who would inherit the property in the event of simultaneous death, in your back-up will. If the property passes under your will, however, it will probably go through probate.

- You can transfer the property to your living trust, and each spouse can name an alternate beneficiary to receive his or her share of the property. It's a bit more paperwork, but you're assured that probate will be avoided even in the event of simultaneous death.

10. Community Property

Arizona	Louisiana	Texas
California	Nevada	Washington
Idaho	New Mexico	Wisconsin

Most community property states have tried to make it easier on surviving spouses who inherit the couple's community property, by letting at least some community property bypass formal probate. In Nevada, for example, the surviving spouse is presumed to inherit community property real estate; he or she only has to fill out and file (with the county recorder) an affidavit (sworn statement) to get ownership of the property transferred to his or her name.[4] So if avoiding probate is your only concern, and you and your spouse each want to leave your community property to the survivor, you may not need to transfer community property to your living trust.

But be aware that although community property may avoid probate when the first spouse dies, if the property is left to the survivor, it's of no help when the second spouse dies. To avoid probate then, the property must be transferred to inheritors via a living trust or other probate-avoidance device.

Community property doesn't avoid probate if both spouses die simultaneously. If you're concerned about what would happen to the property if you and your spouse died simultaneously, you have two choices.

- You can name a beneficiary, who would inherit the property in the event of simultaneous death, in your back-up will. If the property passes under your will, however, it will probably go through probate.

---

[4]Nev. Rev. Stat. § 111.365.

- You can transfer the property to your living trust, and each spouse can name the other as primary beneficiary and name an alternate beneficiary to receive his or her share of the property in case of simultaneous death. It's a bit more paperwork, but you're assured that probate will be avoided even in the event of simultaneous death.

C. How To Describe Trust Property

When *Nolo's Living Trust* asks you to list the property you want to put in your trust, describe each item clearly enough so that the surviving spouse or successor trustee can identify the property and transfer it to the right person. No magic legal words are required.

Think about whom the property will ultimately go to. If you're leaving everything to one person, or a few major items will be divided among a few people, there's less need to go into great detail. But if there will be a number of trust beneficiaries, and objects could be confused, be more specific about each one. When in doubt, err on the side of including more information.

RULES FOR ENTERING DESCRIPTIONS OF TRUST PROPERTY

- Don't use "my" or "our" in a description. Don't, for example, enter "my books" or "my stereo system." That's because once the property is in the living trust, technically it doesn't belong to you anymore—it belongs to the living trust.

- Don't begin a description with a capital letter (unless it must begin with a proper name, like "Steinway"). That's because the descriptions will be inserted into a sentence in the trust document, and it would look odd to see a capital letter in the middle of a sentence.

- Don't end a description with a period. Again, this is because the descriptions will be inserted into a sentence in the trust document.

You may want to identify some items by their location—for example, "the books kept at 335 Forest Way, Denver, CO." But if the property you're describing is valuable—expensive jewelry or artworks, for example—be more specific. Describe the item in detail, in much the same way you would describe it if you were listing it on an insurance policy.

Here are some sample descriptions:

Real estate

- "the house at 321 Glen St., Omaha, NE"

- "the house at 4444 Casey Road, Fandon, Illinois and the 20-acre parcel on which it is located."

Usually, the street address is enough. It's not necessary to use the "legal description" found on the deed, which gives a subdivision plat number or a metes-and-bounds description. If the property has no street address—for example, if it is undeveloped land out in the country—you will need to carefully copy the full legal description, word for word, from the deed.

If you own a house and several adjacent lots, it's a good idea to indicate that you are transferring the entire parcel to your living trust by describing the land as well as the house.

If you own the property with someone else and are transferring only your share, you don't need to specify the share you own. Just describe the property. The trust document will show that you are transferring all your interest in the property, whatever share that is, to the living trust.

Bank and retirement accounts

- "Savings Account No. 9384-387, Arlington Bank, Arlington, MN"

- "Money Market Account 47-223 at Charles Schwab & Co., Inc., San Francisco, CA"

- "IRA Account No. 990-66-221, Working Assets Money Fund, San Francisco, CA"

Household items

- "all the furniture normally kept in the house at 44123 Derby Ave., Ross, KY"

- "the antique brass bed in the master bedroom in the house at 33 Walker Ave., Fort Lee, New Jersey"

- "all furniture and household items normally kept in the house at 869 Hopkins St., Great Falls, Montana"

Sole proprietorship business property

- "Mulligan's Fish Market"

- "Fourth Street Records and CDs"

- "all accounts receivable of the business known as Garcia's Restaurant, 988 17th St., Atlanta, GA"

- "all food preparation and storage equipment, including refrigerator, freezer, hand mixers and slicer used at Garcia's Restaurant, 988 17th St., Atlanta, GA"

As explained in Section B, above, you should both list the name of the business and separately list items of business property.

Partnership interest

- "all interest in the Don and Dan's Bait Shop Partnership owned by the grantor before being transferred to this living trust"

Because a partnership is a legal entity that can own property, you don't need to list items of property owned by the partnership.

Shares in a closely-held corporation

- "the stock of ABC Hardware, Inc."

Shares in a solely owned corporation

- "all shares in the XYZ Corporation"

- "all stock in Fern's Olde Antique Shoppe, Inc., 23 Turnbridge Court, Danbury, Connecticut"

Securities

- "all securities in account No. 3999-34-33 at Smith Brokerage, 33 Lowell Place, New York, NY"

- "200 shares of General Industries, Inc. stock"

- "Good Investment Co. mutual fund account No. 888-09-09"

Life insurance proceeds

- "the proceeds of Acme Co. Life Insurance Policy #9992A"

Miscellaneous items

- "the Macintosh SE30 computer (serial number 129311) with keyboard (serial number 165895)"

- "the medical textbooks in the office at 1702 Parker Towers, San Francisco, CA"

- "the stamp collection usually kept at 321 Glen St., Omaha, NE"

- "the collection of European stamps, including [describe particularly valuable stamps], usually kept at 440 Loma Prieta Blvd., #450, San Jose, CA"

- "the Martin D-35 acoustic guitar, serial number 477597"

- "the signed 1960 Ernie Banks baseball card kept in safe deposit box 234, First National Bank of Augusta, Augusta, IL"

- "the Baldwin upright piano kept at 985 Dawson Court, South Brenly, Massachusetts"

IMPORTANT REMINDER: TRANSFERRING PROPERTY TO THE TRUST

If an item has a title (ownership) document, such as a deed or title slip, its ownership is not transferred to the trust just by listing it in the program. You *must* also change the title document to show the living trust as the legal owner of the property.

YOU SHOULD TRANSFER OWNERSHIP AS SOON AS POSSIBLE AFTER YOU PRINT OUT AND SIGN YOUR DECLARATION OF TRUST.

Instructions are in Chapter 8, *Transferring Property to the Trust.*

PART 5. BENEFICIARIES OF TRUST PROPERTY

Once you've entered a list of the property you're transferring to your living trust, the next step is to say who you want to inherit that property. In the trust document, each spouse must name beneficiaries—the family, friends or organizations who will receive his or her share of the trust property.

Each spouse names beneficiaries separately, because each spouse's trust property is distributed when that spouse dies. When the first spouse dies, his or her trust property will be distributed to the beneficiaries he or she named. If it is left to the other spouse, it stays in the trust. When the second spouse dies, the rest of the property in the trust is distributed to his or her beneficiaries.

EXAMPLE   Roger and Marilyn Foster create a shared living trust. Each puts co-owned and separately owned property in the trust. When Roger dies, Marilyn takes over as sole trustee and distributes Roger's trust property to the beneficiaries he named in the trust document. Her property, including the trust property she inherits from Roger, stays in the living trust.

The beneficiaries you name in your trust document are not entitled to any trust property while both spouses are alive. Just as with a will, you can amend your trust document and change the beneficiaries any time you wish.

Disinheriting a Spouse or Child

If you don't plan to leave at least half of what you own to your spouse, consult a lawyer experienced in estate planning. State law may entitle your spouse to some of your estate, including the property in your living trust.

In most circumstances, you don't have to leave anything to your children. But if you want to disinherit a child, you should make a back-up will and specifically mention the child in it.

See Chapter 2, *About Living Trusts*.

A. How Do You Want Your Property Distributed?

Nolo's Living Trust asks you first whether you want to leave all your trust property to one beneficiary (or more than one, to share it all) or leave different items to different beneficiaries.

This accommodates the desire of many spouses to leave all trust property to the survivor. If you choose that option, the program inserts your spouse's name (entered earlier) as beneficiary of all your trust property. All you have to do is name an alternate beneficiary, who will inherit your trust property if your spouse does not survive you by five days. (Alternates are discussed in Section D, below.)

If you choose to leave different items to different beneficiaries, you will be taken to a screen that displays a list of all the property items you listed earlier. You can choose any number of the items and name beneficiaries (including your spouse, if you wish) for them.

1. Your Spouse

It's common for spouses to leave each other all or a substantial portion of the property transferred to their shared marital trust. In a shared trust, if one spouse leaves the other trust property, the property stays in the living trust when the first spouse dies.

EXAMPLE Max and Joan make a shared marital living trust. Each leaves all his or her trust property to the other. Max dies first. All his interest in trust property stays in what is now Joan's living trust. Joan has the right to amend the trust document to name beneficiaries for the trust property that is now hers. (See Chapter 10, *After a Grantor Dies.*)

2. Children from Prior Marriages

If you or your spouse have children from a prior marriage, you may well want to leave them property in your living trust. A common way to do this is to leave the children specific items—real estate, life insurance policy proceeds, bank accounts or whatever—and leave everything else to your spouse.

Estate planning note. A more complicated way of ensuring that both your spouse and children from an earlier marriage are taken care of is to create a different kind of trust called a "marital life estate trust." Briefly, this type of trust typically gives the surviving spouse the right to use income from (or live in) certain property for his or her life; then the property goes to the children. (These trusts are discussed in Chapter 3, *A Living Trust as Part of Your Estate Plan.*)

3. Minors or Young Adults

If a beneficiary you name is a minor or a young adult who can't yet manage property without adult help, you can arrange for an adult to manage the trust property for the beneficiary. *Nolo's Living Trust* lets you do this after you have named all your beneficiaries. (See Part 7, below.)

4. Your Successor Trustee

It's very common and perfectly legal to make the person you named to be successor trustee (the person who will distribute trust property after the second spouse dies) a beneficiary as well.

EXAMPLE   Nora and Sean name their son Liam as successor trustee of their living trust. Each spouse names the other as sole beneficiary of his or her trust property, and both name Liam as alternate beneficiary. When Nora dies, her trust property goes to Sean and stays in the trust. Unless Sean amends the trust document to name someone else as successor trustee, after Sean's death, Liam, acting as trustee, will transfer ownership of the trust property from the trust to himself.

5. Co-Beneficiaries

You can name more than one beneficiary to share any item of trust property. Simply list their names in the box provided on the screen. Type the names one per line; don't join the names with an "and." (See the User's Manual for Examples.)

Always use the beneficiaries' actual names; don't use collective terms such as "my children." It's not always clear who is included in such descriptions. And there can be serious confusion if one of the people originally included as a beneficiary dies before you do.

Obviously, if you name co-beneficiaries for a piece of property that can't be physically divided—a cabin, for example—give some thought to whether or not the beneficiaries are likely to get along. If they are incompatible, disagreements could arise over taking care of property or deciding whether or not to sell it. If they can't settle their differences, any co-owner could go to court and demand a partition—a court-ordered division and sale—of the property.

Co-beneficiaries will share the property equally unless you state otherwise. You will be asked, after you enter the names, whether or not you want this item of trust property to be shared equally among the beneficiaries.

EXAMPLE   Georgia wants to leave her house to her two children, Ross and Ryan, but wants Ross to have a 75% share of it. She enters their names and then, on a later screen, enters their interests, in fractions: 3/4 for Ross and 1/4 for Ryan.

When the children inherit the property, they own it together. But Ross will be liable for 75% of the taxes and upkeep cost, and entitled to 75% of any income the house produces. If they sell it, Ross will be entitled to 75% of the proceeds.

B. Entering Beneficiaries' Names

When you enter a beneficiary's name, use the name by which the beneficiary is known for purposes such as a bank account or driver's license. Generally, if the name you use clearly and unambiguously identifies the person, it is sufficient.

The name you use doesn't have to be the one that appears on the person's birth certificate. And you don't need to include all the nicknames (Chuck for someone whose real name is Charles, for example) a beneficiary is known by.

If you name an institution (charitable or not) to inherit the property in your trust, enter its complete name. It may be commonly known by a shortened version, which could cause confusion if there are similarly named organizations. Call to ask if you're unsure. (An institution that stands to inherit some of your money will be more than happy to help you.) Also be sure to specify if you want a specific branch or part of a national organization to receive your gift—for example, a local chapter of the Sierra Club.

C. Beneficiaries for Co-Owned Trust Property

As you name your beneficiaries, remember that when it comes to property you and your spouse co-own, you're naming people to receive only your share. When one spouse dies, only his or her interest in the co-owned property will go to the named beneficiary.

EXAMPLE Marcia and Perry transfer all the property they own together into their living trust. Marcia names Perry as the beneficiary of all her interest in the trust property. Perry names Marcia to inherit all of his half except his half-interest in their vacation cabin, which he leaves to his son from a previous marriage, Eric. If Perry dies first, Perry's half-interest in the cabin will go to Eric, who will co-own it with Marcia.

D. Alternate Beneficiaries

Nolo's Living Trust allows you to name an alternate beneficiary for every person you name as a primary beneficiary. The alternate will get the property left to the primary beneficiary if your first choice does not live for more than 120 hours (five days) after your death. This "survivorship" period ensures that if you and a primary beneficiary die simultaneously or almost so, the property will go to the alternate beneficiary you chose, not to the primary beneficiary's heirs.

EXAMPLE Laura leaves all her trust property to her husband Juan-Carlos, and names her daughter from a previous marriage as alternate beneficiary. Laura and Juan-Carlos are seriously injured in a car accident; Juan-Carlos dies a day after Laura does. Because Juan-Carlos did not survive Laura by at least five days, the trust property he would have inherited from Laura goes to Laura's daughter instead.

If there had been no survivorship requirement, the trust property would have gone to Juan-Carlos; when he died a day later, it would have gone to the alternate beneficiaries he had named (or, if she had made no will, to the heirs according to state law).

You don't have to name an alternate for a charitable (or other) institution you name as a beneficiary. If the institution is well established, it is probably safe to assume that it will still exist at your death.

With other beneficiaries, however, there is always the chance that the primary beneficiary may not survive you. If you don't name an alternate, the property that beneficiary would have received will be distributed to the person or institution you name, in the next part of the program, as your "residuary beneficiary." (See Part 6, below.)

You can name more than one person or institution as alternate beneficiaries. If you do, these "co-alternate beneficiaries" will share the property equally.

EXAMPLE Sherry names her husband as beneficiary of her interest in their house, which they have transferred to their living trust. As alternate beneficiaries, she names their three children, Sean, Colleen and Tim.

Sherry's husband dies just before she does, leaving his half of the house to Sherry. Under the terms of the trust document, it stays in the living trust. At Sherry's death, the house goes to the three children equally. All three own equal shares in all of it. If they sell the property, each will be entitled to a third of the proceeds.

PART 6. RESIDUARY BENEFICIARIES

Each spouse must name a residuary beneficiary. The residuary beneficiary of your living trust is the person or organization who will receive:

- any trust property for which both the primary and alternate beneficiaries you named die before you do

- any trust property that you didn't leave to a named beneficiary (this could include property you transferred to the trust later but didn't name a beneficiary for, and trust property that was owned by your spouse, which he or she left you)

- any property you leave to your living trust through your will. (Because property left through a pour-over will doesn't avoid probate, there's usually no reason to use one. See Chapter 3, *A Living Trust as Part of Your Estate Plan.*)

- any property that you actually transferred to your living trust but didn't list in the trust document

Often, the residuary beneficiary of a living trust doesn't inherit anything from the trust. Usually, naming a residuary beneficiary is just a back-up measure, to guard against the extremely small chance that both a primary and alternate trust beneficiary do not survive you.

You may, however, deliberately leave the residuary beneficiary trust property by:

- Adding property to the trust later and not naming a specific beneficiary to receive it after your death.

- Using a pour-over will to leave property to your living trust.

If you name more than one person or institution as residuary beneficiary, they will each get an equal share of any trust property they receive.

EXAMPLE You name your two children, Anne and Alice, as your residuary beneficiaries. If they end up receiving trust property, they will own it together, and both will own an equal share of it.

PART 7. PROPERTY MANAGEMENT FOR TRUST BENEFICIARIES

If any of the beneficiaries (including alternate and residuary beneficiaries) named by either spouse might inherit trust property before they are ready to manage it without an adult's help, that spouse should arrange for someone to manage it for them for a while. There are several ways to go about it:

- **Leave the property to an adult to use for the child.** Many people don't leave property directly to a child. Instead, they leave it to the child's parent or to the person they expect to have care and custody of the child if neither parent is available. There's no formal legal arrangement, but they trust the adult to use the property for the child's benefit.

- **Create a child's subtrust.** You can use *Nolo's Living Trust* to establish a "child's subtrust" in your living trust. If you do, your surviving spouse (or the successor trustee, after both spouses' death) will manage the property you left the child and dole it out for education, health and other needs. The subtrust ends at whatever age you designate (up to 35), and any remaining property is turned over to the child outright.

- **Name a custodian under the Uniform Transfers to Minors Act (UTMA).** In many states, you can name a "custodian" to manage property you leave a child until the child reaches 18 or 21, depending on state law (up to 25 in Alaska or California). If you don't need management to last beyond that age, a custodianship is probably preferable.

Subtrusts and custodianships are explained below.

 Children with special needs. These property management options are not designed to provide long-term property management for a child with serious disabilities. You should see a lawyer and make arrangements geared to your particular situation.

A. Should You Arrange for Management?

It's left to each spouse whether or not to make arrangements, in the trust document, to have someone manage trust property if it is inherited by young beneficiaries. Each spouse chooses whether or not to arrange for management for his or her beneficiaries.

The consequences of forgoing management for trust property inherited by a young beneficiary depend on whether the beneficiary is over or under age 18 at your death.

1. Children Under 18 Years Old

Minors—children under 18—cannot, legally, own or manage significant amounts of property. An adult must be in charge if the minor acquires more than a few thousand dollars' worth of property. (The exact amount depends on state law.)

If your minor beneficiaries won't inherit anything of great value—if you're leaving them objects that have more sentimental than monetary value—you don't need to arrange for an adult to manage the property.

But if a beneficiary inherits valuable trust property while still a minor, and you have not arranged for the property to be managed by an adult, the beneficiary will have to have a court-appointed guardian to manage the property. Contrary to what you might expect, a child's parent does not automatically have legal authority to manage any property the child inherits. So even if one or both of the beneficiary's parents are alive, they will not automatically have authority to manage the property. They will have to ask the court to grant them that authority, and will be subject to the court's supervision. If neither of the beneficiary's parents are alive, there may be no obvious person for the court to appoint as property guardian. In that case, it may be even more important for you to name someone in your living trust.

2. Young Adults 18 to 35 Years Old

If a living trust beneficiary is over 18 when he or she inherits trust property, you do not need, legally, to have anyone manage the property on the beneficiary's behalf. And if you don't make any arrangements, the beneficiary will get the property with no strings attached. But you can arrange for property management to last until a beneficiary turns any age up to 35.

There is no legal requirement that management for a trust beneficiary's property must end at 35, but we think 35 is a reasonable cutoff. If you don't want to let a beneficiary get his or her hands on trust property by the time he or she reaches 35, you probably need to see a lawyer and tailor a plan to the beneficiary's needs.

B. Which Method Is Best: Subtrust or Custodianship?

Using *Nolo's Living Trust*, you can create either a child's subtrust or a custodianship under the Uniform Transfer to Minors Act (if it's available in your state). Both are safe, efficient ways of managing trust property that a young person inherits. Under either system, the person in charge of the young beneficiary's property has the same responsibility to use the property for the beneficiary's support, education and health.

The most significant difference is that a child's subtrust can last longer than a custodianship, which must end at age 18 to 21 (up to 25 in Alaska and California) in most states. For that reason, a child's subtrust is a good choice when a child could conceivably inherit a large amount of property.

Because an UTMA custodianship is easier to administer, it is usually preferable if the beneficiary will inherit no more than about $50,000 worth of trust property ($100,000 or more if the child is quite young). That amount is likely to be used up for living and education expenses by the time the beneficiary is 18 to 21, so there's no need to create a child's subtrust that can continue beyond that age.

STATES THAT HAVE ADOPTED THE UNIFORM TRANSFERS TO MINORS ACT

State	Age at which minor gets property
Alabama	21
Alaska	18-25
Arizona	21
Arkansas	18-21
California	18-25
Colorado	21
District of Columbia	18
Florida	21
Georgia	21
Hawaii	21
Idaho	21
Illinois	21
Iowa	21
Kansas	21
Kentucky	18
Maine	18-21
Maryland	21
Massachusetts	21
Minnesota	21
Missouri	21
Montana	21
Nevada	18
New Hampshire	21
New Jersey	18-21
New Mexico	21
North Carolina	18-21
North Dakota	21
Ohio	21
Oklahoma	18
Oregon	21
Rhode Island	18
South Dakota	18
Utah	21
Virginia	18-21
Washington	21
West Virginia	21
Wyoming	21

A custodianship has other advantages as well:

- Handling a beneficiary's property can be easier with a custodianship than with a trust. A custodian's powers are written into state law, and most institutions, such as banks and insurance companies, are familiar with the rules. Trusts, on the other hand, vary in their terms. So before a bank lets a trustee act on behalf of a beneficiary, it may demand to see and analyze a copy of the Declaration of Trust.

- You can name whomever you wish to be a custodian, and you can name different custodians for different beneficiaries. So if you want to arrange custodianships for grandchildren, for example, you could name each child's parent as custodian. A child's subtrust is not quite so flexible: The surviving spouse, or the successor trustee if you are the second spouse to die, will be the trustee of all children's subtrusts created for your young beneficiaries.

C. Children's Subtrusts

Nolo's Living Trust allows you to set up a separate child's subtrust for each young beneficiary.

1. How a Child's Subtrust Works

In your trust document, you state the age at which the beneficiary should receive trust property outright. If at your death the beneficiary is younger than the age you specified, a subtrust will be created for that beneficiary. (If the beneficiary is older, he or she gets the trust property with no strings attached, and no subtrust is created.) Each beneficiary gets a separate child's subtrust.

Nolo's Living Trust is set up so that the surviving spouse, or the successor trustee after both spouses die, will serve as trustee of all children's subtrusts. If you want different people to manage property inherited by different beneficiaries, you may want to use a custodianship instead of a child's subtrust. (To appoint someone else to be trustee of a child's subtrust, the trust document would have to be changed significantly; see a lawyer.)

Whatever trust property the beneficiary is entitled to receive upon one spouse's death will go into the child's subtrust, if the child is still under the age set for termination of the subtrust. The trustee will manage the subtrust property and use it as necessary for the beneficiary's health, education and support. After the spouse's death, the subtrust cannot be revoked or amended. (Until then, that spouse is free to change his or her mind about having a subtrust set up for a particular beneficiary.)

The child's subtrust will end when the beneficiary reaches the age designated by the spouse in the Declaration of Trust. This can be any age up to and including 35. The trustee will then give the beneficiary what remains of the subtrust property.

EXAMPLE 1 In the trust document that Stanley makes with his wife Natalie, he names his 14-year-old son Michael as beneficiary of $25,000 worth of stock. He specifies that any stock Michael becomes entitled to when Stanley dies should be kept in a subtrust until Michael is 25, subject to the trustee's right to spend it on Michael's behalf.

Stanley dies when Michael is 19. The stock goes into a subtrust for him, managed by Natalie. She is free to use the stock (or the income it produces) to pay for Michael's education and support. Michael will receive what's left of the stock when he turns 25.

EXAMPLE 2 Roger and Victoria create a living trust and leave their trust property to the other. They name their daughters, who are 22 and 25, as alternate beneficiaries, and arrange for any trust property they inherit to stay in children's subtrusts until each daughter reaches 30. They name Victoria's sister, Antoinette, as successor trustee.

Roger and Victoria die in a car accident when one daughter is 28 and the other is 31. The 28-year-old's half of the trust property stays in a subtrust, managed by Antoinette, until she turns 30. The 31-year-old gets her half outright; no subtrust is created for her.

How a Child's Substrust Works

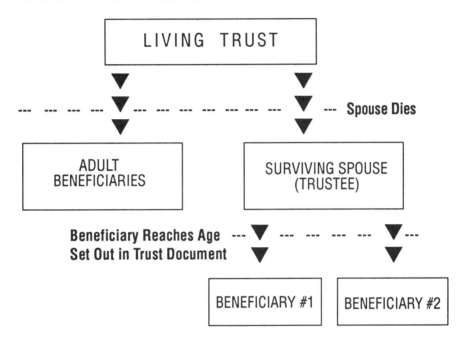

---

2. The Subtrust Trustee's Duties

The subtrust trustee must:

- Manage subtrust property until the beneficiary reaches the age set out in the trust document—which can take years.

- Use subtrust property or income to pay for expenses such as the beneficiary's support, education and health care.

- Keep separate records of subtrust transactions and file income tax returns for the subtrust.

The trustee's powers and responsibilities are spelled out in the trust document. If the subtrust trustee needs to hire an accountant, tax lawyer or other expert, he or she can use subtrust assets to pay a reasonable amount for the help.

The trust document also provides that the trustee of a subtrust is entitled to reasonable compensation for his or her work as trustee. The trustee decides what is a reasonable amount; the compensation is paid from the subtrust assets.

For more on the trustee's responsibilities, see Chapter 10, *After a Grantor Dies*.

D. Custodianships

A custodianship is the preferable alternative for many people. Here's how it works.

1. How a Custodianship Works

In the trust document, the grantor names someone to serve as custodian for a particular beneficiary. That person manages any trust property the young beneficiary inherits from that spouse until the beneficiary reaches the age at which state law says the custodianship must end. (See table in Section B, above.)

EXAMPLE Sandra and Don make a living trust. Sandra leaves 100 shares of General Motors stock to her niece, Jennifer Frankel. She names Hazel Frankel, Jennifer's mother, as custodian under the Illinois Uniform Transfers to Minors Act.

After Sandra's death, Don, as trustee, turns the stock over to the custodian, Hazel. She will manage it for Jennifer until Jennifer turns 21, the age Illinois law says she must be given the property outright.

In some states, you can specify—within limits—at what age the custodianship will end. If your state allows this, the program will ask you to enter an age at which you want the custodianship to end.

EXAMPLE Alexis and Jonathan, who live in New Jersey, make a living trust. They leave each other their trust property and name their young children, Ian and Noel, as alternate beneficiaries. They both specify, in the trust document, that any trust property the children inherit should be managed by the other spouse as custodian, under the New Jersey Uniform Transfers to Minors Act, until the boys turn 21. As alternate custodian, both name Jonathan's mother.

Alexis and Jonathan die simultaneously in an accident. Jonathan's mother takes over management of the trust property for her grandchildren. When each boy turns 21, he will receive whatever of the property hasn't been used for his support or education.

How a Custodianship Works

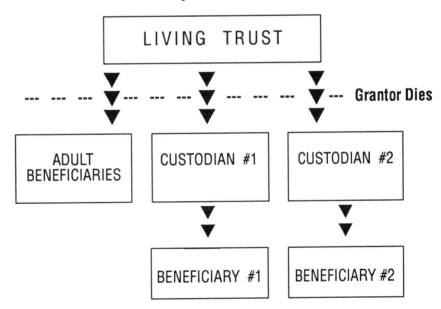

2. The Custodian's Responsibilities

A custodian has roughly the same responsibility as the trustee of a child's subtrust: to manage the beneficiary's property wisely and honestly. The custodian's authority and duties are clearly set out by state law (the Uniform Transfers to Minors Act, as enacted by your state[5]). No court directly supervises the custodian.

The custodian must:

- Manage the property until the beneficiary reaches the age at which, by law, he or she gets the property outright. If the child is a minor at your death, this can be a number of years.

- Use the property or income to pay for expenses such as the young beneficiary's support, education and health care.

- Keep the property separate from his or her own property.

- Keep separate records of trust transactions. The custodian does not have to file a separate income tax return; income from the property can be reported on the young beneficiary's return. (By comparison, the trustee of a child's subtrust must file a separate tax return for the subtrust.)

A custodian who needs to hire an accountant, tax lawyer or other expert can use the property to pay a reasonable amount for the help.

If state law allows it, the custodian is entitled to reasonable compensation and reimbursement for reasonable expenses. The payment, if any is taken, comes from the property the custodian manages for the beneficiary.

---

[5]The UTMA is a model law written by a national panel of experts, but legislatures may make minor modifications in it when they adopt it for their states.

3. Choosing a Custodian

You can name a different custodian for each young beneficiary, if you wish.

In most cases, you should name the person who will have physical custody of the minor child. That's almost always one of the child's parents. If the beneficiary is your child, name the child's other parent unless you have serious reservations about that person's ability to handle the property for the child.

Only one person can be named as custodian for one beneficiary. You can, however, name an alternate custodian to take over if your first choice is unable to serve.

Sample Marital Trust

Signing, Storing and Registering the Trust Document

Before You Sign

Before you sign the trust document, make sure it says exactly what you want it to say and that you understand it all. If you want to make changes, use the program and print out another trust document. (If you need help, see the User's Guide) Don't write any changes on the document.

Get Your Signature Notarized

Sign your living trust document in front of a notary public for your state. Both you and your spouse need to sign the trust document in front of the notary.

Making Copies

If you need copies of the trust document, use a photocopy of the original trust document—the one you signed and had notarized. Do not just print out and sign another copy.

Registering the Trust

Some states (Alaska, Colorado, Florida, Hawaii, Idaho, Maine, Michigan, Nebraska, New Mexico, North Dakota and Tennessee) require that you register your living trust document with the local court. But there are no legal consequences or penalties if you don't. See Chapter 7 for instructions on how to register.

Storing the Trust Document

Store your living trust document and the *Nolo's Living Trust* disk where you keep important papers. Make sure your successor trustee knows where the original trust document is and can get hold of it soon after your death.

Declaration of Trust

Part 1. Trust Name

This revocable living trust shall be known as The Leslie M. Carey and William C. Carey Revocable Living Trust.

Part 2. Declaration of Trust

Leslie M. Carey and William C. Carey, called the grantors, declare that they have transferred and delivered to the trustees all their interest in the property described in Schedules A, B and C attached to this Declaration of Trust. All of that property is called the "trust property." The trustees hereby acknowledge receipt of the trust property and agree to hold the trust property in trust, according to this Declaration of Trust.

Either grantor may add property to the trust.

Part 3. General Administrative Provisions

A. Controlling Law

The validity of this trust shall be governed by the laws of California.

B. Severability of Clauses

If any provision of this Declaration of Trust is ruled unenforceable, the remaining provisions shall stay in effect.

C. Amendments

The term "this Declaration of Trust" includes any provisions added by valid amendment.

Part 4. Character of Trust Property

While both grantors are alive, property transferred to this trust shall retain its original character as community or separate property, as the case may be.

If the trust is revoked, the trustee shall distribute the trust property listed on Schedule A to the grantors as their community property. The trust property listed in Schedule B shall be distributed to Leslie M. Carey as her separate property, and the trust property listed in Schedule C shall be distributed to William C. Carey as his separate property.

Part 5. Amendment and Revocation

A. Revocation by Grantor

Either grantor may revoke this trust at any time, without notifying any beneficiary. Revocation may be made in writing or any manner allowed by law.

B. Amendment by Grantors

While both grantors are alive, this Declaration of Trust may be amended only by both of them acting together. All amendments must be in writing and signed by both grantors.

C. Amendment or Revocation by Other Person

The power to revoke or amend this trust is personal to the grantors. A conservator, guardian or other person shall not exercise it on behalf of either grantor, unless the grantor specifically grants a power to revoke or amend this trust in a Durable Power of Attorney.

Part 6. Payments from Trust During Grantors' Lifetimes

The trustees shall pay to or use for the benefit of the grantors as much of the net income and principal of the trust property as the grantors request. Income not paid to or used for the benefit of the grantors shall be accumulated and added to principal.

Part 7. Trustees

A. Original Trustees

Leslie M. Carey and William C. Carey shall be trustees of this trust. Either alone may act for or represent the trust in any transaction.

B. Trustee on Death of Original Trustee

Upon the death or incapacity of Leslie M. Carey or William C. Carey, the surviving trustee shall serve as sole trustee of this trust and of all children's subtrusts created by it.

C. Trustee's Responsibility

The trustee in office shall serve as trustee of all trusts created under this Declaration of Trust, including children's subtrusts.

D. Terminology

In this Declaration of Trust, the term "trustee" includes successor trustees or alternate successor trustees serving as trustee of this trust. The singular "trustee" also includes the plural.

E. Successor Trustee

Upon the death or incapacity of the surviving spouse, or the incapacity of both spouses, Jeffrey R. Carey shall serve as trustee. If after the death or incapacity of the surviving spouse, Jeffrey R. Carey is unable or unwilling to serve as successor trustee, Susan DiFlorio shall be the trustee.

F. Resignation of Trustee

Any trustee in office may resign at any time by signing a notice of resignation. The resignation must be delivered to the person or institution who is either named in this Declaration of Trust, or appointed by the trustee under Part 7, Section G, to next serve as the trustee.

G. Power to Appoint Successor Trustee

If no one named in this Declaration of Trust as a successor trustee or alternate successor trustee is willing or able to serve as trustee, the last acting trustee may appoint a successor trustee and may require the posting of a reasonable bond, to be paid from the trust property. The appointment must be made in writing, signed by the trustee and notarized.

H. Bond

No bond shall be required for any trustee named in this Declaration of Trust.

I. Compensation

No trustee shall receive any compensation for serving as trustee, unless the trustee serves as a trustee of a child's subtrust created by this Declaration of Trust.

J. Liability of Trustee

With respect to the exercise or non-exercise of discretionary powers granted by this Declaration of Trust, the trustee shall not be liable for actions taken in good faith. Such actions shall be binding on all persons interested in the trust property.

Part 8. Trustee's Management Powers and Duties

A. Powers Under State Law

The trustee shall have all authority and powers allowed or conferred on a trustee under California law, subject to the trustee's fiduciary duty to the grantors and the beneficiaries.

B. Other Powers

The trustee's powers shall also include:

1. The power to borrow money and to encumber trust property, including trust real estate, by mortgage, deed of trust or other method.

2. The power to manage trust real estate as if the trustee were the absolute owner of it, including the power to lease (even if the lease term may extend beyond the period of any trust) or grant options to lease the property, to make repairs or alterations and to insure against loss.

3. The power to sell or grant options for the sale or exchange of any trust property, including stocks, bonds, debentures and any other form of security or security account, at public or private sale for cash or on credit.

4. The power to invest trust property in property of any kind, including but not limited to bonds, debentures, notes, mortgages and stocks.

5. The power to receive additional property from any source and add to any trust created by this Declaration of Trust.

6. The power to employ and pay reasonable fees to accountants, lawyers or investment experts for information or advice relating to the trust.

7. The power to deposit and hold trust funds in both interest-bearing and non-interest-bearing accounts.

8. The power to deposit funds in bank or other accounts uninsured by FDIC coverage.

9. The power to enter into electronic fund transfer or safe deposit arrangements with financial institutions.

Part 9. Incapacity of Grantor

If Leslie M. Carey or William C. Carey becomes physically or mentally incapacitated, whether or not a court has declared the grantor incompetent or in need of a conservator, the other spouse shall be sole trustee until a licensed physician certifies in writing that the grantor is again able to manage his or her affairs. Incapacity must be certified in writing by a licensed physician.

If both spouses become incapacitated, the successor trustee named in Part 7, Section E of this Declaration of Trust shall serve as trustee.

The trustee shall manage the trust property and use any amount of trust income or trust principal necessary for the proper health care, support, maintenance, comfort and welfare of both grantors, in accordance with their accustomed manner of living. Any income not spent for the benefit of the grantors shall be accumulated and added to the trust property.

Part 10. Death of a Grantor

The first grantor to die shall be called the "deceased spouse." The living grantor shall be called the "surviving spouse."

Upon the deceased spouse's death, the trustee shall divide the property of The Leslie M. Carey and William C. Carey Revocable Living Trust listed on Schedules A, B and C into two separate trusts, Trust #1 and Trust #2. The trustee shall serve as trustee of Trust #1 and Trust #2.

Trust #1 shall contain all the property of The Leslie M. Carey and William C. Carey Revocable Living Trust owned by the deceased spouse before it was transferred to the trust, plus accumulated income, except trust property left by the terms of this trust to the surviving spouse. Trust #1 shall become irrevocable at the death of the deceased spouse. The trustee shall distribute the property in Trust #1 to the beneficiaries named in Part 11.

Trust #2 shall consist of all the property of The Leslie M. Carey and William C. Carey Revocable Living Trust owned by the surviving spouse before it was transferred to the trust, plus accumulated income, and any trust property left by the deceased spouse to the surviving spouse. It shall remain revocable until the death of the surviving spouse.

The trustee shall pay out of trust property such amounts as necessary for payment of debts, estate taxes and expenses of the last illness and funeral of the deceased and surviving spouses.

Part 11. Beneficiaries

A. Husband's Beneficiaries

At the death of William C. Carey, the trustee shall distribute the trust property listed on Schedule C, plus accumulated interest; the share of the property on Schedule A owned by William C. Carey before it was transferred to the trust, plus accumulated interest; and if William C. Carey is the second spouse to die, any property listed on Schedule B left to him by the deceased spouse, plus accumulated interest; as follows, subject to provisions in this Declaration of Trust that create children's subtrusts or create custodianships under the Uniform Transfers to Minors Act:

1. Leslie M. Carey shall be given all William C. Carey's interest in all the furniture in the house at 3320 Windmill Road, Andersonville, California, the condominium at 19903 Forest Way #43, Wawona, California and the house at 3320 Windmill Road, Andersonville, California. If Leslie M. Carey does not survive William C. Carey by 120 hours, that property shall be given to Claudia A. Carey.

2. Jonathan Goldfarb shall be given all William C. Carey's interest in brokerage account No. 3301-A94 at International Brokers, San Francisco, California. If Jonathan Goldfarb does not survive William C. Carey by 120 hours, that property shall be given to Melissa Goldfarb.

3. Claudia A. Carey shall be given all William C. Carey's interest in trust property not otherwise specifically and validly disposed of by this Part. If Claudia A. Carey does not survive William C. Carey by 120 hours, The Nature Conservancy shall be given all William C. Carey's interest in trust property not otherwise specifically and validly disposed of by this Part.

B. Wife's Beneficiaries

At the death of Leslie M. Carey, the trustee shall distribute the trust property listed on Schedule B, plus accumulated interest; the share of the property on Schedule A owned by Leslie M. Carey before it was transferred to the trust, plus accumulated interest; and if Leslie M. Carey is the second spouse to die, any property listed on Schedule C left to her by the deceased spouse, plus accumulated interest; as follows, subject to provisions in this Declaration of Trust that create children's subtrusts or create custodianships under the Uniform Transfers to Minors Act:

1. William C. Carey shall be given all Leslie M. Carey's interest in trust property. If William C. Carey does not survive Leslie M. Carey by 120 hours, that property shall be given to Claudia A. Carey.

2. Claudia A. Carey shall be given all Leslie M. Carey's interest in trust property not otherwise specifically and validly disposed of by this Part.

C. Property Left to the Surviving Spouse

Any trust property left by the deceased spouse to the surviving spouse shall remain in the surviving spouse's revocable trust, Trust #2.

Part 12. Children's Subtrusts

A. Beneficiaries for Whom Subtrusts May Be Created

1. If Claudia A. Carey has not yet reached the age of 29 when Claudia A. Carey becomes entitled to any trust property under Part 11.A, that trust property shall be kept in a separate child's subtrust, under the provisions of this Part, until Claudia A. Carey reaches the age of 29.

2. If Claudia A. Carey has not yet reached the age of 29 when Claudia A. Carey becomes entitled to any trust property under Part 11.B, that trust property shall be kept in a separate child's subtrust, under the provisions of this Part, until Claudia A. Carey reaches the age of 29.

B. Powers of Subtrust Trustee

The trustee may distribute as much of the net income or principal of the child's subtrust as the trustee deems necessary for the beneficiary's health, support, maintenance or education. Education includes, but is not limited to, college, graduate, postgraduate and vocational studies, and reasonably related living expenses.

In deciding whether or not to make a distribution to the beneficiary, the trustee may take into account the beneficiary's other income, resources and sources of support. Any subtrust income not distributed by the trustee shall be accumulated and added to the principal of the subtrust.

C. Assignment of Subtrust Assets

The interests of the beneficiary of a child's subtrust shall not be transferable by voluntary or involuntary assignment or by operation of law before receipt by the beneficiary. They shall be free from the claims of creditors and from attachments, execution, bankruptcy or other legal process to the fullest extent permitted by law.

D. Compensation of Trustee

Any trustee of a child's subtrust created under this Declaration of Trust shall be entitled to reasonable compensation out of the subtrust assets for ordinary and extraordinary services, and for all services in connection with the termination of any subtrust.

E. Termination of Subtrusts

A child's subtrust shall end when any of the following events occurs:

1. The beneficiary dies. If the subtrust ends for this reason, the subtrust property shall pass to the beneficiary's heirs.

2. The beneficiary reaches the age specified in Section A of this Part. If the subtrust ends for this reason, the remaining principal and accumulated income of the subtrust shall be given outright to the beneficiary.

3. The trustee distributes all subtrust property under the provisions of this Declaration of Trust.

Part 13. Custodianships Under the Uniform Transfers to Minors Act

1. Any property Melissa Goldfarb becomes entitled to under Part 11.A of this Declaration of Trust shall be given to Jane Goldfarb, as custodian for Melissa Goldfarb under the California Uniform Transfers to Minors Act. If Jane Goldfarb is unable or ceases to serve as custodian, Leslie M. Carey shall serve as custodian.

We certify that we have read this Declaration of Trust and that it correctly states the terms and conditions under which the trust property is to be held, managed and disposed of by the trustees, and we approve the Declaration of Trust.

Dated: _____

_____

William C. Carey, Grantor and Trustee

_____

Leslie M. Carey, Grantor and Trustee

State of _____

County of _____

On _____, 19___, before me, a notary public for the State of California, personally appeared Leslie M. Carey and William C. Carey, known to me to be the grantors and trustees of the trust created by the above Declaration of Trust, and to be the persons whose names are subscribed to the Declaration of Trust, and they acknowledged and executed the same as settlors and trustees.

IN WITNESS WHEREOF, I have set my hand and affixed by official seal.

_____

NOTARY PUBLIC for

the State of California

My commission expires _____, 19___.

Schedule A

1.   All the furniture in the house at 3320 Windmill Road, Andersonville, California.

2.   The condominium at 19903 Forest Way #43, Wawona, California.

3.   The house at 3320 Windmill Road, Andersonville, California.

Schedule B

1. Scudder International Fund Account 993-222-1.

2. The 4-volume American stamp collection kept at 3320 Windmill Road, Andersonville, California.

Schedule C

1. Brokerage account No. 3301-A94 at International Brokers, San Francisco, California.

7 Signing, Storing and Registering the Trust Document

Y ou don't yet have a valid living trust when you've completed the program and printed out your living trust document. Here's what to do next.

A. Before You Sign

When you've printed out the trust document, take plenty of time to read it. Carefully. Make sure it says what you want it to say. Check to be sure you have:

- included all property you want to leave through the trust

- clearly and accurately identified all property (doublecheck any account and serial numbers, for example)

- included all beneficiaries to whom you want to leave property

- spelled beneficiaries' (including alternate and residuary beneficiaries) names correctly and consistently

- made adequate arrangements for management of trust property that young beneficiaries might inherit

If you want to make changes, go back to the part of the program you need to change, enter the new data, and print out another trust document. (If you need help, see the User's Manual.)

Although in most instances it isn't necessary, you may also want to have an experienced estate planning lawyer look over the trust document before you sign it. You may already have consulted a lawyer, if you found yourself in a situation where we recommend that you get expert help—for example, if you haven't left at least half of your estate to your spouse or want to disinherit a minor child.

Now that you have the trust document in your hands, we recommend that you see a lawyer if:

- you're unsure about the legal effect of anything in the trust document, or

- you want to make changes, even if they seem insignificant, to the trust document created by *Nolo's Living Trust*.

The cost of paying an experienced estate planning attorney to review the trust document should be reasonable—especially compared to the cost of having an attorney do the whole thing from scratch. (Chapter 11, *If You Need Expert Help*, discusses how to find a lawyer and get the most help for your legal fees.)

A word of caution: Be aware that a lawyer who has a set way of doing things may disparage your self-help efforts and try to sell you expensive services you don't need. Before you sign up, be sure that the work is really necessary and justifies the expense.

B. Signing Your Trust Document in Front of a Notary

To create your living trust, you must sign the trust document. A living trust document, unlike a will, does not need to be signed in front of witnesses (in Florida, two witnesses are not required but are customarily used.) But you do need to sign your living trust document in front of a notary public for your state. If you and your spouse create a living trust together, both of you need to sign the trust document in front of the notary. If anyone challenges the authenticity of your signature after your death, the notarization will serve as evidence that it is genuine. And some institutions (stock brokerage houses, for example) may require that the signature be notarized before they will transfer assets into the trust.

You can usually find a notary public at a bank, title or escrow company, real estate brokerage or library. Or check the yellow pages under "Notaries Public."

Getting a signature notarized is quite simple. You show some evidence of your identity, and then the notary watches you sign the trust document and signs and dates it, too. The notary also stamps a notarial seal on the document.

The living trust document produced by *Nolo's Living Trust* includes, at the end of the document after the lines for your signature, a place for the notarization. The notarization form should be valid in most places, but if the notary public for your state wants to modify it, that's fine; some states require slightly different wording.

C. Making Copies

You will probably need copies of the trust document to transfer certain kinds of property (stocks, for example) into your living trust. (The details are in Chapter 8, *Transferring Property to the Trust.*) If a broker, bank or other institution wants to see your trust document, use a photocopy of the original trust document—the one you signed and had notarized. Do not just print out and sign another copy. Each copy you actually sign becomes, legally, an original trust document. Later, if you amend or revoke your living trust, you don't want lots of duplicate original trust documents floating around.

You should give a copy of the trust document to anyone you named to be a custodian of trust property inherited by a young beneficiary. The custodian may need it to show his or her authority to manage the property on behalf the beneficiary.

It's possible, but not usually advisable, to give copies of the trust document to beneficiaries. The problem is that if you later revoke or amend the trust but don't collect all the old copies, there will be outdated copies of your trust document floating around.

D. Registering the Trust

STATES THAT PROVIDE FOR REGISTRATION OF LIVING TRUSTS

Alaska	Maine
Colorado**	Michigan
Florida*	Nebraska*
Hawaii	New Mexico
Idaho	North Dakota

*not mandatory

**registration of a revocable living trust not required until the grantor's death; no registration required required if all trust property is distributed to the beneficiaries then

Some states require that the trustee of a trust register the trust with the local court. But there are no legal consequences or penalties if you don't.

Registration of a living trust doesn't give the court any power over the administration of the trust, unless there's a dispute. Registration serves to give the court jurisdiction over any disputes involving the trust—for example, if after your death a beneficiary wants to object to the way your successor trustee distributed the trust property. But if you don't register your trust, the result is the same: the court still has jurisdiction if a disgruntled relative or creditor files suit.[1]

To register a revocable living trust, the trustee must file a statement with the court where the trustee resides or keeps trust records. The statement must include:

- the name and address of the trustee
- an acknowledgement of the trusteeship
- the name(s) of the grantor(s)
- the name(s) of the original trustee(s)
- the date of the trust document

A trust can be registered in only one state at a time.

E. Storing the Trust Document

Store your living trust document, the *Nolo's Living Trust* disk and the manual where you keep important papers such as your will or durable power of attorney. A fireproof box in your home or office is fine. If you want to be extra careful, a safe deposit box is a good choice.

Make sure your successor trustee (or spouse, if you made a shared marital trust) knows where the original trust document is and can get hold of it soon after your death. The new trustee will need it to carry out your instructions on how to manage and distribute trust property. The new trustee will also need the information in Chapter 10, *After a Grantor Dies*, to carry out his or her duties.

---

[1]The only exception is that if a court demands that a trustee register a trust, and the trustee refuses, the trustee can be removed.

The copy of your trust document stored on the disk does not create a valid living trust. The trust document must be printed out and signed to create a trust.

8 Transferring Property to the Trust

After you sign your living trust document, you have a valid living trust. But the trust is of absolutely no use to you until the property you listed in the trust document is actually transferred into the trust's name. Lawyers call this "funding" the trust.

Transferring your property to your living trust is crucial, and takes some time and paperwork, but it's not difficult. You should be able to do it yourself, without a lawyer.

For some types of property, the work is done simply by preparing your trust document. If the property does not have an official title (ownership) document—a deed or title certificate, for example—the trust document itself states that the property is transferred to the trust. That's enough; you don't need another piece of paper that says the same thing. Property that falls into this category includes most furniture, clothing, books, appliances and other household goods.

But for items that have a title document that shows ownership—real estate, bank accounts, securities and much more—you will have to prepare a new document to show that the trust owns the property. This chapter shows you how.

 Take care of this last step promptly. Failing to transfer property to the trust is the most common and serious mistake people make when creating a living trust. If you don't get around to preparing and signing these new documents, the trust document will have no effect on what happens to your property after your death. Instead, the property will go to the "residuary beneficiary" named in your will, if you have one (you should—see Chapter 3, *A Living Trust as Part of Your Estate Plan*). If you don't have a will, the property will go to certain close relatives, according to state law. Either way, it will probably go through probate.

Note that you should transfer ownership into the living trust's name, not the trustee's name. So if your trust is called "The Denise Chapman Revocable Living Trust," you signed it May 19, 1991 and you are the trustee, you should transfer title to "The Denise Chapman Revocable Living Trust dated May 19, 1991," not to "Denise Chapman, trustee of The Denise Chapman Revocable Living Trust." The reason is that trustees may change, but the name of your trust does not.

A. Real Estate

To transfer real estate (also called real property) into the name of your trust, you must prepare and sign a new deed. The deed transfers ownership from you to the trust. You can fill out a new deed yourself; it's not difficult.

Co-op apartments. If you own a co-op apartment, you can't use a deed to transfer your shares in the co-op. You will have to check the co-op corporation's rules to see if the transfer is allowed. Some co-ops resist such transfers because they are afraid a living trust isn't a proper shareholder in the corporation. You can probably overcome any resistance you encounter by reminding the powers that be that for all practical purposes, you and the trust are the same—you have the same tax identification number, for example.

1. Preparing the Deed

First, get a deed form.[1] In many places, you can find blank deed forms in stationery or office supply stores. If you can't find what you need there, try a local law library; look for books on "real property" that have deed forms you can photocopy. You can use a "quitclaim" or "grant" deed form.[2]

Deed forms vary somewhat, but they all require the same basic information. Using a typewriter, fill out your deed like the sample shown below. Type in:

• The current owners' names. If you are the sole owner, or if you and someone else co-own the property and you are transferring just your share, only your name goes here. If you and your spouse own the property together and are transferring it to a shared marital trust, type in both of your names. Use exactly the same form of your name as is used on the deed that transferred the property to you and you used in your living trust document.

---

[1] If you're in California, you can find deed forms and instructions for filling them out in *The Deeds Book*, by Mary Randolph (Nolo Press). Much of the information in *The Deeds Book* is valid in other states as well, but it's best to use a deed form that's in common use in your area.

[2] The type of deed isn't important when you're transferring property to your own living trust. If you use a grant deed, you are promising the new owner (the trust) that you have good title to the property. If you use a quitclaim deed, you are promising only to transfer whatever interest you own in the property. The distinction isn't important when you control the trust.

- The new owner's name. Fill in the trust's name, exactly as it appears in the first paragraph of your trust document, and the date you signed the trust document in front of a notary public.

- The "legal description" of the property. Copy the description exactly as it appears on the previous deed.

If you co-own the property with someone and are transferring only your share to the living trust, you must also state, with the legal description, that you are transferring only that share (a one-half interest, for example) or that you are transferring "all your interest in" the property.

EXAMPLE   Amanda, who owns a house with her sister, wants to transfer her half of the property to her living trust. When she fills out a new deed, she can insert either "a one-half interest in" or "all my interest in" before the legal description.

Recording requested by

  Rose and Michael Morris
  4482 Franklin Ave.
  Fresno, CA 96833

and when recorded mail
this deed and tax statements to:

  same as above

For recorder's use

GRANT DEED

☒ This transfer is exempt from the documentary transfer tax.
☐ The documentary transfer tax is $_____ and is computed on:
    ☐ the full value of the interest or property conveyed.
    ☐ the full value less the value of liens or encumbrances remaining thereon at the time of sale.
The property is located in ☐ an unincorporated area. ☒ the city of: _Fresno_____.

For a valuable consideration, receipt of which is hereby acknowledged,

  Rose Morris and Michael Morris
hereby grant(s) to

  The Rose Morris and Michael Morris Revocable Living Trust
  dated January 13, 1991

the following real property in the City of _Fresno_____, County of _Fresno_____,
California:

  (legal description, exactly as on the previous deed)

Date: _Jan. 15, 1991_   *Rose Morris*

      Jan. 15, 1991   *Michael Morris*

State of California
County of _Fresno_) ss.

On _January 15_ 19_91_ *Rose Morris and Michael Morris*
known to me or proved by satisfactory evidence to be the person(s) whose name(s) is/are subscribed
above, personally appeared before me, a Notary Public for California, and acknowledged that
they executed this deed.

_____*Caroline L. Fishman*_____   [SEAL]
Signature of Notary

After everything is filled in, sign and date the deed in front of a notary public for the state in which the property is located. Everyone you listed as a current owner, who is transferring his or her interest in the property to the trust, must sign the deed.

2. Recording the Deed

After the deed is signed, you need to "record" it—that is, put a copy of the notarized deed on file in the county office that keeps local property records. In most places, the land records office is called the County Recorder's Office, Land Registry Office or County Clerk's office.

Just take the original, signed deed to the land records office. For a small fee, a clerk will make a copy and put it in the public records. You'll get your original back, stamped with a reference number to show where the copy can be found in the public records.

3. Transfer Taxes

In most places, you will not have to pay a state or local transfer tax when you transfer real estate to a revocable living trust. Most real estate transfer taxes are based on the sale price of the property and do not apply when no money changes hands. Others specifically exempt transfers where the real owners don't change—as is the case when you transfer property to a revocable living trust you control.

Before you record your deed, you can get information on transfer tax from the county tax assessor, county recorder or state tax officials.

4. Insurance

After you have transferred ownership of real estate to your living trust, call your insurance agent to report the change. The company will change its records on the policy, but the change won't affect your coverage or the cost of the policy.

5. Due-on-Sale Mortgage Clauses

Many mortgages contain a clause that allows the bank to call ("accelerate") the loan—that is, demand that you pay the whole thing off immediately—if you transfer the mortgaged property. Fortunately, in most instances lenders are forbidden by federal law to invoke a due-on-sale clause when property is transferred to a living trust. The lender can't call the loan if the borrower is a trust beneficiary and the transfer is "unrelated to occupancy" of the premises.[3]

CALIFORNIA PROPERTY TAXES

In California, increases in real estate taxes are limited by constitutional amendment (Proposition 13). The assessed value of the property can't go up more than 2% annually until a piece of property is sold. When the property is sold, however, the house is taxed on its market value. Transferring real property to a revocable living trust—or back to the person who set up the trust—does not trigger a reassessment for property tax purposes. (Cal. Rev. & Tax Code § 62(d).)

You may, however, have to file a form called a Preliminary Change of Title Report with the county tax assessor.

B. Bank Accounts and Safe Deposit Boxes

It should be simple to re-register ownership of a bank account in the name of your living trust or open a new account in the trust's name. Just ask the bank what paperwork you need to submit.

The bank will be concerned with the authority granted to the trustees to act on behalf of the trust. Depending on the kind of account, the bank may want to know if the trustees have the power to borrow money, put funds in a non-interest-bearing account, or engage in electronic transfers. (The trust document created by *Nolo's Living Trust* includes all these powers.)

---

[3]Garn-St. Germain Depository Institutions Act of 1982 (96 Stat. 1505).

To verify your authority, the bank may want to see a copy of your trust document, or have you fill out its own form, often called a Trust Certification.

If you want to transfer title to a safe deposit box to your trust, you'll have to re-register its ownership, too. The bank will have a form for you to fill out.

Estate planning note. Instead of transferring a bank account to a living trust, you may want to turn the account into a pay-on-death account (also called an revocable trust account). It's another, even easier, way to avoid probate of the money in the account. (See Chapter 3, A Living Trust as Part of Your Estate Plan.)

C. Vehicles

Most people don't transfer vehicles to a living trust, for reasons discussed in Part 7 of Chaper 5 or 6. Putting title to the vehicle in joint tenancy with a co-owner (or, if your state allows it, designating a beneficiary on the car registration) is usually a simpler way to avoid probate of the vehicle at your death.

But if you want to put a vehicle in trust, you must fill out a change of ownership document and have title to the vehicle reissued in the trust's name. The title certificate to your vehicle may contain instructions. If you have questions, call your state's Motor Vehicles Department.

D. Securities

How you transfer stocks, bonds and other securities to your living trust depends on whether you hold your stocks in a brokerage account or separately.

1. Brokerage Accounts

If you hold your stocks, bonds or other securities in a brokerage account, either change the account to the living trust's name or open a new account in the living trust's name. Simply contact your broker and ask for instructions. The brokerage company will probably have a straightforward form that you can fill out, giving information about the trustees and their authority.

If not, you will probably need to send the broker:

- a copy of the trust document or an "abstract of trust" (the first and last pages of the trust document, showing your notarized signature), and

- a letter instructing the holder to transfer the brokerage account to the living trust's name (or open a new account in the trust's name).

After you've submitted your request, get written confirmation that the account's ownership has in fact been put in the trust's name.

2. Stock Certificates

If you have the stock certificates or bonds in your possession—most people don't—you must get new certificates issued, showing the trust as owner. Ask your broker for help. If the broker is unwilling or unable to help, write to the "transfer agent" of the corporation that issued the stock. You can get the address from your broker or the investor relations office of the corporation. The transfer agent will give you simple instructions.

You will probably have to send in:

- your certificates or bonds;

- a form called a "stock or bond power," which you must fill out and sign; and

- a copy of the trust document or an "abstract of trust," which is just the first and last pages of the trust document, showing your notarized signature.

The stock or bond power may be printed on the back of the certificates; if not, you can probably find a copy at a stationery store. Send these documents to the transfer agent with a letter requesting that the certificates be reissued in the living trust's name.

Stock in closely-held corporations. See Section F, Business Interests, below.

3. Government Securities

To transfer government securities—for example, Treasury bills or U.S. bonds—have your broker contact the issuing government agency, or do it yourself.

E. Mutual Fund Accounts

Ask the company that issues the mutual fund what it requires for you to re-register ownership of your mutual fund account in your living trust's name. Most will send you an easy-to-use form to fill out. In addition, it will usually want a copy of your trust document or an "abstract of trust," which is just the first and last pages of the trust document.

F. Business Interests

How you transfer small business interests to your living trust depends on the way the business is owned.

1. Sole Proprietorships

An unincorporated business that you own by yourself is the easiest to transfer to a trust. First, list the business, by name, as an item of property in the trust document. That transfers the name to your living trust and whatever customer goodwill goes with it.

Because you own the business assets in your own name (a sole proprietorship, unlike a corporation, is not an entity that can own property), you transfer them to your living trust like you would any other valuable property. (See the Valuable Property Inventory, Chapter 5 or 6.)

If you have a registered trademark or service mark, you must re-register ownership in the living trust's name. For sample forms, see *Nolo's*

Trademark Book: How To Name Your Business and Product, by Kate McGrath and Steve Elias (Nolo Press; available Spring 1992).

2. Solely Owned Corporations

If you own all the stock of a corporation, you shouldn't have any problem transferring it to your living trust. Follow these four steps:

Step 1. Fill out the stock transfer section on the back of the certificate.

Step 2. Mark the certificate "cancelled" and place it in your corporate records book.

Step 3. Resissue a new certificate in the name of the living trust.

Step 4. Show the cancellation of the old certificate and the issuance of the new certificate on the stock ledger pages in your corporate records book.

3. Closely-Held Corporations

Normally, you can transfer your shares in a closely-held corporation to your living trust by following corporate bylaws and having the stock certificates reissued in the living trust's name. But first, check the corporation's bylaws and articles of incorporation, as well as any separate shareholders' agreements, to see if there are any restrictions on such transfers. If an agreement limits or forbids transfers, it will have to be changed before you can put your shares in your living trust.

4. Partnership Interests

To transfer your partnership interest to your living trust, you must notify your business partners and modify the partnership agreement to show that your partnership interest is now owned by your living trust. If there is a partnership certificate, it must be changed to substitute the trust as owner of your share.

Occasionally a partnership agreement limits or forbids transfers to a living trust. If so, you and your partners may want to see a lawyer before you make any changes.

G. Limited Partnerships

Limited partnerships are a form of investment, governed by securities laws. Contact the partnership's general partner to find out what paperwork is necessary to transfer your interest to a living trust.

H. Copyrights

If you want to transfer your interest in a copyright to your living trust, you should list the copyright in the trust document and then sign and file, with the U.S. Copyright Office, a document transferring all your rights in the copyright to the living trust. Sample transfer forms are in *The Copyright Handbook*, by Steve Fishman (Nolo Press).

I. Patents

If you own a patent and want to transfer it to your living trust, you should prepare a document called an "assignment" and record it with the Patent and Trademark Office in Washington, DC. There is a small fee for recording. Sample assignment forms and instructions are in *Patent It Yourself*, by David Pressman (Nolo Press).

J. Property that Names the Trust as Beneficiary

If you name your living trust as beneficiary of a life insurance policy, individual retirement account (IRA) or Keogh account, you don't need to transfer the policy or account itself to the trust. You, not the living trust, are the owner. The living trust is the beneficiary, which will receive the proceeds at your death. The proceeds will be given to the residuary beneficiary of your living trust unless you named someone else, in the trust document, to receive them.

9 Living With Your Living Trust

As a day-to-day, practical matter, it makes little difference that your property is now owned by your revocable living trust. You have no special paperwork to prepare, forms to file or other duties to perform as the trustee of your own revocable living trust.

This chapter discusses what you need to know after your living trust is up and running, and how to change your trust document if you wish.

A. Reporting Income From Trust Property

No separate income tax records or returns are necessary as long as you are the trustee of your own living trust.[1] Income from property in the trust must be reported on your personal income tax return.

B. If You Move to Another State

Your living trust is still valid if you prepare it in one state and then move to another. When you use *Nolo's Living Trust*, you indicate the state that is your legal residence. The trust document produced by the program states that the law of this state applies to any disputes about disposition of the property. So no matter where you are living at your death, the successor trustee will only have to deal with one state's law.

You may, however, need to take some actions after your move:

• Your new state may require you to register your living trust document with the local court. (See Chapter 7, *Signing, Storing and Registering the Trust Document.*)

• You may want to amend the trust document if the new state's laws differ on matters such as marital property rights or property management for young trust beneficiaries. (See Section E, below.)

---

[1]I.R.S. Reg. § 1.671-4.

C. Adding Property to Your Living Trust

If you acquire valuable items of property after you create your living trust, you should promptly add them to the trust so that they won't have to go through probate at your death.

Your trust document specifically gives you the power to add property to the trust. Adding property to the trust is not an amendment of the trust document. There are four steps:

Step 1. Create a revised Property Schedule A, B or C of your trust document, adding the new property. (If you made an individual trust, you have only one schedule, Schedule A. If you and your spouse made a shared marital trust, Schedule A lists your co-owned property, Schedule B lists the wife's property, and Schedule C lists the husband's property.)

You can't use *Nolo's Living Trust* to revise a property schedule until you've printed out a trust document—until then, there's nothing to revise. After you've printed, when you start the program again, it will ask you whether or not you've signed the trust document, creating a legally valid trust. If you have, the program will take you to a screen that allows you to display your Property Schedules. (See User's Manual, Part K.) You can add the new property to a schedule by editing the schedule on the screen. (See Chapter 5 or 6, Part 5, for how to describe different kinds of trust property.)

Step 2. Print out the new schedule and replace the old one on your signed original trust document. That's all you have to do; schedules don't have to be signed.

Step 3. Transfer ownership of the property to the trust, if the property has a title document. (Instructions are in Chapter 8, *Transferring Property to the Trust.*)

Step 4. If you need to name a beneficiary for the property, create a Trust Amendment. (See Section G, below.) You won't need to create a Trust Amendment if your trust document leaves all your trust property to one person or if you want the new property to go to the residuary beneficiary of the trust.

EXAMPLE When Rose and her husband Michael buy a house, they take title in the name of the "Rose and Michael Morris Revocable Living Trust dated January 13, 1991." They then prepare a revised Schedule A (which lists co-owned property) of their trust document, print it out and replace the old Schedule A.

Because their trust document leaves all their property to each other, they do not need to prepare a Trust Amendment.

D. Selling or Giving Away Trust Property

You have complete control over the property you have transferred to the living trust. If you want to sell or give away any of it, simply go ahead, using your authority as trustee. You (or you and your spouse, if you made a shared marital trust) just sign ownership or transfer documents (the deed, bill of sale or other document) in your capacity as trustee of the living trust.

EXAMPLE Mel transfers ownership of his house to his living trust, but later decides to sell it. He transfers the house to the buyer by signing the new deed as "Melvin Owens, trustee of the Melvin Owens Revocable Living Trust dated June 8, 1991."

If you and your spouse made a shared marital trust, either trustee (spouse) has authority over trust property. That means that either spouse can sell or give away any of the trust property—including the property that was co-owned or was the separate property of the other spouse before it was transferred to the trust. In practice, however, both spouses will probably have to consent to transfer real estate out of the living trust. Especially in community property states, buyers and title insurance companies usually insist on both spouses' signatures on transfer documents.

If for any reason you want to take property out of the trust but keep ownership of it, you can transfer it to yourself. So if Mel, in the previous example, wanted to take his house out of his living trust but keep ownership in his own name, he would make the deed out from "The Melvin Owens Revocable Living Trust dated June 8, 1991, Melvin Owens, trustee" to "Melvin Owens." If the item doesn't have a title document—a piece of furniture, for example—no paperwork is necessary to make the transfer.

After you have removed property from the trust (whether or not it has a title document), modify the property schedule of your trust document to reflect the change. (See Section C, above.) If you don't, the schedules will still show that the property is owned by the trust. Legally, the trust no longer owns it, but the discrepancy could be confusing to the people who carry out your wishes after your death. If you named a specific beneficiary to receive the item, you should delete that trust language, using a Trust Amendment. (Section G, below, shows how to create a Trust Amendment.)

EXAMPLE Wendy and Brian made a shared living trust several years ago. Wendy transferred a valuable antique dresser, which she inherited from her grandfather before she was married, to the living trust. It's listed on Schedule B of the trust document. The trust document provides that the dresser will go to her son at her death. But she's changed her mind and wants her daughter to have the dresser right now.

After Wendy gives the dresser to her daughter, she prints out two documents. First, she prepares a new Schedule B, deleting the dresser from the list of property, and replaces the old Schedule B attached to her trust document. Second, she prepares a Trust Amendment, stating that the paragraph that left the dresser to her son is no longer in effect.

E. When To Amend Your Living Trust Document

One of the most attractive features of a revocable living trust is its flexibility: you can change its terms, or end it altogether, at any time. This section discusses several events that should be red flags, alerting you that you may need to amend your living trust. (Instructions for making the Trust Amendment are in Section G, below.)

In most circumstances, you will want to amend your living trust document, not revoke it. It might seem easier to revoke it and start again, as you might with a will. But if you revoke your living trust and create another one, you must transfer all the trust property out of the old living trust and into the new one. (Section H, below, discusses when it is advisable to revoke your living trust and make another.)

1. You Change Your Mind

You may simply change your mind about whom you want to leave certain items of trust property to, or whom you want to serve as your successor trustee. To change these or other terms of your living trust, you'll need to make a Trust Amendment.

2. You Marry or Have a Child

If you marry or have a child, you'll almost certainly want to amend your trust document to provide for your new spouse or offspring. And your estate plan will be influenced by the fact that your spouse or minor child may be entitled, under state law, to a certain portion of your property. (See Chapter 2, *About Living Trusts*.) If you divorce, you should revoke your trust; see Section H, below.

3. You Add Valuable Property to the Trust

If you add property to your living trust, you may need to amend the trust document to name a beneficiary for the property. (See Section C, above.)

4. You Move to Another State

Although your living trust is still valid if you move to another state, you may want to change your living trust in response to your new state's laws. Here are several aspects of an estate plan that may be affected by a move.

a. Marital Property Laws: Who Owns What

If you are married and move from a community property state to a non-community property state, each spouse's ownership rights in the property already acquired stay the same. The new state's law applies to property acquired in the new state.

If you move from a non-community property state to a community property state, however, the move may change which spouse owns what. This is a concern only if one spouse plans to leave a significant amount of property to someone other than the surviving spouse, and that spouse might contest it.

For example, take a married couple's move from New York, a non-community property state, to California, a community property state. In New York, the spouse whose name is listed on a title (ownership) document owns the property. But California views property ownership differently—it treats the property acquired by a married couple in New York as community property, owned equally by each spouse, if it would have been community property had the couple acquired it in California. (The legal term for such property is "quasi-community property.") This means each spouse owns half of this property and can leave only that share at death.

Different community property states have different rules about what happens to spouses' property when they move to that state. If you're concerned, see a lawyer who's knowledgeable about your new state's family law.

b. Property Management for Young Beneficiaries

Your state's law determines the choices you have when it comes to arranging for property management for young trust beneficiaries. In all states, *Nolo's Living Trust* lets you create a "child's subtrust" for any beneficiary who might inherit trust property before he or she is 35. But state law determines whether or not you have another option: appointing someone to be the "custodian" of trust property inherited by a young beneficiary. (All of this is explained in Chapter 5 or 6, Part 7.)

If you move to a state that has the custodianship option, you may want to create a Trust Amendment, changing your trust document to let you take advantage of it.

If you have already created a custodianship, you should amend the trust document to delete the old custodianship clause and add a new one that conforms to your new state's law.

c. Rights of a Surviving Spouse or Child To Inherit

Different states entitle surviving spouses (and in some cases, minor children) to different shares of a deceased spouse's estate. If you haven't left much property to your spouse or child and are concerned that either might challenge your estate plan after your death, you'll want to know what your new state's laws say. (See Chapter 2, *About Living Trusts*.) You may want to amend your trust document to change what you leave to your spouse or child, or see a lawyer.

5. Your Spouse Dies

If you and your spouse made a shared living trust, when one spouse dies the other will probably inherit some, if not all, of the deceased spouse's trust property. The surviving spouse may need to amend his or her trust to name beneficiaries for that property. (See Chapter 10, *After a Grantor Dies*.)

6. A Major Beneficiary Dies

If you left much or all of your trust property to one person, and that person dies before you do, you may well want to amend your trust document. If you named an alternate beneficiary for the deceased beneficiary, there's not an urgent need to amend the trust document; the alternate will inherit the property. But amending it makes sense, so that you can name another alternate beneficiary, who will receive the property if the former alternate (now first in line) dies before you do.

EXAMPLE Marty and Frank make a living trust together. Marty leaves all her trust property to Frank, but he dies before she does. Because she named her daughter Stephanie as alternate beneficiary for her husband, she has already planned for the possibility of Frank's death. But it still makes sense for her to amend her trust, to name an alternate beneficiary for Stephanie.

Remember that your trust document has another back-up device built into it: the residuary beneficiary. If both the primary and alternate beneficiary die before you do, the residuary beneficiary will inherit the trust property.

F. Who Can Amend a Living Trust Document

Who can amend the terms of a living trust document depends on whether you created an individual living trust or a shared one with your spouse.

1. Individual Living Trusts

If you created an individual living trust, you (the grantor) can amend any of its provisions at any time.

2. Shared Marital Living Trusts

While both spouses are alive, both must agree to amend any provision of the living trust document—for example, change a beneficiary, successor trustee or the management set up for a young beneficiary.

After one spouse dies, the shared living trust is split into two trusts, one of which can no longer be amended. (This is explained in Chapter 10, *After a Grantor Dies.*) Basically, the surviving spouse is free to amend the terms of the trust document that deal with his or her property, but can't change the parts that determine what happens to the deceased spouse's trust property.

3. Someone Acting on a Grantor's Behalf

The trust document created by *Nolo's Living Trust* does not allow the trust document to be amended by someone acting on a grantor's behalf, unless the grantor has given that authority in another document.

That means someone who is appointed by a court to handle your affairs (a conservator) or someone you have given authority to act for you in a document called a Durable Power of Attorney (your "attorney-in-fact") cannot amend the trust document absent specific authorization. If you want to give your attorney-in-fact authority to amend your living trust, you must specifically grant this authority in your Durable Power of Attorney.

G. Changing Beneficiaries, Trustees, Subtrusts or Custodianships

It's simple to amend your trust document to change a beneficiary, successor trustee or custodian named in it. Just use *Nolo's Living Trust* to print out a document called a Trust Amendment.

You can't create a Trust Amendment until you've printed out a trust document. After you've printed, when you start the program again, it will ask you whether or not you've signed the trust document, creating a legally valid trust. If you have, the program will take you to a screen with a list of Trust Amendment templates. (See the User's Manual, Part K.)

Pick the template you need and fill it out on the screen; instructions and sample forms for different kinds of amendments are in the sections below. After you print out the Trust Amendment, sign it in front of a notary public and attach it to the signed original trust document. Both spouses must sign a Trust Amendment to amend a shared marital living trust. Then give a copy of the Trust Amendment to anyone who already has a copy of the original trust document.

Changing your changes

If you want to change a provision in a previous Amendment you have printed out and signed, be sure that you work from the language of the Amendment, not the original trust document. You will need to create a new Amendment and type in the language from the earlier amendment that you want to change or delete. (Don't worry that the amendment template says the language is deleted "from the trust document"; any amendments are considered, legally, part of the trust document.)

Do not change any provisions of the trust document except as instructed in the Trust Amendment templates. You could create serious problems for your heirs or even invalidate your trust.

1. Adding a Beneficiary

If you've added property to the trust by amending a property schedule (Part C, above), and you want to name a beneficiary to receive the property, you should create a Trust Amendment. A sample is shown below.

To prepare your Trust Amendment, follow these steps:

Step 1. Select Add One Beneficiary or Add Co-Beneficiaries from the list of templates.

Step 2. Fill in the date you signed the original trust document in the two spaces left blank near the beginning of the form.

Step 3. *One beneficiary:* Type in the name of the beneficiary and the property description. Also name an alternate beneficiary if you wish.

Co-beneficiaries: Choose the option you want to use, depending on whether you want the beneficiaries to inherit equal or unequal shares, and how you want to name alternate beneficiaries for them. Delete the other clauses.

Sample amendments are shown below. The samples are for an individual trust. If you made a shared marital trust with your spouse, the template will look slightly different. The Part number that gives you authority to make the amendment will be Part 5 (not Part 4), and you will be adding language to Part 11.A or 11.B (not Part 10).

Sample Trust Amendment: Add One Beneficiary (Individual Trust)

Amendment to
The Clara Goldman Revocable Living Trust
dated <u>April 14, 1991</u>

Under the power reserved to the grantor by Part 4 of the Declaration of Trust dated <u>April 14, 1991</u>, creating the Clara Goldman Revocable Living Trust, the grantor hereby amends the Declaration of Trust as follows:

The following is added to Part 10 of the trust document:

<u>Richard Tillman</u> shall be given all the grantor's interest in <u>the house at 321 Glen St., Omaha, Nebraska</u>. If <u>Richard Tillman</u> does not survive the grantor by 120 hours, that property shall be given to <u>Michelle Renaud.</u>

_____   _____
Clara Goldman, Grantor   Date

[NOTARIZATION]

Sample Trust Amendment: Add Co-Beneficiaries (Individual Trust)

Amendment to
The Michael Hunter Revocable Living Trust
dated <u>November 29, 1991</u>

Under the power reserved to the grantor by Part 4 of the Declaration of Trust dated <u>November 29, 1991</u>, creating the Michael Hunter Revocable Living Trust, the grantor hereby amends the Declaration of Trust as follows:

The following is added to Part 10 of the trust document:

[CHOOSE ONE OF THE FOLLOWING PARAGRAPHS AND DELETE THE OTHERS:]

[OPTION 1: IN EQUAL SHARES TO SURVIVORS]

1. The grantor's interest in <u>the house at 4448 Pinehaven St., Atlanta, Georgia</u> shall be given in equal shares to those of <u>Richard Gimbel and Joseph Gimbel</u> who survive the grantor by 120 hours.

[OPTION 2: IN UNEQUAL SHARES TO SURVIVORS]

1. Richard Gimbel and Joseph Gimbel shall be given all the grantor's interest in the house at 4448 Pinehaven St., Atlanta, Georgia divided as follows: Richard Gimbel shall receive 3/4. If Richard Gimbel fails to survive the grantor by 120 hours, his or her interest in this property shall be given to the survivors in equal shares. Joseph Gimbel shall receive 1/4. If Joseph Gimbel fails to survive the grantor by 120 hours, his or her interest in this property shall be given to the survivors in equal shares.

[OPTION 3: IN EQUAL SHARES, WITH NAMED ALTERNATES]

1. The grantor's interest in the house at 4448 Pinehaven St., Atlanta, Georgia shall be given in equal shares to Richard Gimbel and Joseph Gimbel. If Richard Gimbel does not survive the grantor by 120 hours, his or her interest in this property shall be given to Kyoka Johnson. If Joseph Gimbel does not survive the grantor by 120 hours, his or her interest in this property shall be given to Francine Gimbel.

[OPTION 4: IN UNEQUAL SHARES, WITH NAMED ALTERNATES]

1. The grantor's interest in the house at 4448 Pinehaven St., Atlanta, Georgia shall be given to Richard Gimbel and Joseph Gimbel as follows. Richard Gimbel shall be given 2/3. Joseph Gimbel shall be given 1/3. If Richard Gimbel does not survive the grantor by 120 hours, his or her interest in this property shall be given to Joseph Gimbel. If Joseph Gimbel does not survive the grantor by 120 hours, his or her interest in this property shall be given to Richard Gimbel.

_____   _____

Michael Hunter, Grantor   Date

[NOTARIZATION]

---

2. Changing a Beneficiary

You may change your mind about leaving certain trust property to a beneficiary you named in the trust document, or a beneficiary may die before you do. If so, you'll need to prepare a Trust Amendment.

EXAMPLE Jim and Toni created their living trust three years ago and named Jim's sister Eileen as beneficiary of some stock that Jim transferred to the trust. But since then Jim and his sister have had a falling out. He wants to amend the trust document to leave the stock to his son, Aaron.

All Jim and Toni need to do is use *Nolo's Living Trust* to prepare an amendment. The amendment shown below deletes the paragraph in the Declaration of Trust that left the stock to Eileen. It also adds a paragraph leaving the stock to Aaron and stating that if Aaron doesn't survive him, that it should go to his nephew David.

(If they eliminated the gift to Eileen but didn't name a new beneficiary for the property, it would go the residuary beneficiary of the trust.)

To prepare your Trust Amendment, follow these steps:

Step 1. Select Change a Beneficiary from the list of templates.

Step 2. Fill in the date you signed the original trust document in the two spaces left blank near the beginning of the form.

Step 3. Copy and paste the language you want to delete from your trust document. (Part K of the User's Manual explains how.)

Step 4. Choose one of the five options, depending on how many beneficiaries you want to name and how you want to name alternate beneficiaries, if any. Delete the other paragraphs.

A sample amendment is shown below. It shows how you would fill out all four options, although when you actually create an amendment you would use only one and delete the others.

The sample amendment below is for a shared marital trust. If you made an individual trust, the template will look slightly different: The Part number that gives you authority to make amendments will be Part 4 (not Part 5), and you will be changing Part 10 (not Part 11.A or 11.B).

Sample Trust Amendment: Change a Beneficiary
(Shared Marital Trust, Husband's Beneficiary)

Amendment to
The James Mansell and Toni Mansell Revocable Living Trust
dated <u>March 2, 1991</u>

Under the power reserved to the grantors by Part 5 of the Declaration of Trust dated <u>March 2, 1991</u>, creating the James Mansell and Toni Mansell Revocable Living Trust, the grantors hereby amend the Declaration of Trust as follows:

The following is deleted from Part <u>11.A</u> of the trust document:

4. Eileen Gruber shall be given all James Mansell's interest in 100 shares of stock in Cliff Industries, Inc.

The following is added to Part <u>11.A</u> of the trust document:

[CHOOSE ONE OF THE FOLLOWING PARAGRAPHS AND DELETE THE OTHERS:]

[OPTION 1: TO ONE BENEFICIARY]

4. <u>Aaron Rice</u> shall be given all <u>James Mansell</u>'s interest in 100 shares of stock in Cliff Industries, Inc. If <u>Aaron Rice</u> doesn't survive <u>James Mansell</u> by 120 hours, that property shall be given to <u>David Stine</u>.

[OPTION 2: TO MORE THAN ONE BENEFICIARY,
IN EQUAL SHARES TO SURVIVORS]

4. <u>James Mansell</u>'s interest in 100 shares of stock in Cliff Industries, Inc. shall be given in equal shares to those of <u>Aaron Rice and Fanny Rice</u> who survive <u>James Mansell</u> by 120 hours.

[OPTION 3: TO MORE THAN ONE BENEFICIARY,
IN UNEQUAL SHARES TO SURVIVORS]

4. <u>Aaron Rice and Fanny Rice</u> shall be given all <u>James Mansell</u>'s interest in 100 shares of stock in Cliff Industries, Inc. divided as follows: <u>Aaron Rice</u> shall receive <u>3/4</u>. <u>Fanny Rice</u> shall receive <u>1/4.</u> If <u>Fanny Rice</u> fails to survive <u>James Mansell</u> by 120 hours, his or her interest in this property shall be given to the survivors in equal shares. If <u>Aaron Rice</u> fails to survive <u>James Mansell</u> by 120 hours, his or her interest in this property shall be given to the survivors in equal shares.

[OPTION 4: TO MORE THAN ONE BENEFICIARY,
IN EQUAL SHARES, WITH NAMED ALTERNATES]

4. James Mansell's interest in 100 shares of stock in Cliff Industries, Inc. shall be given in equal shares to Aaron Rice and Fanny Rice. If Aaron Rice does not survive James Mansell by 120 hours, his or her interest in this property shall be given to Margaret Puckett. If Fanny Rice does not survive James Mansell by 120 hours, his or her interest in this property shall be given to Margaret Puckett.

[OPTION 5: TO MORE THAN ONE BENEFICIARY,
IN UNEQUAL SHARES, WITH NAMED ALTERNATES]

4. James Mansell's interest in 100 shares of stock in Cliff Industries, Inc. shall be given to Aaron Rice and Fanny Rice as follows: Aaron Rice shall be given 3/4. Fanny Rice shall be given 1/4. If Aaron Rice does not survive James Mansell by 120 hours, his or her interest in this property shall be given to Margaret Puckett. If Fanny Rice does not survive James Mansell by 120 hours, his or her interest in this property shall be given to Margaret Puckett.

_____   _____
James Mansell, Grantor   Date

_____   _____
Toni Mansell, Grantor   Date

[NOTARIZATION]

---

3. Changing a Trustee or Custodian

You can amend your trust document if you change your mind about who you want to serve as:

- **Successor trustee** (the person who handles the trust, and any children's subtrusts, after your death or the surviving spouse's death if a shared trust was created)

- **Alternate successor trustee** (the person who takes over as trustee if your first choice can't serve)

- **Custodian** of a child's trust property (the person who manages a young beneficiary's trust property under the terms of the Uniform Transfer to Minors Act, if it's available in your state), or

- **Alternate custodian** (the custodian if your first choice can't serve)

To prepare your Trust Amendment, follow these steps:

Step 1. Select the proper form from the list of templates: Change a Successor Trustee, Change an Alternate Successor Trustee or Change a Custodianship.

Step 2. Fill in the date you signed the original trust document in the two spaces left blank near the beginning of the form.

Step 3. Put the correct number in the blank after "The following is deleted from Part __." If you are changing a successor trustee, the Part number will be 6 or 7. If you are changing a custodian or alternate custodian, the Part number will be 11, 12 or 13. Check your original trust document to find the number of the part you are changing.

Step 4. Copy the language you want to delete from your trust document and paste it here. (Part K of the User's Manual explains how to copy text from the original trust document.)

Step 5. Put the same Part number you used in Step 3 in the blank after "The following is added to Part __." Paste the same deleted language (Step 3) again and then replace the old name with the new one.

The sample amendment shown below is for an individual trust. If you made a shared marital trust with your spouse, the template will look slightly different: The Part number that gives you authority to make the amendment will be Part 5 (not Part 4).

Sample Trust Amendment: Change Successor Trustee
(Individual Trust)

Amendment to
The Geoffrey Spencer Revocable Living Trust
dated <u>May 2, 1991</u>

Under the power reserved to the grantor by Part 4 of the Declaration of Trust dated <u>May 2, 1991</u>, creating the Geoffrey Spencer Revocable Living Trust, the grantor hereby amends the Declaration of Trust as follows:

The following is deleted from Part <u>6</u> of the trust document:

Upon the death or incapacity of Geoffrey Spencer, the trustee of this trust and all subtrusts created by it shall be Philip C. Spencer.

The following is added to Part <u>6</u> of the trust document:

Upon the death or incapacity of Geoffrey Spencer, the trustee of this trust and all subtrusts created by it shall be <u>Scott Castillo</u>.

_____   _____

Geoffrey Spencer, Grantor   Date

[NOTARIZATION]

The sample amendment below is for a shared marital trust. If you made an individual trust, the template will look slightly different: The Part number that gives you authority to make amendments will be Part 4 (not Part 5).

Sample Trust Amendment: Change a Custodianship (Marital Trust)

Amendment to

The Russell Zackman and Sara Zackman Revocable Living Trust

dated <u>October 2, 1991</u>

Under the power reserved to the grantors by Part 5 of the Declaration of Trust dated <u>October 2, 1991</u>, creating the Russell Zackman and Sara Zackman Revocable Living Trust, the grantors hereby amend the Declaration of Trust as follows:

The following is deleted from from Part <u>13</u> of the trust document:

Any property Jeremy Zackman becomes entitled to under Part 11.A of this Declaration of Trust shall be given to Sara Zackman, as custodian for Jeremy Zackman under the Illinois Transfers to Minors Act until Jeremy Zackman reaches the age of 21.

The following is added to Part <u>13</u> of the trust document:

Any property Jeremy Zackman becomes entitled to under Part 11.A of this Declaration of Trust shall be given to <u>Thomas Zackman</u>, as custodian for Jeremy Zackman under the Illinois Transfers to Minors Act until Jeremy Zackman reaches the age of 21.

_____   _____
Russell Zackman, Grantor   Date

_____   _____
Sara Zackman, Grantor   Date

[NOTARIZATION]

---

4. Changing the Age at Which a Beneficiary Gets Property

You may also want to change the age at which a young beneficiary is to receive his or her trust property. Be sure to read the restrictions on your choices in Part 7 of Chapter 5 or 6. Once you're sure your change is allowed by state law, follow these instructions:

Step 1. Select Change a Custodianship or Change Age Subtrust Ends from the list of templates.

Step 2. Fill in the date you signed the original trust document in the two spaces left blank near the beginning of the form.

Step 3. *Shared marital trust only:* Put the number of the part you are changing in the blank after "The following is deleted from Part __," and the same number in the blank after "The following is added to Part __." The Part number will be 12 or 13; check your original trust document.

Step 4. Copy, from your original trust document, the paragraph that sets the age at which the custodianship or subtrust ends. (Part __ of the User's Manual explains how to copy text from the trust document.) Paste it in the space after "The following is deleted from Part __."

Step 5. Paste the deleted language again in the space after "The following is added to Part __," and then change the age. Do not make any other changes in the language of the paragraph.

A sample amendment for an individual trust is shown below. If you made a shared marital trust with your spouse, the template will look slightly different. The Part number that gives you authority to make the amendment will be Part 5 (not Part 4).

**Sample Trust Amendment: Change Age Subtrust Ends
(Individual Trust)**

Amendment to
The Lily Trammell Revocable Living Trust
dated <u>August 12, 1991</u>

Under the power reserved to the grantor by Part 4 of the Declaration of Trust dated <u>August 12, 1991</u>, creating the Lily Trammell Revocable Living Trust, the grantor hereby amends the Declaration of Trust as follows:

The following is deleted from Part 11 of the trust document:

1. If at the grantor's death Lucy Hillman has not yet reached the age of 28, any property Lucy Hillman becomes entitled to under Part 10 shall be kept in a separate child's subtrust, under the provisions of this Part, until Lucy Hillman reaches the age of 28. Lucy Hillman shall be the sole beneficiary of the subtrust.

The following is added to Part 11 of the trust document:

1. If at the grantor's death Lucy Hillman has not yet reached the age of <u>30</u>, any property Lucy Hillman becomes entitled to under Part 10 shall be kept in a separate child's subtrust, under the provisions of this Part, until Lucy Hillman reaches the age of <u>30</u>. Lucy Hillman shall be the sole beneficiary of the subtrust.

_____   _____

Lily Trammell, Grantor   Date

[NOTARIZATION]

5. Adding a Child's Subtrust

You can add a child's subtrust to your trust document, whether or not your original trust document created any subtrusts.

To prepare your Trust Amendment, follow these steps:

Step 1. Select Add Child's Subtrust from the list of templates.

Step 2. Fill in the date you signed the original trust document in the two spaces left blank near the beginning of the form.

Step 3. If your original trust document created a subtrust for a different beneficiary, put that Part number in the blank in "The following is added to

[Part __ of] the trust document:" and delete the brackets. If your original trust document did not create any subtrusts, delete the bracketed language, add a heading (shown on the template) to the trust document, and number it accordingly. (The Part number should be one more than the number of Parts in the original trust document.)

Step 4. Fill in the blanks with the name of the beneficiary and the age at which the subtrust ends (any age up to 35).

Step 5. If your original trust document created subtrusts for other beneficiaries, delete the rest of the language (sections B through E), up to the signature line(s).

The sample amendment shown below is for an individual trust. If you made a shared marital trust with your spouse, the template will look slightly different: The Part number that gives you authority to make the amendment will be Part 5 (not Part 4).

Sample Trust Amendment: Add Child's Subtrust (Individual Trust)

Amendment to
The William Schwegler Revocable Living Trust
dated <u>July 5, 1991</u>

Under the power reserved to the grantor by Part 4 of the Declaration of Trust dated <u>July 5, 1991</u>, creating the William Schwegler Revocable Living Trust, the grantor hereby amends the Declaration of Trust as follows:

The following is added to [Part __ of] *[IF YOUR ORIGINAL TRUST DOCUMENT CREATED A SUBTRUST, FILL IN THE PART NUMBER; OTHERWISE, DELETE BRACKETED LANGUAGE.]* the trust document:

[IF YOUR ORIGINAL TRUST DOCUMENT DID NOT CREATE ANY CHILDREN'S SUBTRUSTS, ADD THE HEADING BELOW AND NUMBER THE NEW PART. OTHERWISE, START AFTER THE HEADING.]

Part <u>12</u>. Children's Subtrusts

A.   Beneficiaries for Whom Subtrusts May Be Created

If <u>Emma Schwegler</u> has not reached the age of <u>30</u> when <u>Emma Schwegler</u> becomes entitled to any trust property under Part 10, that trust property shall be kept in a separate child's subtrust, under the provisions of the Part, until <u>Emma Schwegler</u> reaches the age of <u>30</u>.

[IF YOUR ORIGINAL TRUST DOCUMENT CONTAINS OTHER SUBTRUSTS, DELETE THE FOLLOWING LANGUAGE, UP TO THE SIGNATURE LINE. CHECK YOUR TRUST DOCUMENT.]

B.   Powers of Subtrust Trustee

The trustee may distribute as much of the net income or principal of the child's subtrust as the trustee deems necessary for the subtrust beneficiary's health, support, maintenance or education. Education includes, but is not limited to, college, graduate, postgraduate and vocational studies, and reasonably related living expenses.

In deciding whether or not to make a distribution to the beneficiary, the trustee may take into account the beneficiary's other income, resources and sources of support. Any subtrust income not distributed by the trustee shall be accumulated and added to the principal of the subtrust.

C. Assignment of Subtrust Assets

The interests of subtrust beneficiaries shall not be transferable by voluntary or involuntary assignment or by operation of law. They shall be free from the claims of creditors and from attachments, execution, bankruptcy or other legal process to the fullest extent permitted by law.

D. Compensation of Trustee

Any trustee of a child's subtrust created under this Declaration of Trust shall be entitled to reasonable compensation out of the subtrust assets for ordinary and extraordinary services, and for all services in connection with the termination of any subtrust.

E. Termination of Subtrusts

A child's subtrust shall end when any of the following events occurs:

1. The beneficiary dies. If the subtrust ends for this reason, the subtrust property shall pass to the beneficiary's legal inheritors.

2. The beneficiary reaches the age specified in Section A of this Part.

If the subtrust ends for this reason, the remaining principal and accumulated income of the subtrust shall be given outright to the beneficiary.

3. The trustee distributes all subtrust property under the provisions of this Declaration of Trust.

_____   _____

William Schwegler, Grantor   Date

[NOTARIZATION]

---

6. Adding a Child's Custodianship

You can add a child's custodianship to your trust document, whether or not your original trust document created any custodianships, if your state's law allows custodianships. (See Chapter 5 or 6, Part 7.)

To prepare your Trust Amendment, follow these steps:

Step 1. Select Add Custodianship from the list of templates.

Step 2. Fill in the date you signed the original trust document in the two spaces left blank near the beginning of the form.

Step 3. If your original trust document created a custodianship for a different beneficiary, put that Part number in the blank in "The following is added to [Part __ of] the trust document:" and delete the brackets. If your original trust document did not create a custodianship, delete the bracketed language, add a heading (shown on the template) to the trust document, and number it accordingly. (The Part number should be one more than the number of Parts in the original trust document.)

Step 4. Fill in the blanks with the name of the beneficiary, the age at which the custodianship ends, and the name of the custodian and alternate custodian. To fill in the age, check your state's law in the chart in Part 7 of Chapter 5 or 6.

The sample amendment shown below is for an individual trust. If you made a shared marital trust with your spouse, the template will look slightly different: The Part number that gives you authority to make the amendment will be Part 5 (not Part 4).

Sample Trust Amendment: Add Custodianship (Individual Trust)

Amendment to
The Andrea Freedman Revocable Living Trust
dated <u>November 2, 1991</u>

Under the power reserved to the grantor by Part 4 of the Declaration of Trust dated <u>November 2, 1991</u> creating the Andrea Freedman Revocable Living Trust, the grantor hereby amends the Declaration of Trust as follows:

[IF YOUR ORIGINAL TRUST DOCUMENT CREATED A CUSTODIANSHIP, FILL IN THE PART NUMBER; OTHERWISE, DELETE BRACKETED LANGUAGE.]

The following is added to [Part __ of] the trust document:

[IF YOUR ORIGINAL TRUST DOCUMENT DID NOT CREATE ANY CUSTODIANSHIPS, ADD THE HEADING BELOW AND NUMBER THE NEW PART. OTHERWISE, START AFTER THE HEADING.]

Part <u>11</u>. Custodianships Under the Uniform Transfers to Minors Act

Any property <u>Caitlin Freedman</u> becomes entitled to under Part 10 of this Declaration of Trust shall be given to <u>Lynn Faler</u>, as custodian for <u>Caitlin Freedman</u> under the <u>Illinois</u> Transfers to Minors Act, until <u>Caitlin Freedman</u> reaches the age of <u>21</u>. If <u>Lynn Faler</u> is unable or ceases to serve as custodian, <u>Constance Faler</u> shall serve as custodian.

_____   _____

Andrea Freedman, Grantor   Date

[NOTARIZATION]

7. Deleting a Clause

You may want to delete language from your living trust document:

- a clause leaving certain trust property to a beneficiary, if the trust no longer owns that property

- a provision that created a child's subtrust or custodianship.

 Do not delete other provisions. You could create serious problems for your heirs or even invalidate your trust.

Step 1. Select Delete Clause from the list of templates.

Step 2. Fill in the date you signed the original trust document in the two spaces left blank near the beginning of the form.

Step 3. Fill in the part number of the language you are deleting, and copy and paste the language to be deleted. (Part K of the User's Manual shows how to copy language from the original trust document.)

The sample amendment shown below is for an individual trust. If you made a shared marital trust with your spouse, the template will look slightly different: The Part number that gives you authority to make the amendment will be Part 5 (not Part 4).

Sample Amendment: Delete Clause (Individual Trust)

Amendment to
The Enid O'Brien Revocable Living Trust
dated <u>November 29, 1991</u>

Under the power reserved to the grantor by Part 4 of the Declaration of Trust dated <u>November 29, 1991</u>, creating the Enid O'Brien Revocable Living Trust, the grantor hereby amends the Declaration of Trust as follows:

The following is deleted from Part <u>11</u> of the trust document:

Any property Richard Graham becomes entitled to under Part 10 of this Declaration of Trust shall be given to Noreen Glavin, as custodian for Richard Graham under the Washington Transfers to Minors Act, until Richard Graham reaches the age of 21. If Noreen Glavin is unable or ceases to serve as custodian, Evelyn Glavin shall serve as custodian.

_____   _____
Enid O'Brien, Grantor   Date

[NOTARIZATION]

H. Revoking Your Living Trust

You can revoke your living trust at any time. Revoking a living trust (unlike revoking a will) requires some work: You must transfer ownership of all the trust property out of the living trust.

1. Who Can Revoke a Living Trust

If you create an individual living trust, you can revoke it at any time.

Either spouse can revoke a shared living trust, wiping out all terms of the trust. The trust property is returned to each spouse according to how they owned it before transferring it to the trust.

EXAMPLE Yvonne and André make a shared marital living trust. Each transfers separately owned property to the trust. They also transfer ownership of their house, which they own together, to the trust. Later Yvonne, anticipating a divorce, revokes the living trust. She transfers the property she owned back to herself, and the property her husband owned back to him. The co-owned property goes back to both of them.

The trust document does not allow the trust to be revoked by someone acting on your behalf unless you have specifically granted that authority. (See Section F.3, above.)

2. When To Revoke Your Living Trust

If you're like most people, amending your living trust will take care of your changing circumstances over the years, and you will never need to revoke your trust. Here are two fairly common exceptions to that rule:

a. You Want To Make Extensive Revisions

If you want to make very extensive revisions to the terms of the trust document, you should revoke it and start fresh with a new trust document. If you don't, you risk creating inconsistencies and confusion.

b. You Get Divorced

If you divorce, you should revoke your living trust. In Florida and Tennessee, provisions of your living trust that affect your spouse are automatically revoked by divorce, but you shouldn't rely on these laws.[2]

3. How To Revoke Your Living Trust

To revoke your living trust, follow these steps:

---

[2]Fla. Stat. Ann. § 737.106; Tenn. Code Ann. § 35-50-115.

Step 1. Transfer ownership of trust property from the living trust back to yourself. Basically, you must reverse the process you followed when you transferred ownership of the property to the trust's name. You can make the transfer because of your authority as trustee of the trust.

Step 2. Prepare a Revocation of Trust. After you've printed your trust document, when you start the program again, it will ask you whether or not you've signed the trust document, creating a legally valid trust. If you have, the program will take you to a screen that allows you to bring up a Revocation template, which you can fill in on the screen.

Step 3. Sign the Revocation of Trust in front of a notary public.

The sample revocation shown below is for an individual trust. If you made a shared marital trust with your spouse, the template will look slightly different: The Part number that gives you authority to make the revocation will be Part 5 (not Part 4).

Sample Revocation (Individual Trust)

Revocation of
The Dieter Krups Revocable Living Trust
dated <u>May 19, 1991</u>

I, Dieter Krups, hereby revoke the Dieter Krups Revocable Living Trust, created by Declaration of Trust dated <u>May 19, 1991</u>, according to the power reserved to the grantor by Part 4 of the Declaration of Trust.

All property owned by the trust shall be returned to the grantor.

_____   _____

Dieter Krups, Grantor   Date

[NOTARIZATION]

10 After a Grantor Dies

The benefit of a revocable living trust doesn't come until after the grantor's death, when the trust property is transferred to beneficiaries without probate. The all-important responsibility of handling that transfer falls to your surviving spouse, if you made a shared living trust, or your successor trustee, if you made an individual living trust.

A. What Happens When a Grantor Dies

The process works differently depending on whether you made an individual living trust or a shared trust with your spouse.

1. Individual Trust

When the grantor, who is also the trustee, dies, the successor trustee named in the Declaration of Trust takes over as trustee. The new trustee is responsible for distributing the trust property to the beneficiaries named in the trust document.

The trust continues to exist only as long as it takes the successor trustee to distribute trust property to the beneficiaries. In many cases, a living trust can be wound up in only a few weeks after a grantor's death.

The successor trustee is also in charge of managing any property left to a young beneficiary in a child's subtrust. A subtrust will exist until the beneficiary reaches the age specified in the trust document, so if there's a subtrust the successor trustee may have years of work ahead. (See Section F, below.)

If trust property inherited by a young beneficiary is to be managed by a custodian, under the Uniform Transfers to Minors Act, instead of in a child's subtrust, the person named as custodian will be responsible for that property. The successor trustee may also have been named as the custodian for a young beneficiary's property.

THE SUCCESSOR TRUSTEE'S DUTIES

> • Distribute trust property to beneficiaries named in the trust document .
>
> • Manage trust property left in a child's subtrust, if any.
>
> • File federal and state estate tax returns, if necessary (this is the responsibility of the executor of the estate, if there was a will).

2. Shared Marital Trust

When a married couple creates a shared living trust with *Nolo's Living Trust*, both spouses are the original trustees. When the first spouse dies, the surviving spouse becomes sole trustee.

The trust itself is automatically split into two trusts:

• Trust #1 contains the deceased spouse's share of trust property, excluding any trust property left to the surviving spouse. Its terms cannot be changed, and it cannot be revoked.

• Trust #2 contains the surviving spouse's share, including any of the deceased spouse's share of the trust property that is left to the surviving spouse.[1] The surviving spouse is still free to revoke it or amend its terms.

The survivor is sole trustee of Trust #1, Trust #2 and any children's subtrusts set up for the deceased spouse's young beneficiaries.

It's the surviving spouse's job to distribute the property in Trust #1 to the beneficiaries the deceased spouse named in the trust document. If, as is common, much of the trust property is left to the surviving spouse, that spouse will have little to do—the trust property he or she inherits is already in the living trust and does not need to be transferred.

---

[1]The Declaration of Trust created by *Nolo's Living Trust* provides that trust property left to the survivor does not go to the surviving spouse outright but instead stays in the living trust. If it did not contain such a provision, the property would go to the surviving spouse outright. It would have to be transferred from the living trust to the spouse and then, if the surviving spouse wanted it to avoid probate, back to the living trust again.

Trust #2 goes on as before, as a revocable living trust. It contains only the surviving spouse's property, and the surviving spouse is free to change it as he or she wishes.

When the second spouse dies, the successor trustee named in the trust document takes over as trustee. The process of winding up the living trust is the same as that for an individual trust (section 1, above).

EXAMPLE Harry and Maude, a married couple, set up a revocable living trust to avoid probate. They appoint Maude's cousin Emily as successor trustee, to take over as trustee after they have both died. They transfer ownership of much of their co-owned property—their house, savings accounts and stocks—to the trust. Maude also puts some of her family heirlooms, which are her separate property, in the living trust.

In the trust document, Maude leaves her heirlooms to her younger sister. She leaves her half of the trust property she and Harry own together to Harry.

When Maude dies, Harry becomes the sole trustee. Following the terms of the trust document, he distributes Maude's heirlooms (Trust #1) to her sister, without probate. Maude's half of the property they had owned together stays in the trust (Trust #2); no transfer is necessary. After Maude's death, he decides to amend the trust document to name his nephew, Burt, as successor trustee instead of Maude's cousin Emily. When Harry dies, Burt will become trustee and distribute the trust property following Harry's instructions in the trust document. When all the property is given to Harry's beneficiaries, the trust ends.

Section C, below, has more about transferring property to the surviving spouse.

THE SURVIVING SPOUSE'S DUTIES

• Distribute the deceased spouse's share of the trust property to beneficiaries named in the trust document.
• Manage property left in a child's subtrust, if any.
• File federal and state estate tax returns, if necessary (this is the executor's responsibility, if a will named someone else as executor of the estate).
• Amend living trust to reflect changed circumstances, if necessary.

B. Who Serves as Trustee

With a shared marital trust, it's simple: The surviving spouse serves as trustee after one spouse's death. With an individual trust, or when the surviving spouse dies, the successor trustee is in charge.

WHO SERVES AS TRUSTEE

Individual trust	Shared Marital Trust
1. Successor trustee(s)	1. Surviving spouse
2. Alternate successor trustee(s)	2. Successor trustee(s)
	3. Alternate successor trustee(s)

1. More Than One Successor Trustee

If more than one person is named in the trust document as successor trustee, they all serve together. Each must agree on any action taken with regard to the living trust property.

If one of the trustees cannot serve, the others remain as trustees. The person named as alternate successor trustee does not take over unless all the people named as successor trustees cannot serve.

2. If a Trustee Resigns

A trustee can resign at any time by preparing and signing a resignation statement like the own shown below. The ex-trustee should deliver the notice to the person who is next in line to serve as trustee (see list above).

NOTICE OF RESIGNATION

I, Lucia Freni, current Trustee of The Robert Ambruzzi Revocable Living Trust dated March 3, 1990, resign my position as trustee, effective immediately.

Date: November 19, 1991

_____
Lucia Freni, Trustee
State of _____
County of _____

On _____, before me, a notary public in and for said state, personally appeared _____, personally known to me (or proved to me on the basis of satisfactory evidence) to be the person(s) whose name(s) is/are subscribed to the within instrument and acknowledged to me that he or she executed the same in the capacity(ies) indicated at the signature point.

_____

If no one named in the trust document can serve, the last acting trustee can appoint someone else to take over. The appointment must be in writing, signed and notarized. The trustee can prepare a simple document like the one shown below.

APPOINTMENT OF TRUSTEE

I, Lucia Freni, Trustee of The Robert Ambruzzi Revocable Living
Trust dated March 3, 1990, appoint Clarence Ryan as trustee,
effective immediately. This appointment is made under the
authority granted in Part 7 of the Declaration of Trust.

Date: November 19, 1991

_____

Lucia Freni, Trustee

State of _____

County of _____

On _____, before me, a notary public in and for
said state, personally appeared _____,
personally known to me (or proved to me on the basis of
satisfactory evidence) to be the person(s) whose name(s) is/are
subscribed to the within instrument and acknowledged to me that
he or she executed the same in the capacity(ies) indicated at the
signature point.

                              _____

---

3. Removing a Trustee

Very rarely, a beneficiary becomes seriously unhappy with the way a trustee
handles trust property. For example, the beneficiary of a child's subtrust
might complain that the trustee isn't spending enough of the trust property's income on the beneficiary's education. If the dispute can't be worked
out, the beneficiary can file a lawsuit to try to force the removal of the
trustee.

C. Transferring Property to the Surviving Spouse

As mentioned in Section A, above, a surviving spouse who inherits trust property doesn't need to transfer the property. The property is already owned by the living trust, and the surviving spouse now has sole and complete control over all property in the trust.

The surviving spouse may, however, want to amend the trust document to name beneficiaries for the property.

EXAMPLE Edith and Jacques create a shared living trust. They transfer their house, which they own together, into the trust, and name each other as beneficiaries. Edith names her son as alternate beneficiary.

When Jacques dies, Edith inherits his half-interest in the house. Because of the way the trust document is worded, she doesn't have to change the trust document to name a beneficiary for the other half-interest in the house, which she inherited from her husband. Both halves will go to her son at her death. She may, however, want to amend the trust to make her son the primary beneficiary and name someone else to be alternate beneficiary.

For instructions on how to make a Trust Amendment, see Chapter 9, *Living With Your Living Trust*.

D. Transferring Property to Other Beneficiaries

The procedure for transferring trust property to the beneficiaries who inherit it depends on the kind of property you're dealing with. Generally, a copy of the grantor's death certificate (both grantors' death certificates, if the trust property was originally co-owned) and a copy of the trust document are necessary. In some cases, the trustee will need to prepare some other paperwork.

Specific requirements for transferring property vary slightly from place to place, and the trustee may have to make inquiries to banks, stock brokerages and other institutions about current procedures, but here are the general rules.[2] A trustee who runs into difficulties has the authority to get help—from a lawyer, accountant or other expert—and pay for it from trust assets.

Terminology note. This section refers to whoever takes over as trustee after a grantor's death as the "trustee." If you made an individual trust, the trustee is the person you named as successor trustee. If you made a shared marital trust, the trustee is the surviving spouse or, after both spouses have died, the successor trustee. (See Section B, above.)

1. Property Without Title Documents

For trust property that doesn't have a title document—furniture, for example—the task of the trustee is quite simple. The trustee must promptly distribute the property to the beneficiaries named in the trust. If the trustee thinks it's a good idea, it's appropriate to have the recipient sign a receipt.

2. Bank Accounts

It should be simple for the trustee to transfer the funds in a bank or savings and loan account, already held in the name of the living trust, to the beneficiary. Financial institutions are familiar with living trusts and how they work, and the particular bank probably has the trust document (or a bank form with information about the trust) already on file.

The trustee will need to show the bank or savings and loan:

* a certified copy of the trust grantor's death certificate;

* a copy of the living trust document, if the bank doesn't already have one; and

* proof of his or her own identity.

---

[2]For California residents, *How To Probate an Estate*, by Julia Nissley (Nolo Press) contains instructions on transferring the property of a decedent, including living trust property.

3. Real Estate

The trustee need only prepare and sign a deed to transfer ownership of real estate from the trust to the beneficiary. The signed and notarized deed should also be filed (recorded) with the county land records office. In most places, recording costs no more than a few dollars per page. It's unlikely, but depending on local and state law, there may be a transfer tax to pay. (Recording documents and transfer taxes are discussed in Chapter 8, *Transferring Property to the Trust.*)

EXAMPLE   The deed to Evelyn Crocker's house shows that it is owned by her living trust. The living trust document states that Evelyn's daughter, Amanda, is to inherit the house when Evelyn dies. Amanda is also the successor trustee of the trust.

After Evelyn's death, Amanda prepares and signs a new deed, transferring ownership of the house from the trust to herself. She signs the deed in her capacity as trustee of the trust, and records the deed in the county records office.

A title company, before it will issue title insurance to the new owners, will probably want a copy of the trust document and a certified copy of the death certificate of the trust grantor.

4. Stocks and Bonds

How to transfer stocks or bonds from a trust to the beneficiary depends on whether they were held in a brokerage account or separately.

Stock in closely-held corporations.   See section 6, Small Business Interests, below.

a. Brokerage Accounts

The trustee should contact the broker and ask for instructions. The brokerage company will almost surely already have either a copy of the living trust document or a form that includes relevant information about the trust. (These are necessary to transfer the account to the living trust in the first place.)

If not, the trustee will probably need to send the broker:

- a copy of the trust document or an "abstract of trust" (the first, last and other relevant pages of the trust document, showing the notarized signature), and

- a letter instructing the holder to transfer the brokerage account to the beneficiary's name.

b. Stock Certificates

If the deceased grantor kept the stock certificates or bonds in his or her possession—most people don't—the trustee must get new certificates issued, showing the beneficiary as owner.

The trustee will have to send the securities' transfer agent several documents. It's a good idea to write the transfer agent and ask exactly what is needed. Usually, the name and address of the transfer agent appear on the face of the stock or bond certificate. But because transfer agents change occasionally, the first thing the trustee should do is write or call (or check with a stock brokerage firm) to verify the name and address of the current transfer agent.

The trustee will probably have to send in:

- A certified copy of the grantor's death certificate.

- The certificates or bonds.

- A document called a "stock or bond power," which the trustee must fill out and sign, with the signature guaranteed by an officer of a bank or brokerage firm. The stock or bond power may be printed on the back of the certificates; if not, stationery stores carry them.

- A copy of the trust document or an "abstract of trust," (which is just the first, last and other relevant pages of the trust document, showing the notarized signature) if the transfer agent did not receive one when the securities were transferred into the trust.

- An Affidavit of Domicile (a form available from banks and stock brokers) signed by the trustee, showing what the trust grantor's state of residence was.

- A letter of instructions requesting that the certificates be reissued in the beneficiary's name.

c. Government Securities

To transfer government securities—Treasury bills or U.S. bonds, for example—the trustee should ask the broker to contact the issuing government agency, or contact the government directly.

5. Mutual Fund Accounts

The trustee should ask the company what it requires to re-register ownership of a mutual fund account in the beneficiary's name. Generally, the trustee must send the company the grantor's death certificate, a letter of instructions (or a form that the company provides) and a copy of the trust document.

6. Small Business Interests

How a trustee transfers small business interests owned by a living trust depends on the way the business was organized.

a. Sole Proprietorships

The trustee must transfer business assets to the beneficiary like he or she would transfer any other trust property. The name of the business itself, if owned by the living trust, does not have a title document, so the trustee doesn't need to do anything to transfer it to the beneficiary.

A registered trademark or service mark must be reregistered in the name of the beneficiary. See *Nolo's Trademark Book: How To Name Your Business and Product,* by Kate McGrath and Steve Elias (Nolo Press).

b. Solely Owned Corporations

Corporation officers must prepare the appropriate corporate records to show ownership transferred to the beneficiary, and then have the stock certificates reissued in the beneficiary's name.

c. Closely-Held Corporations

The stock certificates owned by the trust will have to be reissued in the beneficiary's name. The trustee should contact the officers of the corporation; the other shareholders may have the right, under the corporation's bylaws or a separate shareholders' agreement, to buy back the shares.

d. Partnership Interests

The trustee should contact the deceased grantor's partners, who may have the right to buy out the grantor's share. If the beneficiary wants to enter into the partnership, the partnership agreement must be changed to add the beneficiary.

7. Copyrights

To transfer an interest in a copyright to a beneficiary, the trustee should sign and file, with the U.S. Copyright Office, a document transferring all the trust's rights in the copyright to the beneficiary. Sample transfer forms are in *The Copyright Handbook*, by Steve Fishman (Nolo Press).

8. Patents

To transfer a patent from a living trust, the trustee should prepare a document called an "assignment" and record it with the Patent and Trademark Office in Washington, DC. There is a small fee for recording. Sample assignment forms and instructions are in *Patent It Yourself,* by David Pressman (Nolo Press).

9. Other Property With Title Documents

If an item of trust property has a title document that shows ownership in the name of the trust, the trustee must prepare and sign a new title document transferring ownership to the beneficiary. Usually, the trustee will need a copy of the trust document and of the trust grantor's death certificate if the property is in someone else's possession.

If a vehicle was owned by the trust, the trustee should contact the state Department of Motor Vehicles to get the forms required to transfer it to the beneficiary.

E. Preparing and Filing Tax Returns

If a state death tax or federal estate tax return must be filed for the grantor, it is the responsibility of the executor named in the decedent's will; usually, the same person is both executor and trustee.

A federal estate tax return must be filed if the decedent's gross estate was worth more than $600,000. It is due nine months after the decedent's death. The successor trustee can get a helpful 20-page set of instructions, "Instructions for Form 706," from the Internal Revenue Service. Another useful IRS publication is called "Federal Estate and Gift Taxes" (Publication 448). And again, the trustee is entitled to pay for professional help out of the trust assets.

F. Administering a Child's Subtrust

If, in the trust document, the deceased grantor set up a child's subtrust, the trustee will have to manage that property until the beneficiary is old enough to receive it. A child's subtrust comes into being only if the beneficiary has not yet reached the age the grantor specified.

EXAMPLE Carl sets up a living trust and names his two young children as beneficiaries. He specifies that if the children are younger than 30 when he dies, the property
they are to receive from the trust should be kept in a separate children's subtrust for
each child.

When Carl dies, one child is 30; the other is 25. The 30-year-old will receive her trust
property with no strings attached. But a child's subtrust will be created for the 25-
year-old. The successor trustee named in the trust document is responsible for managing the property and turning it over to the child when he turns 30.

The trustee must:

- Take good care of the subtrust property. The trustee must always act honestly and in the best interests of the beneficiary. For example, the trustee
  must not make risky investments with subtrust property.

- Use the income from subtrust property, or the subtrust property itself, to
  pay for the beneficiary's needs. The living trust document created with
  Nolo's Living Trust gives the trustee broad authority to use subtrust assets
  for the beneficiary's health, support, maintenance or education.

- File an annual trust income tax return. The subtrust may also have to pay
  estimated income taxes.

- Give the remaining subtrust property to the beneficiary when he or she
  reaches the age designated in the trust document.

The trustee can use subtrust assets to get professional assistance if necessary.
For example, the trustee might want to pay a tax preparer for help with the
subtrust's income tax return, or consult a financial planner for investment
advice.

The trust document also provides that the trustee of a subtrust is entitled to
reasonable compensation for his or her work as trustee. The trustee decides
what is a reasonable amount; the compensation is paid from the subtrust assets. A beneficiary who disagrees with the trustee's decisions about payment—or other decisions about management or distribution of the subtrust
property—must go to court to challenge the trustee's decisions.

G. Administering a Custodianship

Someone who is is appointed, in the trust document, to be the custodian of trust property inherited by a young beneficiary has about the same management responsibilities as the trustee of a child's subtrust. (See Section F, above.) The specifics are set out in the Uniform Transfers to Minors Act, as adopted by the particular state's legislature.

A custodian, however, does not have to file a separate income tax return. Any income from the beneficiary's property is reported on the beneficiary's own return.

11 If You Need Expert Help

You probably won't need a lawyer's help to make a living trust with *Nolo's Living Trust*.

Many other methods of avoiding probate—joint tenancy and pay-on-death bank accounts, for example—are also safe and straightforward enough to use yourself without consulting an expert. To understand how to draw up a complete estate plan making use of a living trust and other devices, we recommend Nolo's *Plan Your Estate With a Living Trust*, by Denis Clifford.

But you may come up with questions about your particular situation that should be answered by an expert. This is especially likely if you have a very large estate, must plan for an incapacitated minor or have to deal with the assets of a good-sized small business. These and other "red flags" that should alert you to the need for professional advice are highlighted throughout the manual and program.

A. What Kind of Expert Do You Need?

If you have questions, the first thing to decide is what type of expert you should seek out. Questions about estate taxes may be better (and less expensively) answered by an experienced accountant than a lawyer. Or if you're wondering what type of life insurance to buy, you may be better off talking to a financial planner.

Consult a lawyer if you have specific questions about a provision of your living trust or other estate planning device. Also see a lawyer if you want to get into sophisticated estate planning—for instance, if you want to establish a marital life estate trust to save on federal estate taxes or a long-term trust for a disabled child.

B. Legal Advice Over the Phone

Before you sign up as a lawyer's client, consider getting legal advice in a relatively new form: over the phone. A group of lawyers in the Los Angeles area have formed a company, Tele-Lawyer, that offers legal advice for $3/minute ($180/hour). It may sound expensive, but compared to the conventional way of buying legal advice from a lawyer, it can be a bargain.

Tele-Lawyer's staff includes lawyers who specialize in many different areas, including estate planning. You're charged only for the time you spend talking to the lawyer on the phone. So if you have a concrete question that can be answered fairly quickly, it won't cost much. If the lawyer can't answer your question, he or she will find out the answer and call you back.

Tele-Lawyer offers only advice. Its lawyers do not accept cases, and it does not give referrals to lawyers. All conversations are confidential.

To contact Tele-Lawyer, call 800-835-3529 (charged to your credit card) or 900-776-7000 (charged on your phone bill).

C. How To Choose a Lawyer

Finding a competent estate planning lawyer who charges a reasonable fee and respects your efforts to prepare your own living trust may not be easy. Here are some suggestions on how to go about the task.

1. Look Into a Group Legal Plan

Some unions, employers and consumer action organizations offer group legal plans to their members or employees, who can obtain comprehensive legal assistance free or for low rates. If you are a member of such a plan, check with it first. Your problem may be covered free of charge. If it is, and you are satisfied that the lawyer you are referred to is knowledgeable in estate planning, this route is probably a good choice.

Some plans give you only a slight reduction in a lawyer's fee. In that case, you may be referred to a lawyer whose main virtue is the willingness to reduce fees in exchange for a high volume of referrals.

2. Check Out a Prepaid Legal Plan

For basic advice, you may want to consider joining a prepaid legal plan that offers advice, by phone or in person, at no extra charge. (Some of these plans throw in a free simple will, too.) Your initial membership fee may be reasonable, compared to the cost of hiring a lawyer by the hour, but there's no guarantee that the lawyers available through these plans are of the best caliber.

Most plans have renewal fees; you can join a plan for a specific service and then not renew. The plans are sold by companies such as Montgomery Ward and Amway, and are often offered to credit card holders or sold door-to-door.

You should realize that the lawyer you see probably receives at most $2 or $3 a month for dealing with you. Why do lawyers agree to this minimal amount? They hope to find clients who will pay for extra legal services not covered by the monthly premium. The low basic fee means the lawyers have an incentive to complicate, rather than simplify, your problem. So if a plan lawyer recommends an expensive legal procedure, get a second opinion.

3. Ask Businesspeople and Friends

Anyone who owns a small business probably has a relationship with a lawyer. Ask around to find someone you know who is a satisfied client. If that lawyer does not handle estate planning, he or she will likely know someone who does. And because of the continuing relationship with your friend, the lawyer has an incentive to recommend someone who is competent.

Also ask people you know in any social or other organization in which you are involved. They may well know of a good lawyer whose attitudes are similar to yours. Senior citizens' centers and other groups that advise and assist older people may have a list of local lawyers who specialize in wills and estate planning and are well regarded.

4. Consult a Legal Clinic

Law firms with lots of small offices across the country, such as Hyatt Legal Services and Jacoby & Meyers, trumpet their low initial consultation fees. It's true that a basic consultation is cheap, often about $20; anything beyond that isn't cheap at all. Generally, the rates average about the same as those charged by other lawyers in general practice.

If you do consult a legal clinic, often the trick is to quickly extract the information you need and resist attempts to convince you that you need more services. If the lawyer you talk to is experienced in estate planning, however, and you're comfortable with the person and the service, it may be worthwhile. Unfortunately, most of these offices have extremely high lawyer turnover, so you may see a different one every time you visit.

5. Call an Attorney Referral Service

A lawyer referral service will give you the name of an attorney who practices in your area. Usually, you can get a referral to an attorney who claims to specialize in estate planning and will give you an initial consultation for a low fee.

Most county bar associations have referral services. In some states, independent referral services, run by or for groups of lawyers, also operate.

Unfortunately, few referral services screen the attorneys they list, which means those who participate may not be the most experienced or competent. Often, the lawyers who sign up with referral services are just starting out and need clients. It may be possible to find a skilled estate planning specialist through a referral service, but be sure to take the time to check out the credentials and experience of the person to whom you're referred.

Living Trust Seminars

Newspapers, radio and TV are full of ads for free "seminars" on living trusts. Usually, these events are nothing more than elaborate pitches for paying a lawyer $1,000 to $1,500 to write a living trust. Is it worth it? Probably not.

For a relatively small estate, *Nolo's Living Trust* will probably be all you need. For more complicated estate planning, you will almost surely get better, less expensive and more personal advice from a local estate planning specialist.

D. Dealing With a Lawyer

If you decide to speak to a lawyer, find one who specializes in estate planning. Most general practice lawyers are simply not sufficiently educated in this field to competently address complicated problems.

Many lawyers, however, have recently discovered living trusts—or, more accurately, discovered their profit-making potential. Lawyers who know almost nothing about living trusts (it's easy to go through law school without ever hearing of one) have found that they can charge huge fees—$900 to $1500 is common—for a simple document. Some use computer programs to churn out trusts and may or may not take into account your specific needs.

The fee of an experienced specialist may be 10 to 30% higher than that of a general practitioner, but the specialist will probably produce results more efficiently and save you money in the long run.

Lawyer fees usually range from $100 to $350 or more per hour. But price is not always related to quality. It depends on the area of the county you live in, but generally, fees of $100 to $200 per hour are reasonable in urban areas, given the lawyer's overhead. In rural areas and smaller cities, $80 to $150 is more like it.

Be sure you've settled your fee arrangement—preferably in writing—at the start of your relationship. In addition to the hourly fee, you should get a clear, written commitment from the lawyer about how many hours your problem should take to handle.

Before you talk to the lawyer, decide what kind of help you really need. Do you want someone to advise you on a complete estate plan, or just to review your living trust to make sure it looks all right? If you don't clearly tell the lawyer what you want, you may find yourself agreeing to turn over all your estate planning work.

One good strategy is to do some background research and write down your questions as specifically as you can. If the lawyer doesn't give you clear, concise answers, try someone else. If the lawyer acts wise but says little except to ask that the problem be placed in his or her hands—with a substantial fee, of course—watch out. You're either dealing with someone who doesn't know the answer and won't admit it (common) or someone who finds it impossible to let go of the "me expert, you plebeian" philosophy (even more common).

User's Guide Index

A

Alternate beneficiaries, UG/55-60
Alternate custodian, UG/71
Alternate residuary beneficiaries, UG/68
Amendments. *See* Trust amendments
Application disk, UG/3
ASCII file, UG/75-76
AutoSave feature, UG/15, UG/24-25

B

Back-up copy
    of NLT disk, UG/4-7
    of trust data file, UG/26
Backing up from screen to screen,
    UG/17-18
Beneficiaries, of trust property
    alternate residuary, UG/68
    alternates, UG/55-60
    and unequal shares, UG/53-55
    entering names, UG/51-52
    minors, UG/69-72
    more than one, UG/52-55
    naming, UG/46-67
    residuary, UG/68
    young adults, UG/69-72
Bomb messages, UG/88-89
Buttons
    continue, UG/23
    default, UG/23
    dimmed, UG/20
    Go Back, UG/17-18
    OK, UG/23

C

Check marks, UG/20-21
Checklist screen, UG/18-22, UG/36
    jumping back to, UG/18
Clipboard full, UG/87
Commands
    copy, UG/32
    cut, UG/32
    paste, UG/32
    Paste From Names List, UG/29
Continue buttons, UG/23
Copies
    of NLT disk, UG/4-7
    of trust data file, UG/26
Copy command, UG/32
Custodian and custodianship, UG/70,
    UG/71
Customer and Technical Support, iii-vii,
    UG/76
Cut command, UG/32

D

Damaged disk, vi, UG/85
Damaged file, UG/87, UG/90
Declaration of Trust. *See* Trust
    document
Default buttons, UG/23
Dimmed buttons, UG/20
Disk
    application, UG/3
    damaged, vi, UG/85
    locked, UG/86
    not found, UG/87
    too full, UG/85
    unreadable, UG/90

E

Erase all and start over option, UG/67
Error messages, UG/84-88
Escape key, UG/23, UG/24

F

Fast track options, UG/46, UG/47-49,
    UG/60
File
    damaged, UG/87, UG/90
    naming, UG/16, UG/25
    not found, UG/86
    opening too many, UG/86

Legal Manual Index

alternate, 9/17-20

changing, 9/11, 9/17-20

and individual living trust, 5/36, 5/38, 5/42-45

and shared marital trust, 6/45, 6/47, 6/49, 6/52-55

D

Death

of beneficiary, 9/9

of first spouse, in shared marital trust, 6/4, 6/10-11

of original trustee/grantor, 5/4, 5/9-10, 5/33, 6/42-43, 10/2-16

of second spouse, in shared marital trust, 6/6-7, 6/11

simultaneous, 5/24, 5/33, 6/31, 6/32-34, 6/42-43

Death tax returns, 10/14

Death taxes. *See* State inheritance taxes

Declaration of Trust, 1/1, 2/2

samples, 5/47-53, 6/57-69

See also Trust document

Deed forms, 5/23, 8/3-6

preparing, 8/3-6

recording, 8/6

and transfer of real estate to beneficiary, 10/10

Disabled persons, and trusts, 3/35

Disinheritance

of child(ren), 2/15, 3/7, 5/30, 6/39, 9/9

of spouse, 2/12-14, 3/7, 5/30, 6/39, 9/9

Disk, storage of, 7/5-6

Dissolution, 4/3

Divorce, 4/3, 9/29

Domicile. *See* Legal residence

Dower law, 2/14

Due-on-sale mortgage clauses, and transfer of property, 8/6

Durable Power of Attorney for Financial Management, 2/7, 3/33, 6/11, 9/10

and successor trustee, 5/13, 6/15

Durable Power of Attorney for Health Care, 3/33, 6/11, 9/10

E

Estate planning, 3/3-36, 6/40, 8/7

confidentiality of, 2/7

resources, 3/4-5

Estate taxes. *See* Federal gift and estate taxes

F

Family allowance, 2/5

Family residence, inheritance of, 2/14

Federal estate tax returns, 10/14

Federal gift and estate taxes, 2/16, 3/24-31

and joint tenancy, 3/21

reducing, 3/26-31

Flexible trusts, 3/36

Foreign divorces, 4/3

Funding the trust. *See* Property, transfer

G

Gay couples, 4/3

Generation-skipping trusts, 3/31

Gift taxes. *See* Federal gift and estate taxes

Gifts, 3/14, 3/22

of life insurance, 3/28-29

made within three years of death, 3/27

and minor children, 3/28n

non-tax exempt, 3/27

and reducing estate tax liability, 3/26-29

tax-exempt, 3/26-27

Government securities, 8/10, 10/12

Grandchild(ren)

and generation-skipping trusts, 3/31

overlooked, 2/15

Grant deed, 8/3

Grantor/original trustee

death of, 5/4, 5/9-10, 5/33, 6/42-43, 10/2-16

defined, 2/4

for individual living trust, 5/8

for shared marital trust, 6/9-10

Guardian, of minor child, 3/6, 3/7

H

Home of Record, 5/6, 6/8

name of, 8/2
See also Living trusts

U

Unified gift and estate taxes. *See* Federal
gift and estate taxes
Uniform Transfer-on-Death Security
Registration Act, 5/22n, 6/30n
Uniform Transfers to Minors Act (UTMA),
2/8, 10/16
and individual living trust, 5/36, 5/38-
39, 5/44
and shared marital trust, 6/45, 6/47-48
User's Guide. *See separate index preceding
this one*
UTMA. *See* Uniform Transfers to Minors
Act (UTMA)

V

Vehicles. *See* Motor vehicles

W

Wills
back-up, 2/3, 3/6-12
and child(ren), 2/14-15, 3/6, 3/7
pour-over, 3/10-12
WillMaker, 3/8-9

Y

Young adults
and changing age at which gets
property, 9/20-22
and individual living trust, 5/31,
5/35-45
and life insurance proceeds, 5/21, 6/29
and living trust, 2/8, 5/36-37, 6/46
and shared marital trust, 6/40,
6/44-45, 6/46-55
See also Child(ren)

UPDATE SERVICE

ESTATE PLANNING & PROBATE

Plan Your Estate With a Living Trust

Attorney Denis Clifford
National 1st Edition
This book covers every significant aspect of estate planning and gives detailed specific, instructions for preparing a living trust, a document that lets your family avoid expensive and lengthy probate court proceedings after your death. *Plan Your Estate* includes all the tear-out forms and step-by-step instructions to let you prepare an estate plan designed for your special needs.
$19.95/NEST

Nolo's Simple Will Book

Attorney Denis Clifford
National 2nd Edition
It's easy to write a legally valid will using this book. The instructions and forms enable people to draft a will for all needs, including naming a personal guardian for minor children, leaving property to minor children or young adults and updating a will when necessary. Good in all states except Louisiana.
$17.95/SWIL

The Power of Attorney Book

Attorney Denis Clifford
National 4th Edition
Who will take care of your affairs, and make your financial and medical decisions if you can't? With this book you can appoint someone you trust to carry out your wishes and stipulate exactly what kind of care you want or don't want. Includes Durable Power of Attorney and Living Will Forms.
$19.95/POA

How to Probate an Estate

Julia Nissley
California 6th Edition
If you find yourself responsible for winding up the legal and financial affairs of a deceased family member or friend, you can often save costly attorneys' fees by handling the probate process yourself. This book shows you the simple procedures you can use to transfer assets that don't require probate, including property held in joint tenancy or living trusts or as community property.
$34.95/PAE

The Conservatorship Book

Lisa Goldoftas &
Attorney Carolyn Farren
California 1st Edition
When a family member or close relative becomes incapacitated due to illness or age, it may be necessary to name a conservator for taking charge of their medical and financial affairs. *The Conservatorship Book* will help you determine when and what kind of conservatorship is necessary. The book comes with complete instructions and all the forms necessary to file a conservatorship.
$24.95/CON

Everybody's Guide to Small Claims Court

Attorney Ralph Warner
National 5th Edition
California 10th Edition
These books will help you decide if you should sue in small claims court, show you how to file and serve papers, tell you what to bring to court and how to collect a judgment.
National $15.95/NSCC
California $15.95/ CSCC

Dog Law

Attorney Mary Randolph
National 1st Edition
Dog Law is a practical guide to the laws that affect dog owners and their neighbors. You'll find answers to common questions on such topics as biting, barking, veterinarians and more.
$12.95/DOG

Fight Your Ticket

Attorney David Brown
California 4th Edition
This book shows you how to fight an unfair traffic ticket—when you're stopped, at arraignment, at trial and on appeal.
$17.95/FYT

The Criminal Records Book

Attorney Warren Siegel
California 3rd Edition
This book shows you step-by-step how to seal criminal records, dismiss convictions, destroy marijuana records and reduce felony convictions.
$19.95/CRIM

Collect Your Court Judgment

Gini Graham Scott, Attorney
Stephen Elias &
Lisa Goldoftas
California 2nd Edition
This book contains step-by-step instructions and all the forms you need to collect a court judgment from the debtor's bank accounts, wages, business receipts, real estate or other assets.
$19.95/JUDG

How to Change Your Name

Attorneys David Loeb & David Brown
California 5th Edition
This book explains how to change your name legally and provides all the necessary court forms with detailed instructions on how to fill them out.
$19.95/NAME

LEGAL REFORM

Legal Breakdown: 40 Ways to Fix Our Legal System

Nolo Press Editors and Staff
National 1st Edition
Legal Breakdown presents 40 common sense proposals to make our legal system fairer, faster, cheaper and more accessible. It explains such things as why we should abolish probate, take divorce out of court, treat jurors better and give them more power, and make a host of other fundamental changes.
$8.95/LEG

MONEY MATTERS

Barbara Kaufman's Consumer Action Guide

Barbara Kaufman
California 1st Edition
This practical handbook is filled with information on hundreds of consumer topics. Barbara Kaufman, the Bay Area's award-winning host and producer of KCBS Radio's *Call for Action*, gives consumers access to their legal rights, providing addresses and phone numbers of where to complain where things to wrong, and providing resources if more help is necessary.
$14.95/CAG

Money Troubles: Legal Strategies to Cope With Your Debts

Attorney Robin Leonard
National 1st Edition
Are you behind on your credit card bills or loan payments? If you are, then *Money Troubles* is exactly what you need. Covering everything from knowing what your rights are—and asserting them to helping you evaluate your individual situation, this practical, straightforward book is for anyone who needs help understanding and dealing with the complex and often scary topic of debts.
$16.95/MT

How to File for Bankruptcy

Attorneys Stephen Elias, Albin Renauer & Robin Leonard
National 3rd Edition
Trying to decide whether or not filing for bankruptcy makes sense? *How to File for Bankruptcy* contains an overview of the process and all the forms plus step-by-step instructions on the procedures to follow.
$24.95/HFB

Simple Contracts for Personal Use

Attorney Stephen Elias
National 2nd Edition
This book contains clearly written legal form contracts to buy and sell property, borrow and lend money, store and lend personal property, release others from personal liability, or pay a contractor to do home repairs.
$16.95/CONT

FAMILY MATTERS

The Living Together Kit

Attorneys Toni Ihara & Ralph Warner
National 6th Edition
The Living Together Kit is a detailed guide designed to help the increasing number of unmarried couples living together understand the laws that affect them. Sample agreements and instructions are included.
$17.95/LTK

A Legal Guide for Lesbian and Gay Couples

Attorneys Hayden Curry & Denis Clifford
National 6th Edition
Laws designed to regulate and protect unmarried couples don't apply to lesbian and gay couples. This book shows you step-by-step how to write a living-together contract, plan for medical emergencies, and plan your estates. Includes forms, sample agreements and lists of both national lesbian and gay legal organizations, and AIDS organizations.
$17.95/LG

The Guardianship Book

Lisa Goldoftas & Attorney David Brown
California 1st Edition
The Guardianship Book provides step-by-step instructions and the forms needed to obtain a legal guardianship without a lawyer.
$19.95/GB

How to Do Your Own Divorce

Attorney Charles Sherman
(Texas Ed. by Sherman & Simons)
California 17th Edition & Texas 2nd Edition
These books contain all the forms and instructions you need to do your divorce without a lawyer.
California $18.95/CDIV
Texas $14.95/TDIV

Practical Divorce Solutions

Attorney Charles Sherman
California 2nd Edition
This book is a valuable guide to the emotional aspects of divorce as well as an overview of the legal and financial decisions that must be made.
$12.95/PDS

How to Adopt Your Stepchild in California

Frank Zagone & Attorney Mary Randolph
California 3rd Edition
There are many emotional, financial and legal reasons to adopt a stepchild, but among the most pressing legal reasons is the need to avoid confusion over inheritance or guardianship. This book provides sample forms and step-by-step instructions for completing a simple uncontested adoption by a stepparent
$19.95/ADOP

California Marriage & Divorce Law

Attorneys Ralph Warner, Toni Ihara & Stephen Elias
California 11th Edition
This book explains community property, pre-nuptial contracts, foreign marriages, buying a house, getting a divorce, dividing property, and more.
$19.95/MARR

PATENT, COPYRIGHT & TRADEMARK

Patent It Yourself
Attorney David Pressman
National 3rdEdition
From the patent search to the actual application, this book covers everything from use and licensing, successful marketing and how to deal with infringement.
$34.95/PAT

The Inventor's Notebook
Fred Grissom & Attorney David Pressman
National 1st Edition
This book helps you document the process of successful independent inventing by providing forms, instructions, references to relevant areas of patent law, a bibliography of legal and non-legal aids and more.
$19.95/INOT

How to Copyright Software
Attorney M.J. Salone
National 3rd Edition
This book tells you how to register your copyright for maximum protection and discusses who owns a copyright on software developed by more than one person.
$39.95/COPY

BUSINESS

How to Write a Business Plan
Mike McKeever
National 3rd Edition
If you're thinking of starting a business or raising money to expand an existing one, this book will show you how to write the business plan and loan package necessary to finance your business and make it work.
$17.95/SBS

Marketing Without Advertising
Michael Phillips & Salli Rasberry
National 1st Edition
This book outlines practical steps for building and expanding a small business without spending a lot of money on advertising.
$14.00/MWA

The Partnership Book
Attorneys Denis Clifford & Ralph Warner
National 4th Edition
This book shows you step-by-step how to write a solid partnership agreement that meets your needs. It covers initial contributions to the business, wages, profit-sharing, buy-outs, death or retirement of a partner and disputes.
$24.95/PART

How to Form Your Own Nonprofit Corporation
Attorney Anthony Mancuso
National 1st Edition
This book explains the legal formalities involved and provides detailed information on the differences in the law among 50 states. It also contains forms for the Articles, Bylaws and Minutes you need, along with complete instructions for obtaining federal 501 (c) (3) tax exemptions and qualifying for public charity status.
$24.95/NNP

The California Nonprofit Corporation Handbook
Attorney Anthony Mancuso
California 6th Edition
This book shows you step-by-step how to form and operate a nonprofit corporation in California. It includes the latest corporate and tax law changes, and the forms for the Articles, Bylaws and Minutes.
$29.95/NON

How to Form Your Own Corporation
Attorney Anthony Mancuso
California 7th Edition
New York 2nd Edition
Florida 3rd Edition
These books contain the forms, instructions and tax information you need to incorporate a small business yourself and save hundreds of dollars in lawyers' fees.
California $29.95/CCOR
New York $24.95/NYCO
Florida $24.95/FLCO

The California Professional Corporation Handbook

Attorney Anthony Mancuso
California 4th Edition
Health care professionals, lawyers, accountants and members of certain other professions must fulfill special requirements when forming a corporation in California. This book contains up-to-date tax information plus all the forms and instructions necessary to form a California professional corporation.
$34.95/PROF

The Independent Paralegal's Handbook

Attorney Ralph Warner
National 2nd Edition
The Independent Paralegal's Handbook provides legal and business guidelines for those · who want to take routine legal work out of the law office and offer it for a reasonable fee in an independent business.
$19.95/ PARA

Getting Started as an Independent Paralegal

(Two Audio Tapes)
Attorney Ralph Warner
National 1st Edition
Approximately three hours in all, these tapes are a carefully edited version of a seminar given by Nolo Press founder Ralph Warner. They are designed to be used with *The Independent Paralegal's Handbook*.
$24.95/GSIP

How to Buy a House in California

Attorney Ralph Warner, Ira Serkes & George Devine
California 1st Edition
This book shows you how to find a house, work with a real estate agent, make an offer and negotiate intelligently. Includes information on all types of mortgages as well as private financing options.
$18.95/BHC

For Sale By Owner

George Devine
California 1st Edition
For Sale By Owner provides essential information about pricing your house, marketing it, writing a contract and going through escrow.
$24.95/FSBO

The Deeds Book

Attorney Mary Randolph
California 1st Edition
If you own real estate, you'll need to sign a new deed when you transfer the property or put it in trust as part of your estate planning. This book shows you how
$15.95/DEED

Homestead Your House

Attorneys Ralph Warner, Charles Sherman & Toni Ihara
California 7th Edition
This book shows you how to file a Declaration of Homestead and includes complete instructions and tear-out forms.
$9.95/HOME

The Landlord's Law Book: Rights & Responsibilities

Attorneys David Brown & Ralph Warner
California 3rd Edition
This book contains information on deposits, leases and rental agreements, inspections (tenant's privacy rights), habitability (rent withholding), ending a tenancy, liability and rent control.
$29.95/LBRT

The Landlord's Law Book: Evictions

Attorney David Brown
California 3rd Edition
Updated for 1991, this book will show you step-by-step how to go to court and get an eviction for a tenant who won't pay rent— and won't leave. Contains all the tear-out forms and necessary instructions.
$29.95/LBEV

Tenant's Rights

Attorneys Myron Moskovitz & Ralph Warner
California 11th Edition
This book explains the best way to handle your relationship both your landlord and your legal rights when you find yourself in disagreement. A special section on rent control cities is included.
$15.95/CTEN

OLDER AMERICANS

Elder Care: Choosing & Financing Long-Term Care

Attorney Joseph Matthews
National 1st Edition
This book will guide you in choosing and paying for long-term care, alerting you to practical concerns and explaining laws that may affect your decisions.
$16.95/ELD

Social Security, Medicare & Pensions

Attorney Joseph Matthews with Dorothy Matthews Berman
National 5th Edition
This book contains invaluable guidance through the current maze of rights and benefits for those 55 and over, including Medicare, Medicaid and Social Security retirement and disability benefits and age discrimination protections.
$15.95/SOA

JUST FOR FUN

29 Reasons Not to Go to Law School

Attorneys Ralph Warner & Toni Ihara
National 3rd Edition
Filled with humor and piercing observations, this book can save you three years, $70,000 and your sanity.
$9.95/29R

Devil's Advocates: The Unnatural History of Lawyers

by Andrew & Jonathan Roth
National 1st Edition
This book is a painless and hilarious education, tracing the legal profession. Careful attention is given to the world's worst lawyers, most preposterous cases and most ludicrous courtroom strategies.
$12.95/DA

Poetic Justice: The Funniest, Meanest Things Ever Said About Lawyers

Edited by Jonathan & Andrew Roth
National 1st Edition
A great gift for anyone in the legal profession who has managed to maintain a sense of humor.
$8.95/PJ

RESEARCH & REFERENCE

Legal Research

Attorney Stephen Elias
National 2nd Edition
A valuable tool on its own or as a companion to just about every other Nolo book. This book gives easy-to-use, step-by-step instructions on how to find legal information.
$14.95/LRES

Family Law Dictionary

Attorneys Robin Leonard & Stephen Elias
National 2nd Edition
Finally, a legal dictionary that's written in plain English, not "legalese"! *The Family Law Dictionary* is designed to help the nonlawyer who has a question or problem involving family law—marriage, divorce, adoption or living together.
$13.95/FLD

A Dictionary of Patent, Copyright & Trademark Terms

Attorney Stephen Elias
National 2nd Edition
This book explains the terms associated with trade secrets, copyrights, trademarks, patents and contracts.
$15.95/IPLD

Legal Research Made Easy: A Roadmap Through the Law Library Maze

2-1/2 hr. videotape and 40-page manual
Nolo Press/Legal Star Communications
If you're a law student, paralegal or librarian—or just want to look up the law for yourself—this video is for you. University of California law professor Bob Berring explains how to use all the basic legal research tools in your local law library.
$89.95/LRME

SOFTWARE

WillMaker

Nolo Press/Legisoft
National 4th Edition
This easy-to-use software program lets you prepare and update a legal will—safely, privately and without the expense of a lawyer. Leading you step-by-step in a question-and-answer format, *WillMaker* builds a will around your answers, taking into account your state of residence. *WillMaker* comes with a 200-page legal manual which provides the legal background necessary to make sound choices. Good in all states except Louisiana.
IBM PC
(3-1/2 & 5-1/4 disks included)
$69.95/WI4
MACINTOSH $69.95/WM4

For the Record

Carol Pladsen & Attorney Ralph Warner
National 2nd Edition
For the Record program provides a single place to keep a complete inventory of all your important legal, financial, personal and family records. It can compute your net worth and also create inventories of all insured property to protect your assets in the event of fire or theft. Includes a 200-page manual filled with practical and legal advice.
IBM PC
(3-1/2 & 5-1/4 disks included)
$59.95/FRI2
MACINTOSH $59.95/FRM2

California Incorporator

Attorney Anthony Mancuso/Legisoft
California 1st Edition
Answer the questions on the screen and this software program will print out the 35-40 pages of documents you need to make your California corporation legal. Comes with a 200-page manual which explains the incorporation process.
IBM PC
(3-1/2 & 5-1/4 disks included)
$129.00/INCI

The California Nonprofit Corporation Handbook

(computer edition)
Attorney Anthony Mancuso
California 1st Edition
This book/software package shows you step-by-step how to form and operate a nonprofit corporation in California. Included on disk are the forms for the Articles, Bylaws and Minutes.
IBM PC 5-1/4 $69.95/ NPI
IBM PC 3-1/2 $69.95/ NP3I
MACINTOSH $69.95/ NPM

How to Form Your Own New York Corporation & How to Form Your Own Texas Corporation

Computer Editions
Attorney Anthony Mancuso
These book/software packages contain the instructions and tax information and forms you need to incorporate a small business and save hundreds of dollars in lawyers' fees. All organizational forms are on disk. Both come with a 250-page manual.

New York 1st Edition
IBM PC 5-1/4 $69.95/ NYCI
IBM PC 3-1/2 $69.95/ NYC3I
MACINTOSH $69.95/ NYCM

Texas 1st Edition
IBM PC 5-1/4 $69.95/ TCI
IBM PC 3-1/2 $69.95/ TC3I
MACINTOSH $69.95/ TCM

VISIT OUR STORE

If you live in the Bay Area, be sure to visit the Nolo Press Bookstore on the corner of 9th & Parker Streets in West Berkeley. You'll find our complete line of books and software—new and "damaged"—all at a discount. We also have t-shirts, posters and a selection of business and legal self-help books from other publishers.

Hours

Monday to Friday	10 a.m. to 5 p.m.
Thursdays	Until 6 p.m
Saturdays	10 a.m. to 4:30 p.m.
Sundays	10 a.m. to 3 p.m.

950 Parker Street, Berkeley, California

ORDER FORM

Name

Address (UPS to street address, Priority Mail to P.O. boxes)

Catalog Code	Quantity	Item	Unit price	Total
		Subtotal		
		Sales tax (California residents only)		
		Shipping & handling		
		2nd day UPS		
		TOTAL		

SALES TAX
California residents add your local tax.

SHIPPING & HANDLING
$4.00   1 item
$5.00   2-3 items
+$.50   each additional item
Allow 2-3 weeks for delivery

IN A HURRY?
UPS 2nd day delivery is available:
Add $5.00 (contiguous states) or
$8.00 (Alaska & Hawaii) to your regular shipping and handling charges

FOR FASTER SERVICE, USE YOUR CREDIT CARD AND OUR TOLL-FREE NUMBERS:
Monday-Friday, 7 a.m. to 5 p.m. Pacific Time
US   1 (800) 992-6656
CA   (inside 510 area code)   549-1976
General Information   1 (510) 549-1976
Fax us your order   1 (510) 548-5902

METHOD OF PAYMENT
☐ Check enclosed
☐ VISA   ☐ Mastercard   ☐ Discover Card
☐ American Expess

Account #   Expiration Date

Signature

Phone

PRICES SUBJECT TO CHANGE   YRW 1